The Coal Industry In America

A Bibliography and Guide to Studies

Robert F. Munn

WEST VIRGINIA UNIVERSITY LIBRARY
MORGANTOWN
1965

McCLAIN PRINTING COMPANY
PARSONS, WEST VIRGINIA

The publication of this book was
made possible by a grant from the

WEST VIRGINIA UNIVERSITY
FOUNDATION

Contents

Abbreviations

Ag	August
AIME	American Institute of Mining Engineers
Ann Amer Acad	Annals of the American Academy of Political & Social Science
Ap	April
D	December
F	February
GPO	Government Printing Office
Ja	January
JAMA	Journal of the American Medical Association
JASA	Journal of the American Statistical Association
Je	June
Jl	July
ML&W	Mountain Life & Work
MLR	Monthly Labor Review
Mr	March
My	May
N	November
O	October
S	September
USDA	United States Department of Agriculture
USGS	United States Geological Survey

Introduction

The coal industry is probably the most poorly documented of the major American industries. This is not to say that there is any lack of published material on the subject. Quite the contrary. Each major strike produced a vast and generally polemical literature, and many of the periods of labor peace were featured by only slightly less furious debate over the "Kriegsschuldfrage." While much of this writing is colorful and interesting, it is of relatively little help to the serious student of the industry.

There appear to be several reasons why the scholar interested in the development of the coal industry faces so many difficulties. Certainly the bitterness and bloodshed which have characterized the industry have militated against the production of careful and dispassionate studies. Many of the active participants were too involved emotionally to make such contributions themselves or help professional scholars do so. Nor was the emotional involvement of the True Believers the only obstacle. Both management and labor had far too many skeletons in the closet—ranging from collusion to murder—to open their records to scholars.

Historians have, with a few distinguished exceptions, all but ignored the coal industry. The paucity of primary sources has doubtless discouraged many. Also, one suspects that the controversial nature of the subject has made it unattractive to some historians. The careful avoidance of the controversial is especially noticeable in journals devoted to state and local history. For example, in a comprehensive, 154-page index to the historical journals published in West Virginia there is not one reference to John L. Lewis, the United Mine Workers or the great strikes in the coal fields.[1]

Editors of West Virginia historical journals have not been alone in their steadfast determination to avoid potentially controversial matters. A rather close examination of the state and local history journals published in the Southern Appalachian area—a region in which coal has been a major or dominant

---

[1] Munn, Robert F. Index to West Virginiana. Charleston: Education Foundation, 1960. 154p.

industry—reveals few articles indeed on the coal industry. And those few are eminently "safe"; there is nothing which could disturb even the most ancient and conservative patron of the local historical society. Strikes, living conditions, unions and other unpleasant matters are almost never mentioned.

The reluctance of scholars to concern themselves with the development of the coal industry has left much of the field to the mythmaker. As a result, probably more nonsense has been written and believed about the coal industry than any comparable subject. For example, it remains an Article of Faith in the Southern Appalachian coal fields that the region's problems, past and present, have been due almost entirely to the fact that many of the major coal companies were controlled by northern capital. The clear—though rarely stated—assumption is that local owners would have been more generous and humanitarian. As a matter of fact, there is no evidence whatever to support the notion that the locally-owned coal company is, was or would have been a better employer or more concerned with the conservation of resources than one controlled by Philadelphia bankers. (Indeed, an equally good case might be made for the thesis that large corporations with a public image to protect may be more enlightened employers than small local concerns.) This is but one of the many myths which still characterize the coal industry.

Public interest in the coal industry has generally been greater than the academic. However, this interest has been both superficial and erratic. Dramatic events such as strikes—especially if they inconvenienced the public—and major mine disasters have become the topic of the day, only to be forgotten tomorrow. On a somewhat more serious level, long periods of more or less complete indifference have been broken by short-lived campaigns to "do something" to or for the coal miner. Perhaps the most spectacular of these grew out of the discovery in the early 1930's of Harlan County, Kentucky by the American Left. The National Committee for the Defense of Political Prisoners was formed and led by such luminaries as Theodore Dreiser and Anna Rochester. However, this interest waned as suddenly as it appeared, and the miners were left in substantially the same position as before.

There are some indications that the current interest in the problems and prospects of the coal industry may be both more sustained and more productive. The principal cause for optimism lies in the national concern for the Appalachian Region. For the first time in our history, there is a major Federal commitment to improve the quality of life in this area. Quite obviously, no program concerned with the Appalachians can overlook the coal industry. Even social scientists who have no special interest in the Appalachian area *per se* are now attracted to it. For, paradoxically enough, the nation's most backward region was the first to experience the full impact of that most modern phenomenon—automation. Coal was the first major industry to automate. Within a decade, its labor requirements were cut by over sixty percent, and the agonies and dislocations are still much with us. There is some reason to suppose that what happened in coal may take place in many other industries. This fact, if no other, insures the continued interest of scholars and planners in the coal industry.

The literature of the coal industry is widely scattered. Contributions of great importance are found in everything from *Coal Age* to *Mountain Life and Work*. This scattering of the literature has increased rapidly in the past several years, as scholars representing the various academic disciplines have become interested in the industry and the social and economic problems associated with it. It is now common to find significant articles in journals devoted to economics, labor relations, sociology, political science and medicine, to mention only the more obvious. The growing interest among professional scholars has also given rise to an increase in the number of theses and dissertations on the problem. There are also government reports without number. In short, the literature has become vast and almost wildly diffused.

It is clearly desirable that research on the coal industry and the problems associated with it be carried on as efficiently and intelligently as possible. Unfortunately, the scattered nature of the literature militates against this. Even the most conscientious scholar finds it increasingly difficult to keep abreast of the literature in his own field. It is generally quite impossible for him to follow that of other disciplines. Thus it is idle to expect the sociologist to scan medical journals or the economist to master the literature of psychology. And yet, it seems clear that fruitful study of many of the problems associated with the coal industry must utilize a multi-disciplinary approach.

The chief purpose of this guide is to aid in such multi-disciplinary research. The principal emphasis has been placed on the social sciences. The enormous body of literature in the science and technology of mining is, of course, outside the scope of this work. Titles dealing with technology (including geology) are included only if they contain a significant amount of material of potential interest to the historian or social scientist. An effort has been made to include as many pertinent dissertations and theses as possible. Many of these, especially theses, are almost impossible to locate through the conventional bibliographic sources. Every effort has been made to include (1) titles of real significance and (2) works whose bibliographies will serve as a guide to those interested in a specific area or problem.

Whether or not to provide abstracts or annotations presents a difficult problem in works of this nature. They can be of undoubted value in many cases. On the other hand, it must be recognized that historical and descriptive accounts, unlike articles in chemistry or physics, do not really lend themselves to abstracting. Unless the abstract is of prohibitive length, there is danger that it may do violence to the original. A compromise seems the only answer. Annotations have been provided for all entries if the title does not make obvious the subject covered. They have also been provided if, in the opinion of the compiler, they would be more likely to help than mislead the user.

A number of librarians and scholars have contributed greatly to whatever utility this work may have. Mr. Stanley K. Bigman, Chief of the Social Studies Section, Division of Occupational Health of the Department of Health, Education and Welfare provided many useful references on the medical problems of the coal industry. The Staff of the West Virginia University Library was, as ever, both helpful and tolerant. However, all sins of omission and commission are those of the compiler; every bibliographer lives not in the fear but in the certain knowledge that he has overlooked titles of importance.

History

(Including general accounts published before 1870)

1. An address to the inhabitants of Rhode Island on the subject of their coal mines. New York, 1825. 16p.

2. ALLISON, ROBERT
    Early history of coal mining and mining machinery in Schuylkill County. Schuylkill County Historical Society. *Publication* IV: 135-55 1912.

3. AMERICAN INSTITUTE OF MINING AND METALLURGICAL ENGINEERS
    Seventy-five years of progress in the mineral industry. New York, 1947. 817p.

    Contents include: Eavenson, H. N. Seventy-five years of progress in bituminous coal mining, pp223-246; Evans, Cadwallader. Seventy-five years of progress in the anthracite industry. pp247-69.

4. ANSTED, D. T.
    Report on the "Wilson survey," near the great Kanawha River, Virginia. New York: W. C. Bryant, 1853. 16p.

5. ARMES, ETHEL MARIE
    The story of coal and iron in Alabama. Birmingham, 1910. 581p.

6. BARKSDALE, S.
    Coal mining thrives on Virginia's "last frontier". *Commonwealth* Je 1949 30-32.

    The "frontier" is the area between Clintwood and Pound. Article includes material on the history of mining in Virginia.

7. BASSETT, JOHN W. AND HARRY L. WASHBURN
    Early underground coal mining in Kentucky. *Kentucky Engineer.* 12 My 1950 7-10.

8. BASTIN, S. L. AND S. A. MORY
History of coal mining in Laurel County, Kentucky, 1750 to 1944. London, Kentucky, 1944. 16p.

9. BEACHLEY, CHARLES E.
History of the Consolidation Coal Company, 1864-1934. New York, 1934. 100p.

10. BILLINGER, ROBERT D.
History and development of the anthracite industry. Pennsylvania Dept. of Internal Affairs. *Monthly Bulletin* F 1951 3-9; Mr 1951 13-27.

11. BILLINGER, ROBERT D.
Pennsylvania's coal industry. Gettysburg: Pennsylvania Historical Association, 1954. 53p. (Pennsylvania History Studies No. 6).

A general history of the industry.

12. BILLIONS OF TONS OF COAL TAKEN FROM THE WILDERNESS OF ST. ANTHONY
Pennsylvania Dept. of Internal Affairs. *Bulletin* N 1936 3-8.

The anthracite coal region of Pennsylvania was once considered so rough and worthless that it was called the Wilderness of St. Anthony.

13. BINDER, FREDERICK M.
Anthracite enters the American home. *Pennsylvania Magazine of History & Biography* 82: 82-99 1958.

14. BINDER, FREDERICK M.
Pennsylvania coal; an historical study of its utilization to 1860. Ph.D. University of Pennsylvania. 1955.

15. BLANCHARD, D. E.
A concise history of the anthracite coal industry of Pennsylvania. Wilkes-Barre: W. H. Seacord, 1884. 24p.

16. BOWEN, ELI
Coal and the coal trade. Philadelphia and Pottsville, 1862. 36p.

17. BOWEN, ELI
The coal regions of Pennsylvania, being a general, geological, historical and statistical review of the anthracite coal districts. Pottsville, Pennsylvania, 1848. 72p.

18. BOYER, MARY J.
The old Gravois coal diggings. Festus, Missouri, 1952.
107p.

Now a part of Saint Louis, Missouri.

19. BRATTON, SAM T.
Coal in Missouri. *Missouri Historical Review* 22: 150-
56 1928.

A brief history of the discovery of coal and the development of
the industry.

19a. BRIDGES, LEONARD H.
Iron millionaire; life of Charlemagne Tower. Philadelphia; University of Pennsylvania Press, 1952. 322p.

Tower became one of the leading coal operators in the post-Civil
War period in Pennsylvania.

20. BUCH, JOHN W.
Historical summary of conveyor mining. *Mechanization* 5 Ap 1941 59-64.

21. BUCK, WILLIAM J.
History of the early discovery of coal. *Potter's American Monthly* 4: 180-82 1875.

22. "CC&B" CELEBRATE 80TH BIRTHDAY
Black Diamond Ap 12, 1947 22-23.

A brief history of Castner, Curran and Bullitt, one of the oldest
and largest coal merchants in the United States.

23. CAMPBELL, ROY E.
History of the development of the coal industry in Ka-
nawha District, West Virginia. Thesis. West Virginia
University. 1930.

24. CARBON COUNTY HISTORICAL SOCIETY
Centennial anniversary of the first shipment of anthracite coal from the Lehigh region at Lausanne, Pennsylvania, August 9, 1814. Mauch Chunk, Pennsylvania:
The Society, 1914. 17p.

25. CARPENTER, SAMUEL
Report of the engineer in relation to the coal mines of
the Hockhocking Valley. Columbus, 1836. 5p.

26. CARTLIDGE, OSCAR
Fifty years of coal mining. Charleston, West Virginia:
Rose City Press, 1936. 74p.

Largely autobiographical account of mining in the coal fields of
Illinois and West Virginia, 1890-1930.

3

27. CAUDILL, HARRY M.
Night comes to the Cumberlands; a biography of a depressed area. Boston: Atlantic-Little, 1963. 394p.

An account of the development and present status of the "coal counties" of Eastern Kentucky. The author feels that the area has been ruthlessly exploited by the coal industry and its people left to rot. An important and widely-read work.

28. CHAPMAN, MARY L.
The influence of coal in the Big Sandy Valley. Ph.D. University of Kentucky, 1945.

29. CHILDS, C. G.
The coal and iron trade, embracing statistics of Pennsylvania. Philadelphia, 1847. 24p.

"A series of articles published in the Philadelphia Commercial List."

30. CHRISTY, DAVID
Report made at the request of the Raccoon Coal and Iron Company, Cincinnati, 1854. 15p.

31. CIST, JACOB
Account of the mines of anthracite in the region about Wilkes-Barre, Pennsylvania. Wyoming Historical Society. *Proceedings* 10: 98-114 1909.

31a. CLARK, STANLEY
Immigrants in the Choctaw coal industry. *Chronicles of Oklahoma* 33: 440-55 1955/56.

32. CLIFFORD, ALBERT J.
The reorganization of the Philadelphia & Reading Coal & Iron Company. Thesis. University of Pennsylvania. 1952.

33. COAL AND IRON TRADE OF THE OHIO VALLEY
Merchant's Magazine 16: 450-55 1847.

34. COAL AND THE COAL MINES OF PENNSYLVANIA
Harpers 15: 451-69 1857.

35. COAL OF PENNSYLVANIA
American Quarterly Register 1: 97-100 1848.

Largely statistical.

36. COAL PRODUCT OF THE UNITED STATES
De Bow's Review 19: 123-31 1855.

37. COAL REGION OF THE SCHUYLKILL AND WYOMING VALLEY
Merchants' Magazine 14: 539-42 1846.

38. THE COAL TRADE IN PENNSYLVANIA
North American Review 42: 241-56 1836.

39. COATES, HAROLD W.
Cincinnati's early coal trade. *Black Diamond* Ja 15, 1927 23.

40. COBB, WILLIAM H.
The beginning of coal development in Randolph County (West Virginia). Randolph County Historical Society. *Magazine of History and Biography* 5: 50-53 1928.

41. CONLEY, PHIL
Early coal development in the Kanawha Valley. *West Virginia History* 8: 207-15 1947.

42. CONLEY, PHIL
History of the West Virginia coal industry. Charleston: Educational Foundation, 1960. 311p.

43. CORRIGAN, JAMES J.
Early tariff and anthracite region problems. Pennsylvania Dept. of Internal Affairs. *Monthly Bulletin* Ag 1951 3-4, 32.

"Memorial of the freeholders and inhabitants of Carbon and Luzerne Counties, Pennsylvania, engaged in the coal business, demonstrating against the tariff" (1846).

44. CUBBY, EDWIN A.
The transformation of the Tug and Guyandot Valleys; economic development and social change in West Virginia. Ph.D. Syracuse University. 1962.

45. CUMBERLAND (MARYLAND) COAL REGION
Banker's Magazine 4: 394-99 1849/50.

46. DAILY TELEGRAPH. (BLUEFIELD, WEST VIRGINIA)
Pocahontas flat-top coal field. Bluefield, 1896. 78p.

A history and general account of the newly-opened flat-top bituminous coal field.

47. DAUPHIN AND SUSQUEHANNA COAL COMPANY
Report of the stockholders. Philadelphia: T. K. and P. G. Collins, 1848. 16p.

48. DE BOW, JAMES D.
Coal mines of Alabama compared with those of the other states. *De Bow's Review* 10: 73-79 1851.

49. A DEFENCE OF THE LEHIGH COAL AND NAVIGATION COMPANY FROM THE ASSAULTS MADE UPON ITS INTERESTS BY X
Philadelphia: Jesper Harding, 1840. 66p.

50. DESCRIPTION OF THE SYCAMORE COAL MINES
Plan of a mining company now forming in Cincinnati. 2nd ed. Cincinnati, 1850. 12p.

51. EARLY COAL MINING IN DAVIESS COUNTY, INDIANA
Coal 1: 200 1882.

52. EATON, AMOS
Observations on the coal formations in the State of New York. *American Journal of Science* 19: 21-26 1831.

53. EAVENSON, HOWARD N.
Coal through the ages. New York: AIME, 1935. 123p.

54. EAVENSON, HOWARD N.
The early history of the Pittsburgh coal bed. *Western Pennsylvania Historical Magazine* 22: 165-76 1939.

55. EAVENSON, HOWARD NICHOLAS
The first century and a quarter of American coal industry. Pittsburgh: Privately printed, 1942. 701p.

The classic work in the field.

56. EAVENSON, HOWARD N.
Notes on an old West Virginia coal field. *West Virginia History* 5: 83-100 1944.

In the Mason County area.

57. EAVENSON, HOWARD N.
The Pittsburgh coal bed; its early history and development. New York: AIME, 1938. 55p.

Bibliography pp48-55.

58. EAVENSON, HOWARD N.
Some side-lights on early Virginia coal mining. *Virginia Magazine of History and Biography* 50: 199-208 1942.

59. FACTS ILLUSTRATIVE OF THE CHARACTER OF THE AN-
     THRACITE OR LEHIGH COAL FOUND IN THE GREAT MINES
     AT MAUCH CHUNK
     New York: Gray & Bunce, 1825. 18p.

60. FAIRBANKS, W. L. AND W. S. HAMILL
     The coal mining industry of Maryland. Baltimore: Bal-
     timore Association of Commerce, 1932. 271p.

61. FEY, ARTHUR W. (CARL CORLSEN, PSEUD.)
     Buried black treasure; the story of Pennsylvania an-
     thracite. Bethlehem, Pennsylvania, 1954. 112p.

62. FIRMSTONE, WILLIAM
     Sketch of early anthracite furnaces. AIME. *Transac-
     tions* 3: 152-56 1874/75.

     In the Pennsylvania fields.

63. FIRST COAL MINING COMPANY OF THE LEHIGH REGION
     Pennsylvania Magazine of History 39: 170-75 1915.

     Copy of a prospectus dated F 13, 1792 for the Lehigh Coal Mine
     Company.

64. FIRST COAL TOWN MUSEUM
     Stotesbury, West Virginia, 1962. 32p.

     A booklet describing the coal museum at Stotesbury, West Vir-
     ginia. It also contains several articles on the history of coal min-
     ing in the Winding Gulf Field.

65. FISHER, CASSIUS A.
     Geology of the Great Falls coal fields, Montana. Wash-
     ington: GPO, 1909. 85p. (USGS. Bulletin 356).

     Includes much information of historical value.

66. FLEMING, A. B.
     History of the Fairmont (West Virginia) coal region.
     West Virginia Coal Mining Institute. *Proceedings* 1911
     251-68.

67. FLOYD, WILLIE M.
     Thurber, Texas, an abandoned coal field town. *Texas
     Geographical Magazine* 3 No. 2 1939 pp1-21.

68. FREYTAG, R. C.
     The Indiana coal industry's part in World War II. *Indi-
     ana Magazine of History* 41: 265-86 1945.

69. FRICK (H. C.) COKE CO.
     Connellsville coke. Pittsburgh, 189?. 44p.

     "A brief outline of the development of the great Connellsville
     coke region."

70. FRISCH, ISADORE
Twentieth century development of the coal mining industry in eastern Kentucky and its influence upon political behavior of the area. Thesis. University of Kentucky. 1938.

71. FULTON, G.
The bituminous coal mining industry of Pennsylvania. Thesis. Penn State College. 1925.

72. GEORGE'S CREEK COAL AND IRON COMPANY
[Baltimore] 1836. 34p.

Contains acts of incorporation and a report on the land belonging to the company.

73. GIBSON, A. M.
Early mining camps in northeastern Oklahoma. *Chronicles of Oklahoma* 34: 193-202 1956.

74. GINGER, RAY
Company-sponsored welfare plans in the anthracite industry before 1900. Business Historical Society. *Bulletin* 27: 112-20 1953.

75. GLENN, L. C.
The northern Tennessee coal field. Nashville, 1925. 478p. (Tennessee. Division of Geology. Bulletin 33-B).

Although devoted largely to geology, the bulletin includes material on the history and economics of coal mining in the area.

76. GREENE, CHARLES S.
A California coal mine. *Overland Monthly* 31: 518-27 1898.

History and account of mining operations at Tesla.

77. GREGG, ROBERT
Origin and development of the Tennessee Coal, Iron and Railroad Co. New York: Newcomen Society, 1948. 40p.

78. GRIFFITH, WILLIAM
Beginning of anthracite coal trade. *Coal Age* 2: 40-42 1912.

79. GRIFFITH, WILLIAM
The proof that Pennsylvania anthracite coal was first shipped from the Wyoming Valley. Wyoming Historical and Geological Society. *Proceedings* 13: 65-71 1914.

80. GRIFFITH, WILLIAM
Some of the beneficial results of Judge Jesse Fell's experiment with Wyoming coal. Wyoming Historical and Geological Society. *Proceedings* 10: 73-86 1909.

81. GUYANDOTTE LAND COMPANY
Reports and letters relating to the Guyandotte Land Company. London: W. Penney, [1853]. 53p.

In what is now West Virginia.

82. HACK, JOHN T.
Prehistoric coal mining in the Jeddito Valley, Arizona. Cambridge, 1942. 24p. (Papers of the Peabody Museum 35: 2).

83. HAGER, CHARLES J.
Alabama's coal pioneers. *Alabama Engineer* S 1958 3-7.

84. HALBERSTADT, BAIRD
An early coal mine lease in Pottsville. Schuylkill County Historical Society. *Publications* 4: 198-211 1912.

The Greenwood Slope Colliery lease was made in 1839.

85. HARDT, ANTON
A brief history of mining in Tioga County (Pennsylvania). *Mines and Minerals* 26: 484-86 1905/6.

86. HARRINGTON, GEORGE B.
Coal mining in Illinois. New York: Newcomen Society, 1950. 24p.

Deals especially with the Chicago, Wilmington, & Franklin Coal Co.

87. HARVEY, HELEN B.
From frontier to mining town in Logan County, West Virginia. Thesis. University of Kentucky. 1942.

88. HARVEY, KATHERINE A.
The coal miners of Western Maryland; some economic and social developments. Thesis. American University. 1962.

89. HAZARD, ERSKINE
History of the introduction of anthracite coal into Philadelphia . . . and, a letter from Jesse Fell, esq. of Wilkes-Barre, on the discovery and first use of anthracite in the valley of Wyoming. Pennsylvania Historical Society. *Memoirs* 2: 155-64 1827.
9

90. HAZARD, ERSKINE
On the application of anthracite coal to the drying of
tobacco. *Journal of the Franklin Institute* 8: 5-6 1831.

91. HEINRICH, OSWALD J.
The Midlothian Colliery, Virginia. AIME. *Transactions*
1: 346-64 1871/73; 4: 308-16 1875/76.

Account of the largest and one of the oldest mines in the Richmond field.

92. HERMELIN, SAMUEL G.
Report about the mines in the United States of America, 1793. Philadelphia: John Morton Memorial Museum, 1931. 82p.

93. HILDRETH, S. P.
Observations on the bituminous coal deposits of the
valley of the Ohio. *American Journal of Science* 29: 1-
148 1836.

94. HISTORY OF COAL MINING IN IOWA
Annals of Iowa 29: 61-63 1947.

95. HISTORY OF EASTERN GAS AND FUEL ASSOCIATES
Black Diamond Je 30, 1962 28.

96. HUGHES, GEORGE W.
Report of an examination of the coal measures, includ-
ing the iron ore deposits, belonging to the Maryland
Mining Company, in Allegany County; and a survey for
railroad from the mines to the Chesapeake and Ohio
Canal, at Cumberland . . . Together with the memorial
to the Legislature of Maryland, and other documents.
Washington: National Intelligencer Office, 1836. 78p.

97. HURST, MARY B.
Social history of Logan County, West Virginia, 1765-
1923. Thesis. Columbia University. [1924?].

98. ILLINOIS COAL OPERATORS ASSOCIATION
A brief outline of 25 years history and experience, with
special reference to the unusual developments of the
war period and subsequently. [Springfield], 1921. 78p.

99. ILLINOIS. DEPT. OF MINES AND MINERALS
A compilation of the reports of the mining industry of
Illinois from the earliest records to the close of the
year 1930. Springfield, 1931. 177p.

100. IMBODEN, JOHN D.
The coal and iron resources of Virginia; their extent, commercial value and early development. Richmond: Clemmitt & Jones, 1872. 28p.

101. JAMES, THOMAS C.
A brief account of the discovery of anthracite coal on the Lehigh. Pennsylvania Historical Society. *Memoirs* 1: 321-31 1826.

102. JACKSON, CHARLES T.
Report of the coal lands of Egypt, Belmont, Evans, Palmer and Wilcox plantations on Deep River, North Carolina. New York: F. Nesbitt, 1853. 24p.

103. JILLISON, WILLARD R.
The coal industry in Kentucky. Frankfurt: 1924. 164p. (Kentucky Geological Survey. Geologic Reports v20).

Contains much information on mining history, statistics, lists of coal companies etc.

104. JILLSON, WILLARD R.
The coal industry in Kentucky, an historical sketch. Frankfort: State Journal Co., 1922. 87p.

105. JILLSON, WILLARD R.
A history of the coal industry in Kentucky. Kentucky Historical Society. *Register* 20: 21-45 1922.

106. JOHNSON, OLE S.
The industrial store; its history, operations, and economic significance. Atlanta: University of Georgia, Atlanta Division, 1952. 171p.

On "company stores" in the coal fields of the Tri-State area (Ohio, Pennsylvania, West Virginia). Written as a Ph.D. dissertation at the University of Pittsburgh, 1951.

107. JOHNSON, WALTER R.
The coal trade of British America, with researches on the characters and practical values of American and foreign coals. Washington: Taylor & Maury, 1850. 179p.

108. JOHNSON, WALTER R.
Notes on the use of anthracite in the manufacture of iron. Boston, 1841. 156p.

109. JOHNSON, WALTER R.
Report of an examination of the coal and iron ore lands known as the Wilson Survey, lying on the south side of the Great Kanawha River, in the counties of Kanawha and Fayette, State of Virginia. Washington: Buell & Blanchard, 1850. 8p.

110. JOHNSON, WALTER R.
Report on the Bradford coal field (Pennsylvania). *American Journal of Science* 39: 137-49 1840.

111. JOHNSON, WALTER R.
Report on the coal lands of the Deep River Mining and Transportation Company, in Chatham and Moore counties, North Carolina. Albany: Weed, Parsons & Co., 1851. 39p.

112. JONES, ALFRED C.
Remarks on the use of anthracite coal in smith's work. *Journal of the Franklin Institute* 13: 73-74 1834.

113. KEATING, WILLIAM
Considerations upon the art of mining. To which are added reflections on its actual state in Europe and the advantages which would result from an introduction of this art into the United States. Philadelphia: M. Carey, 1821. 87p.

114. KENTUCKY COAL MINING CO.
Act of incorporation, with the report of their engineer, John Pickell, upon their coal property at Henderson, Kentucky, with a general view of the extent, importance and value of the coal fields of Kentucky . . . with some statistics showing the future magnitude of the coal trade of the west. Philadelphia: T. K. & P. G. Collins, 1855. 48p.

115. KENTUCKY. GENERAL ASSEMBLY
Report of the Committee on the coal trade and iron interests of Kentucky. n.p. 184?. 20p. (Reprinted as number 271 in the Kentucky Culture Series).

116. KEYES, CHARLES R.
Aboriginal use of mineral coal and its discovery in the west. *Annals of Iowa* 3rd ser. 10: 431-34 1912.

117. KULP, GEORGE B.
Coal; its antiquity, discovery and early development in the Wyoming Valley. Wilkes-Barre, 1892. 32p. (Appears also in his "Historical Essays" pp57-90).

118. THE LACKAWANNA AND WYOMING COAL REGION
Merchants Magazine 19: 290-94 1848.

119. LANSING, R. R.
Exposition concerning the mineral coal of Michigan. Detroit: E. A. Wales, 1854. 20p.

Author discusses the location, quality, demand, transportation etc. of Michigan coal.

120. LEHIGH COAL AND NAVIGATION CO.
Facts illustrative of the character of the anthracite or Lehigh coal, found in the great mines at Mauch Chunk, in possession of the Lehigh Coal and Navigation Company . . . Boston, 1825. 22p.

121. LEHIGH COAL AND NAVIGATION COMPANY
A history of the Lehigh Coal and Navigation Company. Philadelphia: W. S. Young, 1840. 68p.

122. LEHIGH NAVIGATION COAL COMPANY
The story of the old company. Landford, Pennsylvania, 1941. 58p.

123. LEIGHTON, GEORGE R.
Shenandoah, Pennsylvania; the story of an anthracite town. *Harpers* 176: 131-47 1937.

124. LESLEY, J. P.
Manual of coal and its topography. Philadelphia: Lippincott, 1856. 224p.

"Facts in the geology of the Appalachian Region of the United States of North America."

125. LOGAN COAL OPERATORS ASSOCIATION
The story of Logan County, West Virginia coal. Logan, 1921. unpaged.

126. LOVE, GEORGE H.
An exciting century in coal (1864-1964). New York: Newcomen Society, 1955. 24p.

Account of the Consolidation Coal Company.

127. LYCOMING COAL COMPANY
A brief description of the property belonging to the Lycoming Coal Company, with some general remarks on the subject of the coal and iron business. Poughkeepsie: P. Potter, 1828. 32p.

128. MCAULIFFE, EUGENE
Early coal mining in the West—beginning with 1868. New York: Newcomen Society, 1948. 32p.

13

129. MCAULIFFE, EUGENE
Romance and tragedy of coal. Omaha, Nebraska: Colonial Press, 1931. 97p.

130. MCCAULEY, RAY L.
The natural and cultural factors that have affected coal production in Westmoreland County (Pennsylvania) from 1800 to 1950. Thesis. University of Pittsburgh. 1950.

131. MCCLANE, WILLIAM
Letter on the supply of bituminous coal from North Carolina. New York: George F. Nesbitt, 1854. 12p.

132. MCCORMICK, ALLEN
Development of the coal industry of Grundy County, Tennessee. Thesis. George Peabody. 1934.

132a. MCDONALD, RITA AND M. G. BURLINGAME
Montana's first commercial coal mine. *Pacific Northwest Quarterly* 47: 23-28 1956.

133. MAGUIRE, JOHN
Early Pennsylvania coal mine legislation. Schuylkill County Historical Society. *Publication* 4: 337-40 1914.

134. MARYLAND UNIVERSITY. BUREAU OF BUSINESS AND ECONOMIC RESEARCH
Coal in the Maryland economy, 1736-1965. 20p. (*Its* Studies in Business and Economics 7: 3).

135. MELDER, F. E.
History of the discoveries and physical development of the coal industry in the state of Washington. *Pacific Northwest Quarterly* 29: 151-65 1938.

136. MIESSE, CHARLES
Points on coal and the coal business. Myerstown, Pennsylvania, Feese & Uhrich, 1887. 464p.
Includes "history of the anthracite coal field and its surroundings."

137. MILLER, GEORGE L.
Early dreams of coal in Nebraska. Nebraska State Historical Society. *Proceedings* 15: 189-92 1907.

138. MINER, WILLIAM P.
"Cist versus Fell," or the domestic use of anthracite coal. Wyoming Historical Society. *Proceedings* 7: 31-42 1902.

139. MORGAN, JOHN D.
The domestic mining industry of the United States in World War II. Washington: National Resources Conference Board, 1949. 500p. (Pennsylvania State College. Mineral Industries Experiment Station. Bulletin 51).

139a. MORTON, ELEANOR
Josiah White, prince of pioneers. New York: Stephen Daye, 1946. 300p.

White was an important figure in the development of the anthracite fields of Pennsylvania.

140. MORY, SAMUEL A.
History of coal mining in Laurel County, Kentucky, 1750 to 1944. London, Kentucky: Sentinel-Echo, 1944. 16p.

141. MOSS, ALEX
Highlights in the coal trade during the war period. *Coal Age* 15: 227-32 1919.

142. MOURAT, MARY P.
A history of coal mining in West Virginia to 1933. Thesis. University of Pennsylvania. 1947.

143. NEW YORK COAL COMPANY
Plan for supplying the City of New York with fuel. New York: T. & J. Swords, 1814. 16p.

144. NICOLLS, WILLIAM J.
Above ground and below in the George's Creek coal region. Baltimore: Consolidation Coal Company, 1898. 32p.

History and general account of coal mining in the area.

145. NICOLLS, WILLIAM J.
The story of American coals. Philadelphia: Lippencott, 1897. 405p.

146. THE NORTH AMERICAN (PHILADELPHIA)
Pennsylvania coal and its carriers. Philadelphia: Crissy & Markley, 1852. 35p.

147. NOTICE OF COAL MINES IN ILLINOIS
Journal of the Franklin Institute ns 17: 375 1836.

Short account of the Mount Carbon coal mines near Brownsville.

148. ON COAL AS A FUEL IN AMERICA
Literary Magazine 2: 422-24 1804.

"Would it not be in the interest of the United States to establish a regular coal trade from Virginia to the northern states."

149. PAPANIKOLAS, HELEN Z.
The Greeks of Carbon County. *Utah Historical Quarterly* 22: 143-64 1954.

A large number of Greek immigrants were attracted to the newly-opened coal mining region in Carbon County, Utah.

150. PARKER, W. J.
The great coal schooners of New England, 1870-1909. Mystic, Conn., 1948. 135p. (Publication of the Marine Historical Association 2: 6).

151. PATTERSON, JOSEPH F.
Reminiscences of John Maguire after fifty years of mining. Schuylkill County Historical Society. *Publication* 4: 305-36 1914.

Concerns mining operations in the anthracite coal fields of Schuylkill County, Pennsylvania.

152. PATTERSON, LOUISE H.
Discovery of the great anthracite regions of the middle west. *Journal of American History* 5: 115-20 1911.

Jesse Fell and his discovery of anthracite coal in the Wyoming Valley and its use for heating homes.

153. PEACH ORCHARD COAL COMPANY
Peach Orchard coal lands. Cincinnati, 1853?, 11p.

"The works and lands of the Company are situated in Lawrence county, Ky., on the Big Sandy river . . . " Includes list of stockholders as of November, 1853.

154. PEARCE, ALBERT
The growth and development of the Kentucky coal industry. Thesis. University of Kentucky. 1930.

155. PENNSYLVANIA COAL REGION
Harper 27: 455-67 1863.

Account of a trip through the area.

156. PENNSYLVANIA. DEPARTMENT OF MINES AND MINERAL INDUSTRIES
History of Pennsylvania bituminous coal. 3rd edition. Harrisburg, 1962. 61p.

An excellent source for statistical information; arranged by county.

157. PENNSYLVANIA. GENERAL ASSEMBLY
Acts of the General Assembly of Pennsylvania concerning the Lehigh Coal and Navigation Company; together with the by-laws, etc. Philadelphia: James Kay, 1837. 79p.

158. PENNSYLVANIA. GENERAL ASSEMBLY. SENATE. COMMITTEE ON COAL TRADE
Report of the committee of the State of Pennsylvania, upon the subject of the coal trade. Harrisburg: Henry Welsh, 1834. 126p.

159. PHILLIPPS, G. JENKINS
Systems of mining coal and metalliferous veins fully explained . . . productive, consumption and incidental statistics of coal . . . Philadelphia, 1858. 86p.

160. PIERCE, JAMES
Anthracite region of Pennsylvania. [Hazard's] *Register of Pennsylvania* 1: 310-16 1828.

161. PIERCE, JAMES
In the anthracite region of Pennsylvania. *American Journal of Science* 12: 54-74 1827.

162. POCAHONTAS OPERATORS ASSOCIATION
The story of Pocahontas, 1863-1915; a good coal. Roanoke, 1915. 32p.

163. POMEROY, SAMUEL W.
Remarks on the coal region between Cumberland and Pittsburgh. *American Journal of Science* 21: 342-47 1832.

164. PROPOSED PLAN FOR SMELTING IRON ORE WITH ANTHRACITE COAL
Journal of the Franklin Institute 8: 231-32 1831.

165. PRYDE, GEORGE B.
The Union Pacific Coal Company, 1868-1952. *Annals of Wyoming* 25: 190-205 1953.

166. RANDOLPH, B. S.
History of the Maryland coal region. *Maryland Geological Survey* 5: 529-618 1905.

Includes short accounts of the major coal mining companies operating in the area.

167. RANDOLPH, L. S.
Virginia anthracite coal. *Cassier's Magazine* 27: 328-36 1904/5.

History and general description of the area.

168. RASHLEIGH, ALICE V.
The story of Carbondale and the "black stone." Pennsylvania. Dept. of Internal Affairs. *Monthly Bulletin* N 1951 11-18.

169. RICH, PAUL
Early industries in Perry County, Illinois. Illinois Historical Society. *Journal* 26: 349-53 1934.

Coal mining was the principal industry.

170. RICHARDS, W. B.
The story of coal. *Coal Age* 15: 441-45 1919.

Devoted largely to the early history of coal mining in Pennsylvania.

171. RICHARDSON, RICHARD
Memoir of Joseph White; showing his connection with the introduction and use of anthracite coal and iron . . . Philadelphia: Lippincott, 1873. 135p.

172. RICHMOND, WILLIAM H.
Recollections of ninety-five years in Connecticut and the anthracite regions of Pennsylvania. *Journal of American History* 13: 257-72 1919.

The above is part 2 of the series and is confined to Richmond's experiences in the coal region.

173. RICKARD, THOMAS A.
A history of American mining. New York: McGraw-Hill, 1932. 419p.

174. RIDGWAY, THOMAS S.
Memorial of Prof. Ridgway in relation to the coal field of Rhode Island. Providence, 1870. 12p.

175. ROBBINS, W. B.
Cheap fuel. Louisville, 1855. 16p.

A discussion of the need for "effective organization" in procuring cheap coal from Mason County, Virginia. The newly-chartered Kentucky Fuel Company was advanced as the solution.

176. ROBERTS, W. F.
Abstract of a report on the coal and iron estate of the Little Schuylkill Navigation, Railroad and Coal Company. Philadelphia: John C. Clark, 1846. 21p.

"Great as the coal trade now seems . . . it can scarcely yet be considered as past its infancy."

177. ROBERTS, W. F.
Reports upon the West Hazleton and Cattawissa Falls, and the East Mahanoy coal and iron estates. Philadelphia: John C. Clark. 1846. 22p.

178. ROCKVILLE COAL MINING COMPANY (JEFFERSON COUNTY, OHIO)
Articles of association, constitution and by-laws, articles of agreement. Steubenville, Ohio, 1853. 12p.

179. ROTHERT, OTTO A.
Coal mining and its bearing on local history. Kentucky Historical Society. *Register* 12: 33-36 1914.

180. ROTHERT, OTTO A.
Coal mining history of Muhlenberg County, Kentucky. *Coal Age* 5: 10-11 1914.

181. ROY, ANDREW
The coal mines. Cleveland: Robinson, Savage & Co., 1876. 367p.

A general discussion of the history, technology and current state of the industry.

182. ROY, ANDREW
Coal mining in Ohio. *Ohio Mining Journal* 2: 3-15 1883/84.

183. ROY, ANDREW
A history of the coal miners of the U. S., from the development of the mines to the close of the anthracite strike of 1902, 3rd ed., rev. and enl. Columbus, Ohio: Trouger Printing Co., 1907. 465p. (1903 ed. has 454 p.)

184. ROY, ANDREW
The Jackson shaft coal and the Wellston coal of Jackson County (Ohio). *Ohio Mining Journal* 2: 162-75 1883/84.

Much historical information.

185. ROY, ANDREW
The Ohio coal field. *Ohio Mining Journal* 2: 121-29 1883/84.

A history of the field's development.

186. RUFFIN, EDMUND
Visit to Graham's coal pits. *Farmers Register* 5: 315-19
1837.

In the Virginia coal fields.

187. RUTLAND, ROBERT
The mining camps of Iowa: faded sources of Hawkeye
history. *Iowa Journal of History* 54: 35-42 1956.

188. RUTLEDGE, J. J.
Recollections on early mining in Illinois. Illinois Mining Institute. *Proceedings* 52: 76-84 1944.

189. SALINE COAL AND MANUFACTURING CO.
Report of the president and directors . . . Cincinnati: T.
Wrightson, 1855. 91p.

190. SHAMOKIN COAL AND IRON COMPANY
Brief sketch of the peculiar advantages of the Shamo-
kin Coal and Iron Company. Philadelphia: Brown,
Bicking & Guilbert 1841. 33p.

191. SHURICK, ADAM
The coal industry. Boston: Little, Brown, 1924. 383p.

History, mining methods, distribution, economic and sociological
conditions.

192. SILLIMAN, BENJAMIN
Anthracite coal of Rhode Island. *American Journal of
Science* 11: 78-100 1826.

193. SILLIMAN, BENJAMIN
Notes on a journey from New Haven, Connecticut, to
Mauch Chunk and other anthracite regions of Pennsyl-
vania. *American Journal of Science* 19: 1-21 1831.

194. SLAB FORK COAL COMPANY
Golden Anniversary celebration. Beckley, West Virginia, 1957. 24p.

Slab Fork Coal Co. was the first major producer in the Winding
Gulf smokeless coal field in West Virginia. This booklet contains
much historical information.

195. SMITH, EUGENE
Historical account of coal mining operations in Alabama since 1853. *In* Alabama Geological Survey. Progress Report for 1875, pp. 28-44.

196. SMITH, HAMILTON
Cannelton, Perry County, Ind., at the intersection of the eastern margin of the Illinois coal basin, by the Ohio River; its natural advantages as a site for manufacturing. Louisville: Journal Office, 1850. 108p.

197. SMITH, SAMUEL R.
The black trail of anthracite. Kingston, Pa., 1907. 114p.

198. SMURTHWAITE, WILLIAM
Sketch of the development of the Steubenville shaft mines. *Ohio Mining Journal* 2: 100-5 1883/84.

199. STODDARD, PAUL W.
The knowledge of coal and iron in Ohio before 1835. *Ohio Archaeol. & Historical Quarterly* 38: 219-30 1929.

200. STRONG, HENRY K.
Report to the Legislature of Pennsylvania containing a description of the Swatara mining district. Harrisburg: Boas & Coplan, 1839. 61p.

201. STURGEON, MYRON T.
History of Ohio's northernmost coal mine. *Ohio Journal of Science* 44: 255-64 1944.

In Geauga County.

202. SWANK, JAMES M.
History of the manufacture of iron in all ages . . . Also a short history of early coal mining in the United States. Philadelphia: American Iron & Steel Association 2nd ed. 1892. 554p.

203. SWANK, JAMES M.
Introduction to the history of iron making and coal mining in Pennsylvania. Philadelphia, 1878. 125p.

204. SWISHER, JACOB A.
The rise and fall of Buxton. *Palimpsest* 26: 179-92 1946.

Brief account of the famous coal mining community in Iowa.

205. SYCAMORE COAL MINES
Description of the Sycamore Coal Mines, plan of a mining company now forming in Cincinnati. 2nd ed. Cincinnati, 1850. 12p.

21

206. TAMS, W. P. JR.
The smokeless coal fields of West Virginia; a brief history. Morgantown; West Virginia University Library, 1963. 106p.

Tams was one of the leading operators in the southern West Virginia coal fields. His book is by far the best single source of information for this area.

207. TANKERSLEY, ALLEN P.
Zachariah Herndon Gordon (1796-1886). *Georgia Historical Quarterly* 36: 231-49 1952.

Gordon was, among other things, an operator of coal mines in Georgia and Alabama.

208. TAYLOR, GEORGE
Effect of incorporated coal companies upon the anthracite coal trade of Pennsylvania. Pottsville: Bannan, 1833. 34p.

209. TAYLOR, RICHARD C.
Statistics of coal. Philadelphia: J. W. Moore, 1848. 754p.

"Production, consumption and commercial distribution in all parts of the world; together with their prices, tariffs, duties and international regulations."

210. TAYLOR, RICHARD C.
Two reports on the coal lands, mines and improvements of the Dauphin and Susquehanna Coal Company and of the geological examinations, present condition and prospects of the Stoney Creek Coal Estate. Philadelphia, E. G. Dorsey, 1840. 74p.

211. THARP, MARILYN
Story of coal at Newcastle. *Pacific Northwest Quarterly* 48: 120-26 1957.

Brief history of the early coal industry in the Seattle, Washington area.

212. THOMAS, SAMUEL
Reminiscences of the early anthracite-iron industry. AIME. *Transactions* 29: 901-28 1899.

213. THROOP, BENJAMIN
A half century in Scranton, Pennsylvania, 1895. 335p.

Throop, a physician, came to Scranton in 1840. He gives much on the development of the mining industry.

214. THURMOND, WALTER R.
The Logan Coal Field of West Virginia; a brief history.
Morgantown: West Virginia University Library, 1964.
110p.

The author was a leading coal operator in the Logan Field and was for many years Secretary of the Southern Coal Producers Association.

215. TIPTON, J. C.
Cumberland coal fields and its creators. Middlesboro,
Kentucky. Pinnacle Printery, 1905. 112p.

216. TOWER, JAMES A.
The industrial development of the Birmingham region.
Birmingham, Alabama: Birmingham Southern College,
1953 32p.

Coal and iron.

217. TRACHTENBERG, ALEXANDER
The history of legislation for the protection of coal miners in Pennsylvania, 1824-1915. New York: International Publishers, 1942. 239p.

218. TUOMEY, M.
Notice of the Appomattox coal pits. *Farmers Register*
10: 449-50 1842.

Virginia coal fields.

219. UNION PACIFIC COAL COMPANY
History of the Union Pacific coal mines, 1868 to 1940.
Omaha: Colonial Press. 1940. 265p.

220. UNION POTOMAC COMPANY
Charters . . . with a letter addressed to Duff Green, by
the Hon. Charles Kinsey, on the subject of the coal and
iron mines in the counties of Hampshire, Virginia and
Alleghany, Maryland. Washington: Duff Green, 1836.
43p.

221. U. S. CONGRESS. HOUSE
Coal trade—Richmond. Washington, 1837. 8p. (24th
Cong., 2nd Sess. House. Doc. 93).

Petition of Virginia coal operators against a reduction of duties on coal.

222. U. S. NATIONAL ARCHIVES
Preliminary inventory of the records of the Solid Fuels
Administration for War. (Record Group 245). Washington, 1951. 39p. (*Its* Publication No. 52-6. Preliminary Inventories No. 34).

223. THE VANISHING IOWA COAL MINE
Annals of Iowa 30: 142-43 1949.

224. VERHOEFF, MARY
The Kentucky mountains, transportation and commerce, 1750-1911; a study in the economic history of a coal field. Louisville: Filson Club, 1911. 208p. (Filson Club Publication 26).

225. VISIT TO THE LACKAWANNA MINES
Knickerbocker 15: 102-6 1840.

226. WAGNER, E. C.
The Girard coal lands: a history describing the purchase, attempted development and later successful working of the coal property, which was bequeathed to the City of Philadelphia by Stephen Girard. *Colliery Engineer*. In installments through volumes 8 and 9 (1887-1889).

227. WALKER, ELMORE
The Pennsylvania coal fields and their connection with and relation to Buffalo. Buffalo: Matthews & Warren, 1868. 64p.

228. WALTER, R. A.
Historical sketch of the George's Creek (Maryland) coal region. *Coal Age* 5: 995-1000 1914.

229. WARDLEY, C. S.
The early development of the H. C. Frick Coke Company. *Western Pennsylvania Historical Magazine* 32: 79-86 1949.

Covers the period from approximately 1882 to 1901.

230. WEST VIRGINIA COAL MINING COMPANY, INC.
Charter. Washington: J. T. Towers, 1848. 23p.

231. WHITE, ELIZABETH
Development of the bituminous coal mining industry in Logan County, West Virginia. Thesis. Marshall College. 1956.

232. WHITE, JOSIAH
Josiah White's history, given by himself. [Philadelphia, 1909]. 75p.

"The journal of Josiah White is published, as giving in detail the circumstances which led to the introduction of canal navigation and the use of anthracite coal in Pennsylvania."

233. WHITTLESEY, CHARLES
Discovery of coal in Ohio and early mine work. *Ohio Mining Journal* 2: 15-17 1883/84.

234. WHITTLESEY, CHARLES
History of the coal and iron business from Cleveland as it is, 1872. [Cleveland, 1872]. 8p.

235. WOLKINS, GEORGE G.
The coal panic of 1917-1918. Massachusetts Historical Society. *Proceedings* 65: 582-92 1932/36.

236. WOODWORTH, JAY B.
The history of conditions of mining in the Richmond coal basin, Virginia. AIME. *Transaction* 31: 477-84 1901.

237. WOOLDRIDGE, A. S.
Geological and statistical notice of the coal mines in the vicinity of Virginia. *American Journal of Science* 43: 1-13 1842.

Largely historical in nature, the title to the contrary.

238. YEARLEY, C. K.
Enterprise and anthracite: economics and democracy in Schuylkill County, 1820-1875. Baltimore: Johns Hopkins Press, 1961. 254p. (Johns Hopkins University Studies in Historical and Political Science 79: 1).

Labor Relations

(Labor relations in general, including strikes, wages, hours, etc.)

A vast amount of material has appeared on labor relations in the coal industry. Much of it centered about the great strikes and both reflected and contributed to the passions of the day. From the point of view of sheer bulk, the early 1930's were probably the peak years. During that period the miners, especially those in and around Harlan County, Kentucky, were "adopted" by many liberal groups. Indeed, the plight of the miners became one of the favorite causes of the American Left. There were protest meetings, student marches and polemics without number. Much of this interest waned as suddenly as it had appeared, and the miners were left in substantially the same position as before. As might be imagined, the bulk of the writing produced during this period was polemical, topical or both. Those interested in day-by-day accounts will find much material in the *New York Times Index* and the *Readers Guide to Periodical Literature*.

239. ALABAMA COAL COMMISSION
Message of Thomas E. Kilby, governor . . . with report of Commission to Inquire into the Differences between Operators and Miners. Montgomery: Brown Printing Co., 1920. 13p. (Legislative Doc. #5).

Supplemental report. Montgomery: Brown Printing Co., 1920. 12p. (Legislative Doc. #7).

240. ALABAMA COAL OPERATORS ASSOCIATION
Joint scale convention of the Alabama Coal Operators Association and the United Mine Workers of America . . . and the proceedings of the Board of Arbitration. Birmingham: Roberts & Son, 1903. 947p.

241. ALBRIGHT, CHARLES
The great Mollie Maguire trials in Carbon and Schuylkill Counties, Pennsylvania . . . 1876. Pottsville, Pennsylvania: Chronicle, 1876. 94p.

242. ALLEN, DANIEL
Mine war in Pennsylvania. *Nation* 137: 176-77 1933.

Highly partisan account of the strike in the bituminous coal fields of southwestern Pennsylvania.

243. ALLEN, HARBOR
Coal, steel and "sedition." *Nation* 124: 205-6 1927.

244. ALLEN, HENRY J.
How Kansas broke a strike and would solve the labor problem. *Current Opinion* 68:472-78 1920.

As the result of a coal strike, Kansas established a Court of Industrial Relations to compel settlement of labor disputes.

245. AMERICAN CIVIL LIBERTIES UNION
The Kentucky miners' struggle. New York, 1932. 23p.

245a. AMERICAN CIVIL LIBERTIES UNION.
War on the Colorado miners. New York, 1928. 11p.

246. AMMONS, ELIAS M.
Colorado strike. *North American Review* 200: 35-44 1914.

Author was Governor of Colorado.

247. ANDERSON, GEORGE J.
Labor policy in the bituminous coal industry. New York, 1922. 41p.

248. ANDERSON, L. C.
Mine labor conditions in West Virginia. *Outlook* 82: 861-62 1906.

249. ANGLE, PAUL M.
Bloody Williamson; a chapter in American lawlessness. New York: Knopf, 1952. 300p.

Account of the so-called Herrin Massacre (Sept. 1922) and related violence in the coal fields of southern Illinois.

250. ANSON, CHARLES F.
A history of the labor movement in West Virginia. Thesis. University of North Carolina. 1940.

251. ANTHRACITE BUREAU OF INFORMATION
The anthracite strike of 1922; a chronological statement of the communications and negotiations between the hard coal operators and the United Mine Workers of America. Philadelphia, n.d. 62p.

252. ANTHRACITE BUREAU OF INFORMATION
The anthracite strike of 1925-1926 . . . Philadelphia, 1926. 54p.

27

253. ANTHRACITE COAL CRISIS AND CONDITIONS IN WEST VIR-
GINIA
Outlook 82: 575-78 1906.

254. THE ANTHRACITE MINERS' CONVENTION
Coal Age 1: 1076-77 1911/12.

Report of a tri-district convention of anthracite miners.

255. ANTHRACITE OPERATORS
Before the U. S. Anthracite Coal Commission. Exhibits
of the anthracite operators in reply to exhibits presented by the anthracite mine workers. Scranton, 1920.
Various paging.

256. ANTHRACITE STRIKE: ITS SOCIAL AND RELIGIOUS EF-
FECTS
Outlook 72: 585-89 1902.

257. ANTHRACITE PEACE
Nation 141: 554 1935.

The "peace" is between the UMW and the United Anthracite
Miners of Pennsylvania.

258. ARCHBALD, HUGH
The four hour day in coal; a study of the relation between the engineering of the organization of work and
the discontent among the workers in the coal mines.
New York: H. W. Wilson, 1922. 148p.

259. ARTICLES OF AGREEMENT BETWEEN THE KANAWHA OP-
ERATORS AND THE UMWA
Coal and Coke My 1, 1904 10-13; N 1, 1904 8-9.

Includes wages, hours, working conditions, etc.

260. ASHLEY, WILLIAM J.
The adjustment of wages; a study in the coal and iron
industries of Great Britain and America. London and
New York: Longmans, 1903. 362p.

261. ASSOCIATION FOR THE WELFARE OF NEGROES IN ALA-
BAMA
Appeal to the Colored Mine Workers of Alabama. Ens-
ley, 1920?. 4p.

Negro miners are urged to support the UMWA strike.

262. AURAND, AMMON M.
Historical account of the Mollie Maguires and James "McKenna" McParlan, detective extraordinary; origin, depreciations and decay of a terrorist secret organization in the Pennsylvania coal fields during and following the Civil War. Harrisburg: Priv. print., 1940. 32p.

263. BAKER, RAY S.
The right to work: the story of the non-striking miners. *McClures* 20: 323-36 1902/3.

The Anthracite Strike.

264. BALTIMORE SUN (NEWSPAPER)
Mingo County West Virginia coal strike. Baltimore, 1921. 18p.

Reprint of a series of articles appearing in the Baltimore Sun, January 23-25, 1921.

265. BANCROFT, THOMAS B.
Strikes in the Ohio coal fields. *Ohio Mining Journal* 3: 3 1885 27-40.

Includes copies of agreements and contracts between miners and operators.

266. BANNARD, WILLIAM N.
Weary land, a study of the early labor relations in the anthracite coal fields. n.p., 194-?. 166p. proc.

267. BARATZ, MORTON S.
The union and the coal industry. New Haven: Yale University Press, 1955. 170p. (Yale Studies in Economics 4).

268. BARB, JOHN MILLIKEN
Strikes in the southern West Virginia coal fields, 1912-1922. Thesis. West Virginia University. 1949.

269. BARTHOLOMEW, HARVEY E.
Anarchy in Colorado: who is to blame. Denver: Bartholomew Publishing Company, 1905. 136p.

270. BAUER, FREDERICK L.
Earning in bituminous coal mines, November 1962. *MLR* 86: 1153-56 1963.

271. BAYARD, CHARLES J.
The 1927-1928 Colorado coal strike. *Pacific Historical Review* 32: 235-50 1963.

272. BEAME, EDMOND M.
Jacksonville agreement: quest for stability in coal. *Industrial and Labor Relations Review* 8: 195-203 1955.

The Jacksonville Agreement, signed F 19, 1924, was a three-year contract between the UMW and Operators of the Central Competitive Field.

273. BEMIS, EDWARD W.
Mine labor in the Hocking Valley. Saratoga, New York: American Economic Association, 1888. 15p. (American Economic Association. *Publication* 1888-89. 3: 3 pp27-42).

274. BERLE, A. A.
The Colorado mine war. *Bibliotheca Sacra* 1914: 548-72.

275. BERNSTEIN, IRVING AND HUGH G. LOVELL
Are coal strikes national emergencies? *Industrial & Labor Relations Review* 6: 352-67 1953.

Reviews legal decisions concerning such strikes, 1937-50.

276. BEZANSON, ANNE
Earnings of coal miners. *Ann. Amer. Acad.* 111: 1-11 1924.

277. BIMBA, ANTHONY
The Molly Maguires. New York: International Publishers, 1932. 144p.

Deals with the troubles in the anthracite coal regions of Pennsylvania, circa 1875.

278. BITTNER, VAN A.
Wages in bituminous coal mines as viewed by the miners. *Ann. Amer. Acad.* 111: 39-42 1924.

279. BITUMINOUS COAL STOPPAGE, 1939
MLR 49: 691-703 1939.

Includes text of Appalachian Agreement.

280. BITUMINOUS OPERATORS' SPECIAL COMMITTEE
Letter and brief on the campaign of aggression of the United Mine Workers of America in 1922, in enforcing the domination of their monopoly in the State of Ohio. Washington, 1923. 18p.

281. BITUMINOUS OPERATORS' SPECIAL COMMITTEE
Letter and statement to the United States Coal Commission on Herrin. n.p., [1923]. 50p.

282. BITUMINOUS OPERATORS' SPECIAL COMMITTEE
Maryland; the campaign of violence conducted by the UMWA against the open shop mines in the Georges Creek and Upper Potomac fields. n.p., 1923. 50p.

283. BITUMINOUS OPERATORS' SPECIAL COMMITTEE
United Mine Workers in West Virginia; submitted to the United States Coal Commission, Aug. 1923. n.p., 1923. 121p.

Account of violations of law and order on the part of the UMW and its supporters.

284. THE "BLACK DIAMOND" VS. DEMAGOGISM
Black Diamond 5: 210, 251-52 1889/90.

Attack on labor leaders who hold miners in "demagogic thraldom."

285. BLANKENHORN, HEBER
The strike for union; a study of the non-union question in coal and the problems of the democratic movement. New York: H. W. Wilson, 1923 (1924). 259p.

"Based on the record of the Somerset (Pennsylvania) strike, 1922-23."

286. BLIZZARD, WILLIAM C.
There's never peace in West Virginia's hills. *Nation* 177: 549-49 1953.

Description of conditions at Widen, West Virginia.

287. BLOCH, LOUIS
The coal miners' insecurity. New York: Russell Sage Foundation, 1922. 50p.

Stresses irregularity of employment in the coal industry.

288. BLOCH, LOUIS
Labor agreements in coal mines; a case study of agreements between miners' and operators' organizations in the bituminous coal mines of Illinois. New York: Russell Sage Foundation, 1931. 513p.

289. BLUE EAGLE AND THE MINERS
New Republic 77: 34-5 1933.

NRA officials said to favor J. L. Lewis in his struggle with the Progressive Miners of America in Illinois.

290. BOARD OF REFERENCE REPORTS ON WAGE DISPUTE IN ANTHRACITE INDUSTRY
MLR 36: 815-18 1933.

291. BOUGHTON, EDWARD J.
Coal strike and rebellion in Colorado. Chicago: National Founders' Association, 1915. 27p.

292. BOWDEN, WITT
The changing status of bituminous coal miners, 1937-1946. Washington: GPO, 1946. 10p. (Bureau of Labor Statistics. Bulletin 882).

Appeared also in *MLR* 63: 165-76 1946.

293. BOWDEN, WITT
Two alternatives in the settlement of the Colorado coal strike. *Survey* 31: 320-22 1913.

294. BRADLEY, JOSEPH G.
The coal operator and the coal miner—a partnership. n.p., West Virginia Mining Institute, 1922. 16p.

294a. BROEHL, WAYNE G.
The Molly Maguires. Cambridge: Harvard University Press, 1964. 409p.

295. BROOKS, JOHN G.
An impression of the anthracite coal troubles. *Yale Review* 6: 306-11 1897/98.

Strike of 1897.

296. BROOKS, JOHN G.
The public and the anthracite coal strike. *Economic Journal* 13: 364-72 1903.

297. BROPHY, JOHN
A miner's life. Madison: University of Wisconsin Press, 1964. 320p.

Autobiography of one of the more important leaders in the American labor movement.

297a. BROPHY, JOHN
Report of John Brophy, president, to the membership of District 2, UMWA. March, 1927. n.p., 1927. 20p.

298. BROWN, P. AND A. KOUZIAN
Wage structure in bituminous coal mining, fall of 1945. *MLR* 62: 550-59 1946.

299. BRUERE, ROBERT W.
Mind of the anthracite miners. *Survey* 55: 16-19 1925.

300. BUCHANAN, JOHN A.
A survey of labor requirements in northern West Virginia coal mines in 1957. Thesis. West Virginia University. 1960.

301. CAPTIVE COAL MINE STRIKE AND SETTLEMENT
MLR 54: 94-7 1942.

302. CARTER, CHARLES F.
Murder to maintain coal monopoly. *Current History* 15: 597-603 1922.

" . . . twenty-three years of arson, assault and assassination in West Virginia."

303. CARTER, CHARLES F.
The West Virginia coal insurrection. *North American Review* 198: 457-69 1913.

304. CASHMAN, JOSEPH T.
America asleep; the menace of radicalism. New York: National Security league, 1923. 15p.

Attack on the UMWA.

305. [CAUSES AND SETTLEMENT OF COAL STRIKE]
Review of Reviews 26: 515-527 1902.

306. CENTRAL PENNSYLVANIA COAL PRODUCERS' ASSOCIATION
Bituminous coal mining lectures. Altoona, Pennsylvania, 1949. 148p.

Contains sections on labor relations and economics.

307. CHAMBERLAIN, J. G.
Are the avenues to a higher social, industrial and political position increasing or diminishing with the miner. *Ohio Mining Journal* 5: 2 1887 68-73.

308. CHAMBERLAIN, J. G.
Social possibilities of the miner. *Ohio Mining Journal* 2: 73-79 1883/84.

Operators should help miners own their own homes and become "solid" citizens.

309. CHAMBERLAIN, NEIL W. AND JANE M. SCHILLING
The impact of strikes; their social and economic costs. New York: Harper, 1954. 257p.

Chapters 4-6 deal with coal strikes, 1939-1950.

33

310. THE CHANGING STATUS OF BITUMINOUS COAL MINERS 1937-46
Washington: GPO, 1946. 10p. (Bureau of Labor Statistics. Bulletin 882).

311. CHAPLIN, HERMAN W.
The coal mines and the public. Boston, New York: J. B. Millet, 1902. 63p.

"A popular statement of the legal aspects of the coal problem, and of the rights of consumers." Deals with the anthracite strike of 1902.

312. CHILDS, MARQUIS W.
Illinois mine battle. *New Republic* 72: 121-23 1932.

313. CHRISTENSON, CARROLL L.
The impact of labor disputes upon coal consumption. *American Economic Review* 45: 79-112 1955.

314. CHRISTENSON, CARROLL L.
The theory of the offset factor: the impact of labor disputes upon coal production. *American Economic Review* 43: 513-47 1953.

315. CLARK, J. M.
Coal production and the strike settlement. *Journal of Political Economy* 28: 80-84 1920.

316. CLAYTON, E. E.
An economic analysis of labor conditions in the Indiana coal industry in 1932. Thesis. Indiana University. 1941.

317. COAL AND KENTUCKY
Commonweal 30: 129-30 1939.

A collection of editorial opinion on the coal strike of 1939.

318. COAL MINERS' COMBINATION
Scientific American 20: 377 1869.

Editorial against the "excessive" demands of the miners.

319. COLE, E. L.
Anthracite coal strike situation. *Coal Age* 1: 601-3 1911/12.

320. COLEMAN, JAMES W.
Labor disturbances in Pennsylvania, 1850-1880. Ph.D. Catholic University. 1936.

A study of the labor disturbances in the Pennsylvania coal regions led by the Molly Maguires. (Published without thesis notes as: The Molly Maguire riots).

321. COLEMAN, JAMES W.
The Molly Maguire riots; industrial conflict in the Pennsylvania coal region. Richmond: Garrett & Massie, 1936. 189p.

322. COLEMAN, MCALISTER
Men and coal. New York: Farrar & Rinehart, 1943. 350p.

Deals largely with labor relations and working conditions in the coal industry. Part of the "Labor in Twentieth Century America" series.

323. COLEMAN, MCALISTER
A week in West Virginia. *Survey* 53: 532-34 1925.

Account of labor unrest in the southern West Virginia coal fields.

324. COLLECTIVE BARGAINING AND COLORADO
Survey 33: 426-30 1915.

Exchange of letters between J. D. Rockefeller, Jr.; W. L. M. King and J. F. Welborn.

325. COLORADO INDUSTRIAL COMMISSION
The United Mine Workers of America, District No. 15, employees of the Colorado Fuel & Iron Co. *vs.* the Colorado Fuel & Iron Co. Findings and award. [Denver, 1917?] 25p.

326. COLORADO INDUSTRIAL COMMISSION
Report (extract). *MLR* 26: 1131-36 1928.

327. COLORADO MINE OPERATORS' ASSOCIATION
Criminal record of the Western Federation of Miners, Coeur D'Alene to Cripple Creek 1894-1904. [Denver], 1904. 32p.

328. COLORADO NATIONAL GUARD. COMMANDING GENERAL
The military occupation of the coal strike zone of Colorado by the Colorado National Guard, 1913-1914. Denver: Smith-Brooks Printing Co., 1914. 119p.

329. COLORADO. SPECIAL BOARD OF OFFICERS TO INQUIRE INTO THE ARMED CONFLICT, APRIL 20, 1914
Report. Denver: Williamson-Hafner Co., 1914. 29p.

330. COLORADO STATE FEDERATION OF LABOR
Militarism in Colorado. Denver, 1914. 16p.

331. COLORADO STRIKE
Coal Age 5: 770-77, 809-11, 851-52, 885-86, 891-92, 929-30 1914.

332. COMMITTEE OF COAL MINE MANAGERS
Facts concerning the struggle in Colorado for industrial freedom. Denver, 1914. 72p.

   A reissue of "The struggle in Colorado for industrial freedom" bulletins 1-15, June 22 to Sept. 4, 1914.

333. COMPLETED WAGE SCHEDULE FOR BITUMINOUS COAL INDUSTRY
MLR 37: 1073-81 1933.

334. THE CONNELLSVILLE SCALE
Black Diamond 6: 470-71 1890/91.

   Includes wage demands of union and reply of operators.

335. COOLIDGE, WILLIAM H.
Brief in behalf of Island Creek Coal Company. Boston 1921. 16p.

   "In the matter of the hearing before the Committee on Education and Labor of the United States Senate to investigate conditions in the coal fields of West Virginia and the territory adjacent to Kentucky."

336. CORNELL, ROBERT J.
The Anthracite coal strike of 1902. Washington: Catholic University of American Press, 1957. 279p.

   Bibliography: p.260-270. The work was submitted as a Ph.D. dissertation at the Catholic University.

337. CORT, JOHN C.
Lewis and the miners. *Commonweal* 38: 118-22 1943.

   The "miner's side" of the 1943 strike.

338. COSTELLO, E. J.
The shame that is Kentucky's. Chicago: General Defense Committee, 1932. 27p.

   The "war" in Harlan County.

339. COSTIGAN, EDWARD P.
Conditions in the coal mines of Colorado. Washington: GPO, 1914. 60p.

   "Brief for the striking miners."

340. COWLEY, MALCOLM
Kentucky coal town. *New Republic* 70: 67-70 Mr 2, 1932.

Town is Pineville. Replies to this article appeared in the same journal, issues of Mr 30 and My 18.

341. CRAWFORD, CHARLES B.
The mine war on Cabin Creek and Paint Creek, West Virginia in 1912-13. Thesis. University of Kentucky. 1939.

342. CREEL, GEORGE
High cost of hate. *Everybody's Magazine* 30: 755-70 1914.

Colorado coal strike.

343. CULIN, STEWART
A trooper's narrative of service in the anthracite coal strike, 1902. Philadelphia: G. W. Jacobs, 1903. 91p.

344. CUMMINGS, JOHN
The passing of the coal strike. *Journal of Political Economy* 11: 55-74 1902.

345. DAVENPORT, WALTER
Lewis strikes steel. *Colliers* Ag 21, 1937 12-13.

346. DAVIS, JEROME
Human rights and coal. *Journal of Social Forces* 3: 102-6 1924.

Author finds little in the way of human rights for the coal miner in the West Virginia and southern coal fields.

347. DAVIS, W. T.
Southern Colorado coal strike. *Outlook* 106: 24-26 1914.

348. DAVIS, W. T.
Strike war in Colorado. *Outlook* 107: 67-73 1914.

349. DEANS, PARKE P.
Coal mining and workmen's compensation (with discussion). U. S. Bureau of Labor Statistics. *Bulletin* 511: 279-91 1930.

350. DENNETT, TYLER
Walking delegate; a story of the trouble at Hattie's Gulch. *Outlook* 114: 338-41 1916.

351. DENNISON, HENRY S. AND OTHERS
Labor relations in the anthracite industry. Washington, 1923. 66p.

352. DEWEES, FRANCIS P.
The Molly Maguires; the origin, growth and character of the organization. Philadelphia: Lippincott, 1877. 380p.

353. DRUM, FRANCIS J.
Labor relations from the standpoint of the union. *Ann. Amer. Acad.* 111: 120-24 1924.

354. DRURY, HORACE B.
Social cost of irregular employment in coal mining. *American Labor Legislation Review* 14: 81-89 1924.

355. DRURY, HORACE B.
Wages in the coal industry as compared with wages in other industries. *Ann. Amer. Acad.* 111: 314-343 1924.

356. DURAND, E. DANA
The anthracite coal strike and its settlement. *Political Science Quarterly* 18: 385-414 1903.

357. EAVENSON, HOWARD N.
Data about labor employed in various bituminous mines. AIME. *Transactions* 70: 805-25 1924.

358. EBERLING, ERNEST J.
The issues of the anthracite problem. *Current History* 24: 247-53 1926.

359. EIGHT HOURS' DAY IN COAL
Quarterly Review 208: 155-72 1908.

360. EMMET, BORIS
Labor relations in the Fairmont, West Virginia bituminous coal field. Washington: GPO, 1924. 86p. (Bureau of Labor Statistics. Bulletin 361).

361. EMPLOYMENT IN RELATION TO MECHANIZATION IN THE BITUMINOUS COAL INDUSTRY
MLR 36: 256-78 1933.

362. EVANS, CHRIS
History of United Mine Workers of America. Indianapolis [1918-1920] v1 1860-1890, v2 1890-1900.

363. FEDER, BERNARD
      The collective bargaining and the legislative policies of
      the United Mine Workers of America. 1933-1947. Ph.D.
      New York University. 1957.

364. FEDERAL COUNCIL OF THE CHURCHES OF CHRIST IN
      AMERICA. COMMISSION ON THE CHURCH AND SOCIAL
      SERVICE
      The coal controversy . . . New York: The Council,
      1922. 63p. (*Its* Bulletin No. 2).

365   FEDERAL COUNCIL OF THE CHURCHES OF CHRIST IN
      AMERICA. DEPT. OF RESEARCH AND EDUCATION
      The coal strike in western Pennsylvania. New York:
      The Council, 1928. 99p. (*Its* Research Bulletin No. 7).

366. FEDERATION OF MINERS AND MINE LABORERS OF WEST
      VIRGINIA
      Report of convention. *Black Diamond* Ag 1, 1888 p7.

367. FENOLI, JOHN R.
      Era of conflict in Southern Illinois coal fields since
      1890. Thesis. Southern Illinois University. 1962.

368. FINK, WALTER H.
      The Ludlow massacre. [Denver: Williamson-Haffner,
      1914] 91p.

369. FISHER, WALDO E.
      Collective bargaining in bituminous coal. *Personnel
      Journal* 27: 367-76 1949.

370. FISHER, WALDO E.
      Collective bargaining in the bituminous coal industry;
      an appraisal. Philadelphia: University of Pennsylvania
      Press, 1948. 43p.

371. FISHER, WALDO E. AND ANNE BENZANSON
      Wage rates and working time in the bituminous coal in-
      dustry 1912-1922. Philadelphia: University of Pennsyl-
      vania Press, 1932. 374p.

372. FITCH, JOHN A.
      Law and order; the issue in Colorado. *Survey* 33: 241-
      58 1914.

373. FITCH, JOHN A.
      What Rockefeller knew and what he did. *Survey* 34:
      461-72 1915.

374. FLYNN, ELIZABETH G.
Coal miners and the war. New York: Workers Library, 1942. 15p.

375. FOSTER, WILLIAM Z.
The coal miners; their problems in war and peace. New York: New Century Publishers, 1945. 24p.

376. FOWLER, CHARLES B.
Collective bargaining in the bituminous coal industry. New York: Prentice Hall, 1927. 161p.

377. FRANK, B.
Miners unite, for one class struggle union. New York: Workers Library, 1934. 47p.

Violent attack on John L. Lewis.

378. FRANKLIN D. ROOSEVELT AND JOHN L. LEWIS
Catholic World 145: 385-9 1937.

379. FRAZIER, EDWARD K.
Annual earnings in the bituminous coal industry. *MLR* 45: 29-37 1937.

380. FRIEDMAN, MORRIS
The Pinkerton labor spy. New York: Wilshire Book Co., 1907. 229p.

Deals largely with activities of Pinkerton agents, especially in Colorado and Wyoming.

381. GAGLIARDO, DOMENICO
Labor legislation for Kansas coal mines. Lawrence: University of Kansas, 1936. 49p. (Kansas Studies in Business 17).

382. GANNES, HARRY
Kentucky miners fight. New York: Workers International Relief, 1932. 31p.

383. GAY, KATHERINE
Background of the Gallup riot. *Nation* 140: 511-12 1935.

Account of conditions in Gallup, New Mexico leading to the murder of a sheriff while evicting an unemployed miner.

384. GAY, KATHERINE
Fascism enters New Mexico. *Nation* 141: 537-38 1935.

The Gallup case.

385. GEBHART, JOHN G.
The economic impact of an industry-wide strike: a case study of the 1949-50 coal strike. New York: 1950. 15p. (National Assoc. of Manufacturers. Economic Policy Division. Series 27).

386. GENERAL POLICIES COMMITTEE OF ANTHRACITE OPERATORS
Need for greater democracy in the union. Philadelphia, 1923. 11p.

387. GENERAL POLICIES COMMITTEE OF ANTHRACITE OPERATORS
The union ultimatum; the checkoff or no anthracite. Philadelphia, 1923. 12p.

388. GEORGE, HENRY
Tragedy of the great Pennsylvania coal strike. New York, 1902. 24p.

389. GEORGE, JOHN E.
The coal miners' strike of 1897. *Quarterly Journal of Economics* 12: 186-208 1898.

390. GEORGE, JOHN E.
Settlement in the coal mining industry. *Quarterly Journal of Economics* 12: 447-60 1898.

The strike of 1897.

391. GLASSER, CARIE
Union wage policy in bituminous coal. *Industrial & Labor Relations Review* 1: 609-23 1948.

392. GOMPERS, SAMUEL
Core of the miners' strike. *American Federationist* 27: 57-60 1920.

General attack on the coal industry—"the worst managed of any industry".

393. GOMPERS, SAMUEL
President Gompers on labor, the courts and the law. Washington: AFL, 1921. 72p.

"Being the testimony of Mr. Gompers before the United States Senate Committee on Manufacturing in its hearings on production and profits in coal."

394. GOMPERS, SAMUEL
Strikes and the coal miners. *Forum* 24: 27-33 1897.

395. GOODRICH, CARTER
Machine and the miner. *Harper* 154: 649-54 1927.

The introduction of machines will mean "an end to the unique and traditional freedom of the mines."

396. GOODRICH, CARTER
Nothing but a coal factory: machinery in coal mining. *New Republic* 44: 91-93 1925.

Author maintains that the introduction of machines means end to miners' freedom.

397. GOODRICH, CARTER
The miners' freedom. Boston: Marshall Jones, 1925. 189p.

"A study of the working life in a changing industry."

398. GRAUMAN, LAWRENCE
That little ugly running sore (Kentucky coal fields, 1931-32). *Filson Club History Quarterly* 36: 340-54 1962.

"Some observations on the participation of American writers in the investigations of conditions in the Harlan and Bell County, Kentucky, coal fields in 1931-32."

399. GRAY, GEORGE
Arbitration as a factor in the mining industry. American Mining Congress. *Proceedings* 11 pt. 2: 230-34 1908.

400. THE GREAT COAL STRIKE AND ITS LESSONS
Arena 29: 1-25 1903.

401. GREENE, VICTOR R.
Attitude of Slavic communities to the unionization of the anthracite industry before 1903. Ph.D. University of Pennsylvania. 1963.

402. GREENE, VICTOR R.
Study in Slavs, strikes and unions: the anthracite strike of 1897. *Pennsylvania History* 31: 199-215 1964.

403. GREEN, WILLIAM
Does the U. S. want a labor dictator? *Readers Digest* D 1937 104-7.

Attack on John L. Lewis.

404. GREEN, WILLIAM
Mr. Green's reply to the miners. *American Federationist* 45: 249-57 1938.

Letter to Thomas Kennedy, UMWA Secretary-Treasurer, concerning the UMWA's demand that Green resign.

405. GREENBAUM, FRED
A "new deal" for the bituminous coal miners; the United Mine Workers of America and national labor relations policy, 1933-1941. Thesis. University of Wisconsin. 1953.

406. GREENSLADE, RUSH V.
The economic effects of collective bargaining in bituminous coal mining. Ph.D. University of Chicago. 1952.

407. GRONER, ISAAC N.
John L. Lewis; a study in the dynamics of unionism. Thesis. New York University. 1942.

408. GUTMAN, HERBERT G.
The Braidwood Lockout of 1874. Illinois State Historical Society. *Journal* 53: 5-28 1960.

Early labor problems in the Illinois coal fields.

409. GUTMAN, HERBERT G.
The Buena Vista affair. *Pennsylvania Magazine of History and Biography* 88: 251-93 1964.

Account of the first major use of Italian laborers as strikebreakers in the bituminous coal fields. Location of the trouble was southeast of Pittsburgh.

410. GUTMAN, HERBERT G.
Two lockouts in Pennsylvania, 1873-1874. *Pennsylvania Magazine of History and Biography* 83: 307-26 1959.

Labor struggles in the Johnstown and Tioga County areas.

411. GUYER, JOHN P.
Pennsylvania Cossacks and the state's police. Reading: People's Publishing Co., 1923. 96p.

412. HACKAMACK, LAWRENCE C.
Cooperation-conflict in labor-management relations; a study of contrasting cases (women's garment industry and bituminous coal industry). Ph.D. State University of Iowa. 1956.

413. HANFORD, BEN
The labor war in Colorado. New York: Socialist Cooperative Publishing Assoc., 1904. 48p.

414. HAPGOOD, POWERS
In non-union mines: the diary of a coal digger in central Pennsylvania, August-September 1921. New York: Bureau of Industrial Research, 1922. 48p.

415. HARD, WILLIAM
Class policy in coal. *New Republic* 20: 352-55 1919.

"The injunction against the miners . . . is our historic declaration of the class war at home."

416. HARD, WILLIAM AND PAUL R. LEACH
Labor in a basic industry, studies in coal production—effects of the miner's environment upon his mode of thought. Chicago: Chicago Daily News, 1920. 34p.

417. HARGER, CHARLES M.
Kansas's volunteer coal-digging army. *Outlook* 123: 538-39 1919.

Volunteers dug coal after a strike threatened to cut off the fuel supply.

418. HARRIS, HERBERT
Labor in America (the United Mine Workers). *Current History* N 1937 75-83; D 1937 66-74.

419. HARRISON, S. M. AND P. U. KELLOG
Westmoreland strike. *Survey* 25: 345-66 1910.

Labor disputes in the coal fields of Westmoreland County, Pennsylvania.

420. HARVEY, KATHERINE
The coal miners of western Maryland: some economic and social developments, 1850-1910. Ph.D. American University. 1962.

421. HERLIHY, ANN
Work stoppages, bituminous coal mining industry. Washington: GPO, 1955. 18p. (Bureau of Labor Statistics. BLS Report 95).

422. HERLING, JOHN
Building a militant mine union. *World Tomorrow* 16: 162-63 1933.

The Progressive Miners of America.

423. HERRINGTON, FRED
Conditions in the coal mines of Colorado. Washington: GPO, 1914. 81p.

"Brief of the coal mining operators."

424. HICKEN, VICTOR
The Virden and Pana mine wars of 1898. Illinois State Historical Society. *Journal* 52: 263-78 1959.

Account of some of the clashes "between coal feudalism and the rising labor movement in Illinois."

425. HIGH PRICES NOT SO HIGH FOR THE MINER
Literary Digest D 20, 1919 69-74.

Study in southern West Virginia shows that prices have not advanced so much as to require a large increase in wages.

426. HINDS, ROY W.
The last stand of the open shop. *Coal Age* 18: 1037-40 1920.

Account of labor unrest in Mingo County, West Virginia and Pike County, Kentucky.

427. HINRICHS, ALBERT F.
United Mine Workers of America and the non-union coal fields. New York: Columbia, 1923. 194p. (Columbia University. Studies in History, Economics and Public Law 246).

428. HOLBROOK, STEWART H.
The Rocky Mountain revolution. New York: Holt, 1956. 318p.

Albert Horsley and the International Union of Mine, Mill & Smelter Workers.

429. HOLLOWAY, RICHARD B.
The labor problem in the coal mining industry of Kansas. Thesis. University of Kansas. 1920.

430. HOLMES, CHARLES
Colorado plays the red game. *Technical World Magazine* 21: 648-53 1914.

Account of the violence surrounding the "Ludlow Massacre."

431. HOLT, HOMER A.
Message to the miners of West Virginia. Charleston, 1939? 79p.

A general attack by the Governor of West Virginia on the leadership of the UMWA.

432. HUDSON, HARRIET D.
The progressive Mine Workers of America; a study in rival unionism. Urbana: University of Illinois, 1952. 152p. (Bureau of Economic and Business Research. Bulletin 73).

433. HUGHES, FRANCIS W.
Commonwealth versus Patrick Hester, Patrick Tully, and Peter McHugh. Philadelphia, 1877. 114p.

Trials for murder arising from labor troubles in the anthracite fields.

434. HUGHES, MARY M.
United Mine Workers of America as a social control.
Ph.D. University of Pittsburgh. 1937.

435. HUMBLE, JOHN
Time My 15, 1939 18-19.

John L. Lewis and the 1939 coal strike.

436. HUTSON, ANDREW C.
The coal miners' insurrections of 1891 in Anderson
County, Tennessee. East Tennessee Historical Society.
Publication 7: 103-21 1935.

437. HUTSON, ANDREW C.
The overthrow of the convict lease system in Tennessee. East Tennessee Historical Society. *Publication* 8:
82-103 1936.

Free labor resorted to violence to force the abolition of the "un-
fair competition" of convict coal miners.

438. ICKES, HAROLD L.
Crisis in coal. *Colliers* S 4, 1943 17, 56-8.

The 1943 strike.

439. ILLINOIS COAL OPERATORS ASSOCIATION
Statement, brief and exhibits on behalf of the Coal Operators Association of Illinois. n.p., 1928. 55p.

Submitted to the Illinois Joint Wage Commission.

440. ILLINOIS COAL OPERATORS ASSOCIATION
Union mine labor in Illinois and the determination of
wage scales and working conditions. n.p., 1923. 85p.

"Submitted to the United States Coal Commission by the Illinois coal operators."

441. ILLINOIS, SPECIAL COMMISSIONERS TO INVESTIGATE THE
COAL MINER'S STRIKE AND LOCK-OUT
Report. Springfield, 1889. 30p.

442. INDUSTRIAL WORKERS OF THE WORLD
Coal mines and coal miners. Chicago, 1922. 109p.

443. INDUSTRIAL WORKERS OF THE WORLD
Coal mine workers and their industry. Chicago, 1922.
108p.

444. INTERNATIONAL LABOR LEAGUE
The battle of Virden, Illinois. Chicago. [1899]. 28p.

445. IRWIN, N. O.
How modern employment practices assure contented and efficient personnel. *Coal Age* 19: 1077-80 1921.

Practices at the Benham, Kentucky mines of the Wisconsin Steel Co.

446. ITES, ALFRED
A presidential make-believe and a sinister precedent contained in the method of the hard coal strike settlement. Washington: Neale Publishing Co., 1904. 38p.

447. ITTER, WILLIAM A.
Early labor troubles in the Schuylkill anthracite district. *Pennsylvania History* 1: 28-37 1934.

Covers the period 1825-1860.

448. JOHN L. AND AFTER
Fortune N 1954 73-4.

Speculations as to the fate of the UMW after the death of Lewis.

449. JOHN L. LEWIS, BUSINESSMAN
U. S. News Je 29, 1956 58-60.

Account of the UMWA's "huge business empire."

450. JOINT CONFERENCE OF COAL OPERATORS AND COAL MINERS
Proceedings of Joint conference of coal operators and coal miners of western Pennsylvania, Ohio and Indiana. January 25 to February 2, and March 20 to 29, 1906. [Joliet, Ill.] 1906. 272p.

A stenographic report of the proceedings.

451. JOINT CONFERENCE OF COAL OPERATORS AND COAL MINERS
Proceedings of informal and formal conferences. April 5-6, April 12-17, 1917. n.p., 1917.

452. JONES, DAVID R.
The mining conflict: being an exposition of the grievances of the miners. Pittsburgh: Thomas, 1880. 74p.

453. JUSTI, HERMAN
The coal mine operator versus the public. Chicago: Illinois Coal Operators Association, [1904]. 23p.

Address with similar title appeared in *Mines & Minerals* 25: 195-99 1904/5.

454.   JUSTI, HERMAN
Counciliation and arbitration in the coal mining industry. Chicago, [1902]. 40p.

455.   KANAWHA LABOR AGREEMENT
Coal Age 6: 188-90 1914.

Text of the agreement ending the long strike in the Kanawha (West Virginia) field.

456.   KARASKA, GERALD J.
The pattern of settlements in the southern and middle anthracite regions of Pennsylvania. Ph.D. Penn State University. 1962.

457.   KARSH, BERNARD AND JACK LONDON
The coal miners: a study of union control. *Quarterly Journal of Economics* 68: 415-36 1954.

458.   KEELY, JOSIAH
The psychology of strikes at coal mines. *Coal Age* 8: 294-96 1915.

459.   KEHOE, JOHN, DEFENDANT
Report of the case of the Commonwealth vs. John Kehoe et al, members of the Ancient Order of Hibernians, commonly known as Molly Maguires. Pottsville, Pennsylvania, 1876. 262p.

460.   KENNEDY, THOMAS
Wages, hours and working conditions in the anthracite industry. *Ann. Amer. Acad.* 111: 43-52 1924.

461.   KENNELL, H. RICHARD AND OTHERS
Panel on problems of employment and retraining. *In*: United States. Congress. Senate. Subcommittee on problems of the aged and aging. Part 5. 1960 p1095-1113.

Discussion of the problems involved in retraining older workers —largely unemployed coal miners—for other occupations.

462.   KENT, RAYMOND P.
Labor issues in the captive bituminous coal mines. Thesis. University of Pittsburgh. 1934.

463.   KILLEEN, JOHN F.
Coal industry—the leader. *Social Order* 11: 23-28 1961.

Author lauds the introduction of the Vocational Group concept into the coal industry's labor-management relationship.

464. KING, F. A.
Check-off system and the closed shop among the United Mine Workers. *Quarterly Journal of Economics* 25: 730-41 1911.

465. KING, LAWRENCE T.
Peace in the mines. *Commonweal* 65: 506-9 1957.

466. KIRBY, RICHARD M.
The wage policy of the United Mine Workers of America. Ph.D. Harvard. 1943.

467. KRAFFT, FRED A.
Possibilities of an industrial relations program in the coal industry. West Virginia Coal mining Institute. *Proceedings* 1935 40-57.

468. LABOR AND THE N.R.A.
New Republic 77: 282 1934.

The United Anthracite Miners of Pennsylvania.

469. LACEY, JOHN W.
Attitudes of coal miners toward their union. Thesis. West Virginia University. 1962.

470. LANE, JOHN Q. AND S. W. PETITT
Arguments before the investigating committee of the Pennsylvania Legislature, July 28-31, 1875, showing the illegality and criminal conspiracy of the anthracite monopoly. Philadelphia: Zeising, 1875. 94p.

471. LANE, WINTHROP D.
Civil war in West Virginia; a story of the industrial conflict in the coal mines. New York: Huebach, 1921. 128p. (On cover: The Freeman Pamphlets).

472. LANE, WINTHROP D.
The denial of civil liberties in the coal fields. New York, 1924. 44p.

473. LANE, WINTHROP D.
Labor spy in West Virginia. *Survey* 47: 110-12 1921.

C. E. Lively, a Baldwin Felts agent, was the spy.

474. LANGDON, EMMA F.
The Cripple Creek strike; a history of industrial wars in Colorado, 1903-4-5. Denver: Great Western, 1904-5. 463p.

475. LANGDON, EMMA F.
Labor's greatest conflict. Denver: Great Western, 1908. 167p.

476. LAUCK, REX (EDIT.)
John L. Lewis and the International Union, United Mine Workers of America: the story from 1917 to 1952. Washington: UMWA, 1952. 255p.

477. LAUCK, W. J.
Bituminous coal miner and coke worker of Western Pennsylvania. *Survey* 26: 34-51 1911.

478. LEHIGH COAL AND NAVIGATION COMPANY
Answer of the Lehigh Coal and Navigation Company. Philadelphia, [1902]. 23p.

In reply to the Anthracite Coal Strike Commission.

479. LEISERSON, WILLIAM M.
Labor conditions in the mines of the Pittsburgh district. *Ann. Amer. Acad.* 33: 316-25 1909.

479a. LEWIS, ARTHUR H.
Lament for the Molly Maguires. New York: Harcourt, Brace, 1964. 308p.

480. LEWIS, JOHN L.
Anthracite coal facts. *American Federationist* 32: 1008-16 1925.

481. LEWIS, JOHN L.
The anthracite controversy: an address by John L. Lewis, international president United Mine Workers of America at the Altamont Hotel, Hazelton, Pennsylvania, August 25th, 1925. Washington: American Federation of Labor, 1925. 12p.

482. LEWIS, JOHN L.
Guests at labor's table [speech]. *Vital Speeches* 3: 731-3 1937.

483. LEWIS, JOHN L. AND J. B. WARRINER
A half century of successful labor-management relations, 1903-1953. [Hazelton, Pennsylvania?]: Anthracite Board of Conciliation, 1953. 24p.

Addresses . . . at 50th anniversary dinner, Anthracite Board of Conciliation, Oct. 1, 1953.

484. LEWIS, JOHN L.
      Jobs, peace, unity. Washington, 1940. 16p. (CIO Publication No. 40).

485. LEWIS, JOHN L.
      Labor and the National Recovery Administration. *Ann. Amer. Acad.* 172: 58-63 1934.

486. LEWIS, JOHN L.
      The little NRA. *American Labor Legislation Review* 25: 133-35 1935.

      Article supporting the Bituminous Coal Stabilization Act.

487. LEWIS, JOHN L.
      Miners' achievement. *American Federationist* 29: 645-46 1922.

      "The United Mine Workers have fought and won the industrial struggle of the age."

488. LEWIS, JOHN L.
      Miners' service to all labor. *American Federationist* 29: 740-41 1922.

489. LEWIS, JOHN L.
      The miners' fight for American standards. Indianapolis: Bell, 1925. 189p.

490. LEWIS, JOHN L.
      More machines, fewer men, a union that's happy about it. *U. S. News* N 9, 1959 60-64.

      An interview with Lewis concerning the UMWA's attitude toward automation.

491. LEWIS, JOHN L.
      Proposed NLRA amendments. *Fortune* Ap 1939 p76.

492. LEWIS, JOHN L.
      Should the Wagner collective bargaining proposal be adopted? *Congressional Digest* 14: 119-22 1935.

493. LEWIS, JOHN L.
      A union's non-union mine. *Nation* 120: 287 1925.

      An attack on Warren S. Stone and the Brotherhood of Locomotive Engineers for refusing to employ union miners at the Coal Run Collieries, owned by the Brotherhood.

494. LEWIS, JOHN L.
      United Mine Workers demands [address Mr 12, 1946]. *Reference Shelf* 19 No. 4 180-95 1946.

      The 1946 strike.

495. LEWIS, JOHN L.
United Mine Workers of America. *American Federationist* 38: 1211-18 1931.

495a. LEWIS, JOHN L.
What democracy means to me. *Scholastic* My 21, 1938. p33.

496. LEWIS, THOMAS L.
Arbitration as a factor in the mining industry. American Mining Congress. *Proceedings* 11 pt. 2: 235-38 1908.

497. LEWIS, THOMAS L.
Settlement of disputes among the mine workers. *Ann. Amer. Acad.* 36: 333-39 1910.

498. LIBBY, JOHN H.
Bituminous wages from the point of view of an operator. *Ann. Amer. Acad.* 111: 32-38 1924.

499. LILIENTHAL, DAISY M.
The meaning of unionism; a study of the perspectives of members of the plumber's union, of the United Mine Workers, and of the United Automobile Workers of America. Thesis. University of Chicago. 1956.

500. LINTON, RON M.
Kentucky's tragic strike. *Nation* 188: 471-73 1959.

501. LLOYD, HENRY D.
A strike of millionaires against miners; or, the story of Spring Valley. 2nd ed. Chicago: Belford-Clarke, 1890. 299p.

Labor troubles in the Illinois coal fields.

501a. LOAF, T.
Der Kampf der Kohlenarbeiter in den Vereinigten Staaten von Nordamerika. Hamburg: Verlag der Kommunistischen Internationale, 1922. 68p.

501b. LOGAN, SAMUEL C.
A city's danger and defense; or issues and results of the strikes of 1877. Scranton, Pennsylvania, 1877. 355p.

502. LOVEJOY, OWEN R.
Child labor in the soft coal mines. *Ann. Amer. Acad.* 29: 26-34 1907.

503. LOVEJOY, OWEN R.
Coal mines of Pennsylvania. *Ann. Amer. Acad.* 38: Supp. 133-38 1911.

Child labor in the mines.

504. LOVEJOY, OWEN R.
The extent of child labor in the anthracite coal industry. *Ann. Amer. Acad.* 29: 35-49 1907.

505. LOWITT, RICHARD (EDIT.)
Frostburg, 1882: German strikers vs. German strikebreakers. Society for the History of Germans in Maryland. *Report* 28: 72-79 1953.

The dispute between the Knights of Labor and the Consolidation Coal Co.

506. LUCY, ERNEST W.
The Molly Maguires of Pennsylvania, or Ireland in America. London: G. Bell, 1882. 152p.

507. LYNCH, LAWRENCE R.
The West Virginia coal strike. *Political Science Quarterly* 29: 626-63 1914.

508. MCCABE, JAMES D. (EDWARD W. MORTON, PSEUD.)
The history of the great riots. Being a full and authentic account of the strikes and riots on the various railroads of the United States and in the mining regions. Philadelphia: National Publishing Co., 1877. 516p.

509. MCCARTHY, JUSTIN
Brief history of the United Mine Workers of America. Washington: UMW Journal, 1956. 18p.

510. MCCLURG, DONALD J.
The Colorado coal strike of 1927; tactical leadership of the IWW. *Labor History* 4: 68-92 1962/63.

511. MCCONAGHA, WILLIAM A.
The history and progress of the United Mine Workers of America. Ph.D. University of Illinois. 1925.

512. MCCONNELL, GEORGE W.
"We demand"; anthracite and the high cost of cheap labor. *World's Work* 31: 645-51; 32: 85-96 1916.

513. MCCORMICK, KYLE
The National Guard of West Virginia during the strike period of 1912-1913. *West Virginia History* 22: 34-35 1960.

514. McCORMICK, KYLE
The New-Kanawha River and the mine war of West
Virginia. Charleston: Matthews Printing Co., 1959.
176p.

515. McDONALD, DAVID J. AND EDWARD A. LYNCH
Coal and unionism; a history of the American coal min-
ers' unions. Silver Spring, Md., and Indianapolis, Ind.,
Cornelius Press, 1939. 226p.

516. McGOLDRICK, JOSEPH
College students and Kentucky miners. *American
Scholar* 1: 363-5, 1932.

The expulsion of "invading" students by the authorities of east
Kentucky mining counties.

517. McGOVERN, GEORGE S.
The Colorado coal strike, 1913-14. Ph.D. Northwestern
University. 1953.

518. MAHANY, ROWLAND B.
The slaughter of unarmed miners at Lattimer, Pennsylvania. Washington: GPO, 1898. 6p.

519. MARBLE, SAMUEL W.
Justice and coal. *Christian Century* 45: 77-79 1928.

The Colorado coal strike of 1927-1928. For a sharp reply to the
above see p149 of the same volume.

520. MARKHAM, EDWIN
The hoe-man in the making: little slaves of the coal
mines. *Cosmopolitan* 42: 20-28 1906.

521. MARLEY, HAROLD P.
Cowbells shall not ring tonight. *Survey Graphic* 24:
385-87 1935.

Account of labor trouble in the Kentucky coal fields. Men un-
popular with the miners were "belled" and driven from the
area.

522. MARTIN, JOHN B.
What the miners say about John L. Lewis. *Sat. Eve.
Post* Ja 15, 1949 26-7.

523. MARY EVANGELA, SISTER
Bishop Spaulding's work on the Anthracite Coal Strike
Commission. *Catholic Historical Review* 28: 184-205
1942.

524. MATHEWS, WILLIAM G.
Martial law in West Virginia, an address . . . Washington: GPO, 1913. 21p. (63d Congress, 1st Session. Senate Document 230).

525. MATTHIESSEN, F. O.
New Mexican workers' case. *New Republic* 82: 361-63 1935.

The Gallup, New Mexico affair.

526. MAURER, CHARLES E.
The bituminous coal industry of the central states. American Mining Congress. *Proceedings* 25: 93-98 1922.

Deals largely with labor relations.

527. MEADE, EDWARD S.
Investor's interest in the demands of the anthracite miners. *Ann. Amer. Acad.* 21: 36-45 1903.

528. MENEFEE, SELDON C.
Why they follow John L. Lewis. *Nation* 156: 477-9 1943.

1943 strike.

529. MERRICK, MARY A. (SISTER)
A case in practical democracy; settlement of the anthracite coal strike of 1902. Notre Dame, Ind., 1942. 86p. (Ph.D. Notre Dame University).

530. MERRITT, WALTER G.
Coronada Coal Company vs. United Mine Workers; an analysis of the decision of the United States Supreme Court. New York: League of Industrial Rights, 1922. 6p.

531. MERRITT, WALTER G.
Issues in the anthracite strike of 1925. Philadelphia: Anthracite Operators' Conference, 1925. 19p.

532. MICHELSON, M.
Feudalism and civil war in the United States. *Everybody's Magazine* 28: 615-28 1913.

Description of labor troubles in the coal fields of the Paint Creek (West Virginia) area.

533. MILLER, GLENN W.
Recent struggles among the coal miners' organizations in bituminous fields. Thesis. University of Illinois. 1935.

534. MILLER, RICE
      Some problems in labor relations in the coal industry
      as viewed by operators. *Ann. Amer. Acad.* 111: 115-19
      1924.

535. MILLET, PHILIPPE
      Trial in a coal mine. *Outlook* 89: 296-301 1908.
      Account of an arbitration meeting in the Illinois coal field.

536. MILLS, C. WRIGHT
      Case for the coal miner. *New Republic* 108: 695-8
      1943.
      1943 strike.

537. MINERS' AND OPERATORS' MEETINGS
      Black Diamond 5: 740 1889/90.
      Account of joint meetings of miners and operators in Columbus
      Ohio, St. Louis and Chicago.

538. MINERS' MEETING; TROUBLES WITHIN
      Newsweek F 7, 1938 p32-4.
      Internal problems of the UMWA.

539. MITCHELL, JOHN
      The coal strike. *McClures* 20: 219-24 1902/3.

540. MITCHELL, JOHN
      The great coal strike. *Independent* 52: 2613-16 1900.

541. MITCHELL, JOHN
      Mine worker's life and aims. *Cosmopolitan* 31: 622-30
      1901.

542. MITCHELL, JOHN
      Organized labor; its problems, purposes and ideals.
      Philadelphia: American Book and Bible House, 1903.
      436p.

543. MITCHELL, JOHN
      Recognition of trade unions. *Independent* 53: 1895-98
      1901.

544. MITCHELL, JOHN
      The wage earner and his problems. Washington: P. S.
      Risdale, 1913. 186p.

545. MOFFAT, MAURICE P.
      Collective bargaining in the anthracite coal industry:
      a study of social movement. Ph.D. New York Univer-
      sity. 1942.

546. MORONY, IVES GUY
Attitude of coal miners toward union and coal industry. Thesis. West Virginia University. 1959.

Study made in Northern West Virginia.

547. MORRIS, HOMER L.
The plight of the bituminous coal miner. Philadelphia: University of Pennsylvania Press, 1934. 253p.

Study is centered chiefly in the coal fields of Kentucky and West Virginia.

548. MOSES, HARRY M.
The facts about the United Mine Workers' false case to extract a royalty on coal. Washington, 1946. 6p.

549. MURRAY, PHILIP
The case of the anthracite coal mine workers: opening statement and closing argument . . . before the U. S. Anthracite Coal Commission. Baltimore: UMWA, 1920. 95p.

550. MURRAY, PHILIP
The case of the West Virginia coal mine workers: Opening statement . . . Before the Committee on Education and Labor of the U. S. Senate, October, 1921. Washington: UMWA, 1921. 74p.

551. MURRAY, PHILIP
Unemployment in the coal industry. *American Labor Legislation Review* 12: 37-40 1922.

552. MYERS, ROBERT J.
Experience of the UMWA Welfare and Retirement Fund. *Industrial and Labor Relations Review* 10: 93-100 1956.

553. MYERS, ROBERT J.
Further experience of the UMWA Welfare and Retirement Fund. *Industrial and Labor Relations Review* 14: 556-62 1961.

554. NATIONAL COAL ASSOCIATION
The Herrin conspiracy. Washington, 1922. 38p.

555. NATIONAL COAL ASSOCIATION
Petition of coal operators located in Division V of the code of fair competition for the bituminous coal industry, for the restoration of the eight-hour day and the privilege of working six days per week when work is available, to the National Recovery Administration. Washington, 1934. 9p. proc.

556. NATIONAL COMMITTEE FOR THE DEFENSE OF POLITICAL
PRISONERS
Harlan miners speak; report on terrorism in the Kentucky coal fields. New York. Harcourt, Brace, 1932. 348p.

The famous report by Theodore Dreiser, Anna Rochester, etc.

557. NATIONAL INDUSTRIAL CONFERENCE BOARD
The cost of living among wage earners, anthracite region of Pennsylvania, February 1922. New York, 1922. 41p. (*Its* Special Report 21).

558. NATIONAL INDUSTRIAL CONFERENCE BOARD
Wages and hours in anthracite mining, June, 1914-October, 1921, inclusive . . . New York, 1922. 67p. (*Its* Research Report 47).

559. NATIONAL SAVE THE MINERS UNION
Save the Miners Union from the coal operators and the corrupt Lewis machine. Pittsburgh, 1928. 15p.

560. NEW YORK (CITY). COMMITTEE ON LABOR CONDITIONS
AT THE BERWIND-WHITE COMPANY'S MINES IN SOMERSET AND OTHER COUNTIES, PENNSYLVANIA
Statement of facts and summary. New York: M. B. Brown, 1922. 35p.

561. NEWCOMB, HARRY T.
Anthracite Coal Strike Commission. Philadelphia, 1903. 104p.

Argument on behalf of the Philadelphia & Reading Coal & Iron Co.

562. NICHOLLS, T. D.
Anthracite Board of Conciliation. *Ann. Am. Acad.* 36: 366-72 1910.

563. NORTHERN WEST VIRGINIA COAL ASSOCIATION
Classification index of labor decisions, Northern West Virginia Coal Association and District No. 31, United Mine Workers of America, from October 2, 1933 to June 1, 1948. [Fairmont, W. Va., 1948] 64p.

564. OHIO. GENERAL ASSEMBLY. HOCKING VALLEY INVESTIGATION COMMITTEE
Proceedings. Columbus, 1885. 324p.

Committee was established "to make an investigation into and ascertain the causes of the strike in the Hocking Valley."

58

565.   OLDER, CORA (MRS. FREMONT)
Answering a question: martial law in West Virginia. *Colliers* Ap 19, 1913 26, 28.

Paint Creek strike.

566.   OLDER, CORA (MRS. FREMONT)
Last day of the Paint Creek court martial. *Independent* 74: 1085-88 1913.

Account of the trial of Mother Jones and others during the "mine war" in the Paint Creek (West Virginia) area.

567.   OLMSTED, HARRY
Statement of Harry Olmsted, chairman of the labor committee of the Operators' Association of Williamson field, to the Senate Investigating Committee, July 14, 1921. Washington: W. F. Roberts Co., [1921]. 55p.

568.   OPERATORS' ASSOCIATION OF THE WILLIAMSON FIELD
Statement before the Sub-Committee of the Committee on Education and Labor of the United States Senate. n.p., 1921. 59p.

The purpose of the hearing was to "investigate conditions in the coal fields of West Virginia in the territory adjacent to Kentucky."

569.   OWENS, JOHN W.
Gunmen in West Virginia. *New Republic* 28: 90-92 1921.

570.   PALMER, FRANK L.
Solidarity in Colorado. *Nation* 126: 118-20 1928.

Account of the Colorado coal strike of 1927/28.

571.   PALMER, FRANK L.
War in Colorado. *Nation* 125: 623-4 1927.

572.   PARKER, EDWARD W.
The anthracite question: the operators' standpoint. *Current History* 24: 416-19 1926.

A reply by the Secretary of the Anthracite Operators' Conference to the article by E. J. Eberling (See No. 358).

573.   PARKER, EDWARD W.
Conciliation in the anthracite region. American Mining Congress. *Proceeding* 22: 309-16 1919.

Strike of 1919.

574. PARKER, U. S.
Collective bargaining in the soft coal industry. *Journal of Political Economy* 12: 546-54 1904.

575. PARSONS, FLOYD W.
Employment of women in mining. *Coal Age* 13: 859 1918.

Author deplores successful efforts to prevent women from being employed above ground in the Pennsylvania anthracite fields.

576. PATTERSON, JOSEPH F.
Old W.B.A. days. Schuylkill County Historical Society. *Publications* 2: 355-84 1909.

The Workingmen's Benevolent Association. An interesting account of labor relations in the Pennsylvania anthracite fields.

577. PEARSE, BEN
What has John L. Lewis done with his $400,000,000? *Sat. Eve. Post* Ag 30, 1952 26-7.

The Welfare and Retirement Fund.

578. PENNSYLVANIA. COMMISSION ON SPECIAL POLICING IN INDUSTRY
Report to Governor Gifford Pinchot. Harrisburg, 1934. 31p. (Dept. of Labor & Industry. Special Bulletin 38).

Deals largely with mine police.

579. PENNSYLVANIA. COMMISSIONERS TO INVESTIGATE THE BITUMINOUS COAL MINES
Report. Harrisburg: B. F. Meyers, 1875. 50p.

580. PENNSYLVANIA. GENERAL ASSEMBLY. SENATE
Report . . . in relation to the Anthracite coal difficulties, with accompanying testimony. Harrisburg: B. Singerly, 1871.

581. PERRY, VERNON F.
The labor struggle at Wilder, Tennessee. Thesis. Vanderbilt University. 1934.

582. PETRAS, GEORGE S.
Wage policies of the United Mine Workers of America. Thesis. New York University. 1947.

583. PINKERTON, ALLAN
The Molly Maguires and the detectives. New and enl. ed. New York: G. W. Dillingham, 1905. 552p.

584. PINKOWSKI, EDWARD
John Siney, the miner's martyr. Philadelphia: Sunshine Press, 1963. 335p.

Pp. 259-322 bibliographical essay and notes.

584a. PINKOWSKI, EDWARD
Lattimer massacre. Philadelphia: Sunshine Press, 1950. 40p.

The killing of striking coal miners by sheriff's deputies. Luzerne County, Pennsylvania, 1897.

585. POLLAK, KATHERINE H.
What a union did for the coal miners. Katonah, New York: Brookwood Labor College, 1931. 32p.

"A picture of life in the coal fields 35 years ago and of the changes brought through a union in such a state as Illinois."

586. POLLARD, SPENCER D.
Some aspects of the problem of democracy in its application to the government of labor unions, with special reference to the United Mine Workers of America and the United Automobile Workers. Ph.D. Harvard 1940.

587. PORTER, EUGENE O.
The Colorado coal strike of 1913—an interpretation. Historian 12: 3-27 1949.

588. POSEY, THOMAS E.
The labor movement in West Virginia. Ph.D. University of Wisconsin. 1948.

589. POSEY, THOMAS E.
Unemployment compensation and the coal industry in West Virginia. Southern Economic Journal 7: 347-61 1941.

589a. PRITCHARD, PAUL W.
William B. Wilson, master workman. Pennsylvania History 12: 81-108 1945.

Account of Wilson's early career as a miner and union organizer in Pennsylvania.

589b. PRITCHARD, PAUL W.
William B. Wilson; the evolution of a central Pennsylvania mine union leader. Ph.D. University of Pennsylvania. 1942.

590. PURCELL, WILLIAM J.
Study of the methods of decision used by arbitrators in fifty cases involving the United Mine Workers of America. Thesis. University of Illinois. 1950.

591. RANDALL, JAMES G.
Miners and the law of treason. *North American Review* 216: 312-22 1922.

The West Virginia "treason trial."

592. RASKIN, A. H.
John L. Lewis and the mine workers. *Atlantic* My 1963 53-58.

The UMWA's efforts to increase the efficiency of the coal industry have without question helped the industry survive. However, this is little comfort to thousands of unemployed miners, many of whom "fight off the union they once fought to build."

593. RAUSHENBUSH, STEPHEN
Coal without strikes. *Harper* 194-492-99 1947.

Long-term labor contracts are among the suggested reforms.

594. READ, THOMAS L.
Is the coal crisis permanent. *Sat. Eve. Post* S 25, 1943 22, 109-10.

595. RENEWAL OF APPALACHIAN AGREEMENT IN BITUMINOUS COAL INDUSTRY
MLR 41: 1576-80 1935.

596. REPORT OF PRESIDENT'S COMMITTEE ON PORTAL-TO-PORTAL TRAVEL TIME IN BITUMINOUS COAL MINING
MLR 59: 81-3 1944.

597. REYNOLDS, ROBERT J.
Coal kings come to judgment. *American Heritage* Ap 1960 54-61.

"When the anthracite miners downed tools in 1902, economic feudalism went on trial."

598. REYNOLDS, SIM C.
Carpet bagging: its effects on mining. *Coal Age* 2: 387 1912.

Deplores the "aimless drift from employer to employer" on the part of many miners.

599. RHODES, JAMES F.
Molly Maguires in the anthracite region of Pennsylvania. *American Historical Review* 15: 547-61 1910.

600. RICE, MILLARD M.
Bloody Monday again in Colorado. *Independent* 119: 655-6 1927.

Brief review of the history of labor violence in the coal fields of Colorado.

601. RIMLINGER, GASTON
International differences in the strike propensity of coal miners. *Industrial & Labor Relations Review* 12: 389-405 1959.

Study of the frequency of strikes in France, Germany, Great Britain and the United States.

602. ROBERTS, PETER
The anthracite coal strike in its social aspects. *Economic Journal* 13: 20-29 1903.

603. ROBINSON, NEIL
West Virginia on the brink of a labor struggle. Charleston: West Virginia Mining Association, 1912. 7p.

604. ROCHESTER, ANNA
Labor and coal. New York: International, 1931. 225p.

605. ROCKEFELLER, JOHN D.
The Colorado industrial plan. New York, 1916. 94p.

Includes a copy of the plan of representation and agreement adopted at the coal and iron mines of the Colorado Fuel and Iron Company.

606. RINGER, STRAWDER A.
History of the United Mine Workers of America. Thesis. University of Pittsburgh, 1929.

607. ROOSEVELT, FRANKLIN D.
Production of coal will not be stopped [radio address]. *Vital Speeches* 9: 450-52 1943.

1943 strike.

608. ROUSE, ELAINE
Union economic policies and union discipline in the bituminous wage dispute of 1949-1950. Thesis. West Virginia University, 1953.

609. ROY, ANDREW
The origin and results of miners' unions. *Ohio Mining Journal* 2: 113-20 1883/84.

610. ST. CLAIR COAL COMPANY
Answer of the St. Clair Coal Company before the Anthracite Coal Strike Commission. Scranton, Pennsylvania, 1902. 42p.

611. SALIERS, EARL A.
The coal miner; a study of his struggle to secure regulated wages in the Hocking Valley. Bethlehem, Pennsylvania, 1912. 65p.

612. SAUER, NORA
Some attitudes of the United Mine Workers of America on international affairs affecting its membership. Thesis. University of Illinois. 1944.

613. SAXON, GEORGE
From the miners' point of view. *Modern Review* 1: 409-21 1947.

"The revolt of the miner is the revolt against the atomization of the individual in production."

614. SCHLEGEL, MARVIN W.
The Workingmen's Benevolent Association: first union of anthracite miners. *Pennsylvania History* 10: 243-67 1943.

615. SCOTT, GEORGE H.
A study of the United Mine Workers of America Welfare and Retirement Fund. Thesis. West Virginia University, 1951.

616. SCOTT, KARL M.
The coal industry and the coal miners' unions in the United States since the World War. Ph.D. University of Illinois, 1931.

617. SCOTT, NELL
Social workers and labor unions. National Conference of Social Work. *Proceedings* 56: 354-64 1928.

Family case work among members of the United Mine Workers during the strike of 1927-28.

618. SELEKMAN, BENJAMIN M., AND MARY VAN KLEECK
Employes' representation in coal mines. New York: Russell Sage Foundation, 1924. 454p.

A study of the representation plan of the Colorado Fuel and Iron Co.

619. SELEKMAN, BENJAMIN M.
Miners and murder; what lies back of the labor feud in anthracite. *Survey* 60: 150-55 1928.

620. SETTLEMENT OF THE CLEARFIELD STRIKE
Black Diamond 6: 183-184A 1890/91.

Includes exchange of correspondence between the union and officials of the Cresson & Clearfield Coal & Coke Company, Pennsylvania.

621. SHALLOO, JEREMIAH P.
Private police, with special reference to Pennsylvania. Philadelphia: American Academy of Political and Social Sciences. 1933. 224p. (Monograph No. 1 of the Academy).

622. SHANE, MICHAEL
Why coal miners strike. *Common Sense* 12: 243-46 1943.

"They suffer from the industry's poverty and slothfulness".

623. SKINNER, B. F.
A digest of decisions of the Anthracite Board of Conciliation. Scranton, Pennsylvania, 1928. 258p.

624. SIXTY-TWO YEARS OF UMW
Business Week Je 7, 1952 132-38.

625. SLOCUM, WILLIAM J.
Love comes to the soft coal fields. *Nation's Business.* Jl 1950 27-8.

The threat of oil has brought and will enforce "love" between miner and operator.

626. SMITH, FRANK G.
Handling labour grievances in the bituminous coal industry. *Harvard Business Review* 19: 352-63 1941.

627. SMITH, GEORGE O.
Human relations in the coal industry. National Conference of Social Work. *Proceedings* 1922: 287-99.

628. SOMERS, GERALD G.
Grievance settlement in coal mining. Morgantown: West Virginia University, 1956. 44p. (West Virginia University Business and Economic Studies 4: 4).

629. SOUTHERN APPALACHIAN COAL OPERATORS' ASSOCIATION
Statement to the United States Coal Commission. n.p., 1923. 26p.

630. SPERO, STERLING D. AND JACOB ARONOFF
War in the Kentucky mountains. *American Mercury* 25: 226-33 1932.

631. STANLEY, LOUIS
Miners' rebellion. *Nation* 130: 356-57 1930.

A highly partisan account of the Springfield Convention of the UMWA.

632. STOCKING, GEORGE W.
Labor problems in the American bituminous coal industry. *Economic Journal* 37: 213-25 1927.

633. STOCKTON, RICHARD
Underground in Illinois; how coal miners live, work and struggle for unity. Chicago: National Research League, 1935?. 32p.

634. STODDARD, C. E.
Bituminous coal strike. *MLR* 9: 1725-42 1919.

A general history of the 1919 strike. Pertinent documents are reproduced.

635. STRIKE IN THE ANTHRACITE REGION
Colliery Engineer 8: 45-46 1887.

Includes a copy of the wage demands of miners.

636. STRIKE IN WEST VIRGINIA
Coal & Coke Jl 15, 1902 12-13; Ag 15, 1902 12-13; S 15, 1902 12-13.

637. STRIKES IN THE HISTORY OF COAL MINING IN PENNSYLVANIA
Coal 1: 237-38, 247-48, 255, 263-65 1882.

638. STUDY OF THE UNEMPLOYED IN THE BITUMINOUS COAL INDUSTRY.
MLR 39: 639-42 1934.

639. SUFFERN, ARTHUR E.
Coal miners' struggle for industrial status. New York: Macmillan, 1926. 462p.

640. SUFFERN, ARTHUR E.
Conciliation and arbitration in the coal industry of America. Boston: Houghton Mifflin, 1915. 376p.
66

641. SWAIN, GEORGE T.
The incomparable Don Chafin: review of the life of
Logan's dauntless and indomitable sheriff, who pre-
vented the invasion of Logan County on two occasions
by armed miners from the Kanawha Valley coal fields.
Charleston, West Virginia, 1962. 40p.

642. SYDENSTRICKER, EDGAR
Collective bargaining in the anthracite coal industry.
Washington: GPO, 1916. 171p. (Bureau of Labor Sta-
tistics. Bulletin 191).

643. SYDENSTRICKER, EDGAR
Settlement of disputes under agreements in the anthracite industry. *Journal of Political Economy* 24: 254-83
1916.

644. TAYLOR, PAUL F.
The Coal Mine War in Harlan County, Kentucky,
1931-32. Thesis. University of Kentucky. 1955.

645. THOMPSON, CRAIG
Reign of terror at Widen, West Virginia. *Saturday Evening Post* F 20, 1954 17-19.

646. TIPPETT, THOMAS
Horse Shoe Bottoms. New York: Harpers, 1935. 298p.

Account of mining conditions and labor relations in the Illinois
coal fields. 1870's and 1880's.

647. TIPPETT, THOMAS
Miners fight their leaders. *American Mercury* 32: 129-
37 1934.

A bitter attack on John L. Lewis.

648. TOOHEY, PAT
N.R.A., martial law, "insurrection"; the miners strike in
New Mexico. New York: Workers Library, 1934. 62p.

649. TRAIL, WILLIAM R.
History of the United Mine Workers in West Virginia,
1920-1945. Thesis. New York University. 1950.

650. TRESTER, DELMER J.
Unionism among Ohio miners in the 19th Century.
Thesis. Ohio State University, 1947.

651. TROUBLE IN THE COAL MINES, 1889
Documents of an incident at Newcastle, W.T. *Pacific
Northwest Quarterly* 37: 231-57 1946.

652. TRYON, F. G.
The effect of competitive conditions on labor relations in coal mining. *Ann. Amer. Acad.* 111: 82-95 1924.

653. UNITED MINE WORKERS CONVENTION, 1944
MLR 59: 1195-1202 1944.

A review of the proceedings.

654. UNITED MINE WORKERS OF AMERICA
Attempt by communists to seize the American labor movement. Prepared by the United Mine Workers of America and published in newspapers of the United States. Washington: GPO, 1924. 43p. (68th Congress, 1st Session. Senate Document 14).

655. UNITED MINE WORKERS OF AMERICA
The case of the bituminous coal mine workers, as presented by the United Mine Workers of America to the President's Coal Commission, appointed December, 1919. Washington, 1920. 78p.

656. UNITED MINE WORKERS OF AMERICA
Minutes of special convention to consider the anthracite strike, July 17, 18 and 19, 1902. Indianapolis: Hollenbeck Press, 1902. 55p.

657. UNITED MINE WORKERS OF AMERICA
Official records—containing correspondence between the president's office and Warren S. Stone. Indianapolis, 1924. 30p.

Stone was president of the Brotherhood of Locomotive Engineers and also an official in a non-union mine.

658. UNITED MINE WORKERS OF AMERICA
Official statement by the International Executive Board, United Mine Workers of America, in regard to the Kansas controversy. Indianapolis, 1921. 15p.

659. UNITED MINE WORKERS OF AMERICA
Statement to the United States Coal Commission on anthracite accounting and finance. Washington, 1923. 86p.

Cover title: Anthracite accounting and finance.

660. UNITED MINE WORKERS OF AMERICA
Statement to the United States Coal Commission, 1923, by the anthracite representatives of the United Mine Workers of America. Washington, 1923. 32p.

Cover title: The anthracite monopoly.

661. UNITED MINE WORKERS OF AMERICA
The truth about Coal River Collieries, of which Warren S. Stone is Chairman of the Board of Directors. Indianapolis, 1925. 16p.

Stone was president of the Brotherhood of Locomotive Engineers at the time.

662. UNITED MINE WORKERS OF AMERICA
The United Mine Workers of America and the United States Coal Commission, containing copies of the communications filed with the Commission by the miners' union. Indianapolis, 1923?. 47p.

663. UNITED MINE WORKERS OF AMERICA
Wage agreements, bituminous coal industry, division No. 1, consisting of districts No. 2-3-4-5-6-16-17-19-24-28-30-31; together with the Code of Fair Competition and the Appalachian Agreement. Washington, 1934. 594p.

664. UNITED MINE WORKERS OF AMERICA
Wage agreements, bituminous coal industry, 1935-1937, together with Guffey-Snyder Coal Stabilization Act and the Appalachian Agreement. Indianapolis, 1935?. 824p.

665. UNITED MINE WORKERS OF AMERICA. DISTRICT 1. TRI-DISTRICT CONVENTION
Scale resolutions. Hazleton, Pennsylvania, 1930. 48p.

666. UNITED MINE WORKERS OF AMERICA. DISTRICT 2
The government of coal. Clearfield, Pennsylvania. [1921]. 24p.

667. UNITED MINE WORKERS OF AMERICA. DISTRICT 6
Proceedings of special convention. Columbus, 1906?. 103p.

668. UNITED MINE WORKERS OF AMERICA. DISTRICT 19
Officers' report to special convention. Knoxville, Tennessee, 1919. 21p.

669. UNITED MINE WORKERS OF AMERICA. WELFARE AND RETIREMENT FUND
A Chronology of the U.M.W.A. Welfare and Retirement Fund, covering the period between 1945 and April 26, 1951. [Washington, 1951]. 31p.

670. U. S. ANTHRACITE COAL STRIKE COMMISSION
Report to the President on the Anthracite Coal Strike
of May-October 1902. Washington: GPO, 1903. 257p.

Appeared also as Bulletin 43 of the Commissioner of Labor.

671. U. S. BUREAU OF LABOR
Report on the miners' strike in bituminous coal field
in Westmoreland County, Pennsylvania, in 1910-11.
Washington: GPO, 1912. 255p. (62nd Congress, 2nd
Session. House Document 847).

672. U. S. CHILDREN'S BUREAU
Child labor and the welfare of children in the anthra-
cite coal mining district. Washington: GPO, 1922. 94p.
(Bureau Publication 106).

673. THE UNITED STATES COAL STRIKE AND ITS MEANING
Engineering Magazine 31: 255-61 1906.

An attack on the "arrogance" of the UMW.

674. U. S. COLORADO COAL COMMISSION
Labor difficulties in the coal fields of Colorado, letter
from the President of the United States, transmitting
report of the Colorado Coal Commission on the labor
difficulties in the coal fields of Colorado during the
years 1914 and 1915. Washington: GPO, 1916. 16p.
(64th Cong., 1st Sess. House Doc. 859).

675. U. S. COMMISSION ON INDUSTRIAL RELATIONS
Report on the Colorado Coal Strike. Washington: the
Commission, 1915. 189p.

"By George West."

676. U. S. COMMISSION ON INDUSTRIAL RELATIONS
Final Report and Testimony. Washington: the Commission, 1916. 11 volumes.

677. U. S. COMMISSIONER OF LABOR
A report on labor disturbances in the State of Colorado, from 1880 to 1904. Washington: GPO, 1904.
365p. (58th Cong., 3d Sess. Senate Doc. 122).

678. U. S. CONGRESS. HOUSE. COMMITTEE ON LABOR TROU-
BLES IN PENNSYLVANIA
Labor troubles in the anthracite regions of Pennsylva-
nia, 1887-88. Washington: GPO, 1889. 783p. (50th
Cong., 2d Sess. House. Report 4147).

Concerned largely with the activities of the Reading Railroad.

679. U. S. CONGRESS. HOUSE. COMMITTEE ON MINES AND MINING
Conditions in the coal mines of Colorado. Washington: GPO, 1914. 2916p.

680. U. S. CONGRESS. HOUSE. COMMITTEE ON MINES AND MINING
Report on the Colorado Strike Investigation. Washington: GPO, 1915. 53p. (63rd Congress, 3d Session. House. Doc. 1630).

681. U. S. CONGRESS. HOUSE. SELECT COMMITTEE ON EXISTING LABOR TROUBLES IN PENNSYLVANIA
Labor troubles in the anthracite regions of Pennsylvania, 1887-88. Washington: GPO, 1889. 783p. (50th Congress, 2nd Session. House. Report 4147).

682. U. S. CONGRESS. SENATE. COMMITTEE ON EDUCATION AND LABOR
Investigation of Paint Creek coal fields of West Virginia . . . Report. Washington: GPO, 1914. 41p. (63d Cong., 2d Sess. Senate. Report 321).

Running title: Paint Creek coal fields of West Virginia.

683. U. S. CONGRESS. SENATE. COMMITTEE ON EDUCATION AND LABOR
West Virginia coal fields. Hearings . . . to investigate the recent acts of violence in the coal fields of West Virginia and adjacent territory and the causes which led to the conditions which now exist in said territory. Washington: GPO, 1921-22. 1078p.

684. U. S. CONGRESS. SENATE. COMMITTEE ON EDUCATION AND WELFARE
West Virginia coal fields. Personal views of Senator Kenyon and views of Senators Sterling, Phipps and Warren . . . Washington: GPO, 1922. 30p. (67 Congress, 2d Session. Senate. Report 457).

685. U. S. CONGRESS. SENATE. COMMITTEE ON INTERSTATE COMMERCE
Conditions in the coal fields of Pennsylvania, West Virginia, and Ohio. Hearings before the Committee on interstate commerce, U. S. Senate, Seventieth Congress, first session, pursuant to S. Res. 105, a resolution to investigate conditions in the coal fields of Pennsylvania, West Virginia, and Ohio . . . Printed for the use of the Committee on interstate commerce. Washington: GPO, 1928. 2 volumes.

686. U. S. CONGRESS. SENATE. COMMITTEE ON LABOR AND PUBLIC WELFARE
Causes of unemployment in the coal and other domestic industries. Washington: GPO, 1955. 772p.

687. U. S. CONGRESS. SENATE. COMMITTEE ON LABOR AND PUBLIC WELFARE
Causes of unemployment in the coal and other specified industries. Washington: GPO, 1950. 512p.

688. U. S. CONGRESS. SENATE. COMMITTEE ON MANUFACTURES
Conditions in coal fields in Harlan and Bell counties, Kentucky. Washington: GPO, 1932. 286p.

689. UNITED STATES INDUSTRIAL COMMISSION
Report. Washington: GPO, 1900-1902. 19v.
    v12 On the relations and conditions of capital and labor employed in the mining industry. 747p.
    v15: 389-420 Foreign born in the coal mines.
    v17 Reports on labor organizations, labor disputes and arbitration. Chapter 8: Labor organizations of mine workers.

690. U. S. TAKES OVER THE COAL MINES
Life My 10, 1943 23-29.
1943 strike.

691. VAN KLEECK, MARY
Miners and management; a study of the collective agreement between the United Mine Workers of America and the Rocky Mountain Fuel Company, and an analysis of the problem of coal in the U. S. New York: Russell Sage, 1934. 391p.

692. VEAL, PHIL
Obstructionists in the United Mine Workers. New York: New York Labor News, 1911. 16p.
"Crippling hand of false leadership—how it keeps most powerful craft union in the land at mercy of employers."

693. VIRTUE, G. O.
The anthracite mine laborers. U. S. Department of Labor. *Bulletin* 13: 728-74 1897.
A very useful history of labor relations and unionization in the anthracite industry.

694. VIRTUE, G. O.
The anthracite miners' strike of 1900. *Journal of Political Economy* 9: 1-23 1900.
72

695. VORSE, MARY H.
Illinois miners. *Scribners* 93: 169-72 1933.

The Progressive Miners of America and its struggle with the United Mine Workers.

696. WALKER, CHARLES R.
Red blood in Kentucky; why 100 percent Americans turn Communist. *Forum* 87: 18-23 1932.

The "mine wars" in Harlan County.

697. WALLACE, GEORGE SELDEN
In the matter of the Hearing before a subcommittee of the Committee on education and labor of the United States Senate, pursuant to Senate Resolution 37, authorizing the appointment of a Committee to make an investigation of conditions in the Paint Creek district, West Virginia. Brief of George S. Wallace for the state of West Virginia, dealing with the fourth section of the investigation. Charleston, West Virginia, Tribune Printing Co. [1913]. 63p.

698. WALSH, WILLIAM J.
The United Mine Workers of America as an economic and social force in the anthracite territory. Ph.D. Catholic University of America. 1931.

699. WARFARE IN THE COAL FIELDS
U. S. News Ag 28, 1953 54-57.

Account of the bitter struggle between the UMWA and J. G. Bradley, the owner of mines in the Widen, West Virginia area.

700. WARNE, COLSTON E.
Armistice or peace in coal. *Current History* ns4: 242-48 1943.

The 1943 strike.

701. WARNE, COLSTON E.
Coal dispute enters its second year. *Current History* ns6: 2-7-13 1944.

The 1944 strike.

702. WARNE, FRANK J.
The anthracite coal strike. *Ann. Amer. Acad.* 17: 15-52 1901.

703. WARNE, FRANK J.
Coal mine workers; a study in labor organization. New York: Longmans, 1905. 252p.

704. WARNE, FRANK J.
Miner and operator; a study of labor conditions in the anthracite coal fields. *Outlook* 82: 643-56 1906.

705. WARNE, FRANK J.
The miners' union, its business management. *Ann. Amer. Acad.* 25: 67-86 1905.

706. WARNE, FRANK J.
Trade agreement in the coal industry. *Ann. Amer. Acad.* 36: 340-48 1910.

707. WARNE, FRANK J.
The Slav invasion and the mine workers; a study in immigration. Philadelphia: Lippincott, 1904. 211p.

708. WARNE, FRANK J.
Union movement among coal mine workers. Washington: GPO, 1904. (U. S. Bureau of Labor. Bulletin 51 pp. 380-414).

709. WARNER, ARTHUR
West Virginia—industrialism gone mad. *Nation* 113: 372-3 1921.

710. WARRINER, SAMUEL D.
The Anthracite Board of Conciliation. AIME. *Transactions* 42: 390-402 1911.

711. WEBB, JOHN N.
Unemployment in a depressed coal-mining area in southern Illinois. *MLR* 49: 1295-1310 1939.

712. WEITZELL, E. H.
Industrial relations in coal mines. American Mining Congress. *Proceedings* 25: 78-85 1922.

713. WELLMAN, WALTER
Fairmont coal region, a treatise; by Walter Wellman . . . [Chicago, 1902]. 48p.

Reprint from Chicago Record-Herald.

714. WEST, HAROLD E.
Civil war in the West Virginia coal mines. *Survey* 30: 37-50 1913.

A letter by the secretary of the West Virginia Mining Association protesting this article appears on p.8 of the same issue.

715. WEST VIRGINIA. ATTORNEY GENERAL'S OFFICE
Conditions in the Paint Creek district of West Virginia. Investigation by Sub-Committee of the Committee of Education and Labor of the United States Senate. Senate Resolution No. 37. Brief of John B. Morrison and J. E. Brown, Charleston, Assistant Attorneys General on behalf of the state of West Virginia. Tribune Printing Co., [1913]. 133p.

716. WEST VIRGINIA. GOVERNOR'S COMMISSION ON LOGAN COUNTY SITUATION
Report and digest of evidence taken by Commission appointed by the Governor of West Virginia in connection with the Logan County situation. Charleston, West Virginia: [Tribune Print. Company, 1919]. 69p.

The "situation" was the labor unrest in the coal fields of southern West Virginia.

717. WEST VIRGINIA. GOVERNOR'S INVESTIGATING COMMITTEE
Report and proceedings of Widen Strike Committee. Charleston, 1953. 184p. (Appears in West Virginia. Legislature. House of Delegates. Journal. Appendix Mr 2, 1953).

718. WEST VIRGINIA. MINING INVESTIGATION COMMISSION, 1912
Report of West Virginia Mining Investigation Commission, appointed by Governor Glasscock on the 28th day of August, 1912 . . . [Charleston, W. Va., Tribune Printing Co., 1912]. 24p.

719. WESTERN FEDERATION OF MINERS
Category of crime of the Mine Operators' Association. Denver: The Federation, 1904. 31p.

"A partial list, showing 851 men murdered in less than four years." Cover title reads: Reply of the Western Federation of Miners to the "Red Book" of the Mine Operators' Association.

720. WHITE, THOMAS E.
Development and operation of the welfare and retirement fund in the bituminous coal industry. Ph.D. University of Pittsburgh, 1954.

721. THE WHITE SLAVES OF MONOPOLIES: OR, JOHN FITZ PATRICK, THE MINER, SOLDIER AND WORKINGMAN'S FRIEND
A history of his struggles with mine owners, corporations . . . Harrisburg: L. S. Hart, 1884. 371p.

722. WIEBE, ROBERT H.
The anthracite strike of 1902; a record of confusion. *Mississippi Valley Historical Review* 48: 229-51 1961.

723. WIECK, EDWARD A.
The American Miners' Association; a record of the origin of coal miners' unions in the United States. New York: Russell Sage, 1940. 330p.

Contemporary documents illustrating the development of mine unions are reproduced on pages 217-309.

724. WIECK, EDWARD A.
Coal miners journal. *Atlantic Monthly* 134: 5-16 1924.

Describes the activities of a member of the pit committee in a bituminous coal mine.

725. WIECK, EDWARD A.
General Alexander Bradley. *American Mercury* 8: 69-74 1926.

Account of Bradley's activity during the labor disputes in the Illinois coal fields, 1897.

726. WIECK, EDWARD A.
The miners' case and the public interest; a documented chronology. New York: Russell Sage, 1947. 92p.

727. WILLCOX, DAVID
Comments upon suggestions presented by a committee in behalf of some of the employees to the producers of anthracite coal. New York, 1906. 26p.

728. WILLIAMS, GERTRUDE M.
Twenty-nine men in contempt. *Nation* 140: 443-45 1935.

Account of the struggle of the United Anthracite Miners in the area around Wilkes-Barre, Pennsylvania.

729. WILLIAMS, TALCOTT
The Anthracite coal crisis. *Atlantic* 87: 447-56 1901.

730. WILLIAMS, WHITING
What's on the worker's mind; by one who put on overalls to find out. New York: Scribner, 1921. 329p.

731. WILLITS, JOSEPH H.
The conclusions and recommendations of the U. S. Coal Commission as to labor relations in bituminous coal mining. *Ann. Amer. Acad.* 111: 96-107 1924.

732. WILSON, HELEN
Child labor and the welfare of children in an anthracite coal mining district. Washington: GPO, 1922. 94p. (Children's Bureau. Publication 106).

The Shenandoah area of Pennsylvania.

733. WILSON, WILLIAM B.
Speech of W. B. Wilson, Secretary-Treasurer, United Mine Workers of America. Delivered at Ashland . . . October, 1901. Indianapolis: Hollenbeck Press, 1901. 20p.

734. WOLFE, GEORGE
Survey of conditions of operators and production in so-called open-shop districts of West Virginia. American Mining Congress. *Proceedings* 23: 315-22 1920.

Miners are happier in non-union fields; thus "the United Mine Workers of America will not have very much chance to gain a foothold in our midst."

735. WOLL, MATTHEW
Injunctions in West Virginia. *American Federationist* 32: 572-78 1925.

736. WOLTMAN, FREDERICK AND W. L. NUNN
Cossacks. *American Mercury* 15: 399-406 1928.

The "cossacks" are local officials in general and the Pennsylvania State Police in particular.

737. WORK OR IDLENESS IN THE BITUMINOUS COAL INDUSTRY
New York: Consolidation Coal Company, 1925. 13p.

"A correspondence between John D. Rockefeller, Jr., C. W. Watson, President, Consolidation Coal Company, and John L. Lewis, President, United Mine Workers of America."

738. WRIGHT, CARROLL D.
Importance of arbitration as a factor in the advancement of the mining industry. American Mining Congress. *Proceedings* 11 Pt. 2: 52-56 1908.

739. WRIGHT, HELEN S.
Coal's worst year. Boston: R. G. Badger, 1924. 202p.

The anthracite strike of 1922.

740. YOUNG, DALLAS M.
A history of the Progressive Miners of America. Ph.D. University of Illinois. 1940.

741. YOUNG, DALLAS M.
      Origin of the Progressive Mine Workers of America.
      Illinois State Historical Society. *Journal* 40: 313-30
      1947.

742. ZIEGLER, MARTIN
      Social legislation for the protection of coal miners in
      Pennsylvania. Thesis. Penn State College. 1947.

Economics

(Management, costs, prices, sales, etc.)

743. ADAMIC, LOUIS
Great bootleg coal industry. *Nation* 140: 46-49 1935.

Account of the small non-union mines worked by unemployed miners in the Pennsylvania anthracite area.

744. ADAMS, JOHN W.
Costs and efficiency in the wholesaling and retailing of coal. *Ann. Amer. Acad.* 111: 145-54 1924.

745. ADAMS, ROBERT T.
Technology and productivity in bituminous coal. *MLR* 84: 1081-86 1961.

746. ADAMS, RUSSELL K.
A study of marginal coal mines in southern West Virginia. Thesis. University of Pennsylvania. 1954.

747. ADDERFER, EVAN
Paleozoic pains in Pennsylvania. Federal Reserve Bank of Philadelphia. *Business Review* F 1963 3-13.

A general review of the economic problems of coal and related industries.

748. AGOR, JOSEPH
Bootleg coal industry. *American Mercury* 34: 416-21 1935.

In the anthracite region of Pennsylvania.

749. ALFORD, NEWELL G.
Analysis of bituminous coal mines suspended from 1923 to 1932, inclusive. AIME. *Transactions* 108: 476-88 1934.

750. AMERICAN ENGINEERING COUNCIL
Industrial coal; purchase, delivery and storage. New York: Ronald Press, 1924. 419p.

751.   ANKENY, MARLING J.
A look at coal's future markets. *Public Utilities Fortnightly* 70: 413-17 1962.

A generally optimistic view by the director of the U. S. Bureau of Mines.

752.   ANTHRACITE COAL PRODUCTION CONTROL PLAN
University of Pennsylvania Law Review 102: 368-94 1954.

A history and analysis of the Plan, in effect since 1941.

753.   APPALACHIAN COALS INC. ORGANIZES
Coal Age 37: 123 1932.

Includes a "summary of progress in the formation of district sales agencies."

754.   ARCHBALD, HUGH
The problem of efficiency and cost reduction in coal mining. *Ann. Amer. Acad.* 111: 181-190 1924.

755.   ASHBURNER, CHARLES A.
Coal trade and miners' wages in the United States in the year 1888. AIME. *Transactions* 18: 122-39 1889/90.

756.   ASHLEY, GEORGE H.
New coal age. *Economic Geology* 44: 161-68 1949.

Author sees a bright future for the coal industry. His optimism based on a sharp increase in the need for power and the assumed unavailability of other power sources in significant quantities at competitive prices.

757.   ASHMEAD, DEVER C.
Can anthracite mines be operated profitably on more than one shift. AIME. *Transactions* 68: 332-59 1922.

758.   AVRIL, LAWRENCE P.
Variations in the financial experience of bituminous coal companies. Thesis. Indiana University. 1950.

759.   AYER, THOMAS P.
Coal prices: a selected bibliography. *Ann. Amer. Acad.* 111: 344-62 1924.

760.   BACKMAN, JULES
Bituminous coal wages, profits and productivity. [Washington], 1950. 128p.

Prepared for the Southern Coal Producers Association.

761. BAKERMAN, THEODORE
Anthracite coal; a study of advanced industrial decline. Ph.D. University of Pennsylvania. 1956.

762. BALLERT, ALBERT G.
The coal trade of the Great Lakes and the Port of Toledo. *Geographical Review* 38: 194-205 1948.

763. BALLERT, ALBERT G.
The Great Lakes coal trade; present and future. *Economic Geography* 29: 48-59 1953.

764. BALSLEY, HOWARD L.
A political-economic solution to the coal problem. *Western Political Quarterly* 3: 620-28 1950.

Excess production could be controlled by the proper use of government power—especially taxation.

765. BARGER, HAROLD AND S. H. SCHURR
The mining industries, 1899-1939. A study of output, employment and productivity. New York: National Bureau of Economic Research, 1944. 452p. (*Its* Publication No. 43).

766. BEDDOW, W. W.
Coal company organization. *Coal Age* 13: 788-80 1918.

Author urges better coordination of departments in the management of coal companies.

767. BELL, JOHN F. L. AND GOODSPEED, ALLEN W.
Managing forest lands for profit. *Coal Age* Ja 1956 74-77.

The Island Creek Coal Co. conducts an active and progressive forest management program on its holdings.

768. BERNHEIMER, F. P.
Study of the Pennsylvania anthracite coal tax. Thesis. University of Pennsylvania. 1925.

769. BITUMINOUS COAL; RICHEST MAN ON POOR STREET
Forbes Ja 1, 1958 67-70.

"Coal management rarely makes its riches pay their way."

770. BITUMINOUS OPERATORS' SPECIAL COMMITTEE.
Comparative efficiency of labor in the bituminous coal industry under union and non-union operation. Submitted to the United States Coal commission by the Bituminous Operators' Special Committee, September 10, 1923. [Washington, 1923]. 253p.

771. BLANKENSHIP, RONDAL C.
Appalachian Coals, Inc.; a bituminous coal producers' marketing agency. Thesis. West Virginia University. 1949.

772. BOCKUS, C. E.
Bituminous coal problems. *Harvard Business Review* 1: 290-99 1923.

773. BOECKLIN, WERNER
The coal industry of Greater New York. *Engineering Magazine* 35: 893-905 1908.

774. BOOTLEG MINING OF ANTHRACITE
MLR 45: 1323-26 1937.

775. BOOZ, ALLEN & HAMILTON, INC.
Survey of opportunities to stimulate coal utilization. Washington: Office of Coal Research, Dept. of Interior, 1962. 2 vols.

776. BORSODI, WILLIAM
Coal advertising; a collection of selling phrases, descriptions and illustrated advertisements. New York: Advertizers' Cyclopedia Company, 1910. 128p.

777. BOSTON. CHAMBER OF COMMERCE. COMMITTEE ON FUEL SUPPLY
The buying and handling of steam coal; report by the Committee on Fuel Supply of the Boston Chamber of Commerce, November, 1909. [Boston? 1909]. 48p.

778. BOWDEN, WITT
Wage and price structure in the bituminous coal industry. *MLR* 53: 293-313 1941.

779. BOWMAN, MARY J. AND W. W. HAYNES
Resources and people in East Kentucky: Problems and potentials of a lagging economy. Baltimore: Johns Hopkins, 1963. 448p.

This is by far the most comprehensive study of the economic and social problems of East Kentucky.

780. BRADLEY, JOSEPH G.
Southern coal production and distribution in relation to American industry. American Mining Congress. *Proceedings* 25: 86-92 1922.

781. BRITISH COAL MINING PRODUCTIVITY TEAM
Coal; report of a productivity team representing the British coal mining industry which visited the United States of America in 1951. London: Anglo-American Council on Productivity. 1951. 107p.

782. BURKE, STEPHEN P.
"Price-fixing" in the bituminous coal industry; a legal-economic problem. Fairmont, West Virginia, 1935. 40p.

783. BURROWS, JOHN S.
Results of purchasing coal under government specifications. Washington: GPO, 1909. 44p. (USGS. Bulletin 378).

784. BYERS, W. L.
Connellsville coke selling problems. *Coal Age* 3: 872-75 1913.

785. CALDWELL, NAT AND GENE S. GRAHAM
The strange romance between John L. Lewis and Cyrus Eaton. *Harpers* D 1961 25-32.

"The first full report on a case revealing a conspiracy in which a big union and a big capitalist got together to force little coal mines out of business and thousands of miners out of work."

786. CAMPBELL, THOMAS C.
Competition in the bituminous coal industry. West Virginia Academy of Sciences. *Proceedings* 23: 128-32 1951.

"There is little doubt that the bituminous coal industry is almost perfectly competitive."

787. CANNEL COAL COMES INTO USE AS A SUBSTITUTE FUEL
Pennsylvania Dept. of Internal Affairs. *Monthly Bulletin* F 1943 9-11.

788. CARLSON, OLIVER
Bootleg coal. *Harpers* 170: 613-22 1935.

The anthracite region of Pennsylvania.

789. CARTER, EDWARD W.
Price fixing in the bituminous coal industry. *Ann. Amer. Acad.* 193: 120-29 1937.

790. CASSANO, JAMES
Mechanization of western coal mines. Colorado School of Mines. *Quarterly* 45 No. 2B (1950) 13-25.

791.   CHAMBERLIN, J. W.
Coal shipping on the Great Lakes. *Coal Age* 4: 188-91,
222-26, 268-70, 298-300, 1913.

792.   CHANCE, H. M.
Appraisal of coal lands for taxation. AIME. *Transactions* 50: 625-39 1914.

793.   CHANCE, H. M.
Appraisal of coal properties. AIME. *Transactions* 74:
443-55 1926.

794.   CHANCE, H. M.
Valuation of coal land. AIME. *Transactions* 47: 111-46
1913.

795.   CHAPLIN, RONALD L.
Spatial changes in coal employment within Southern Illinois. Thesis. Southern Illinois University. 1961.

796.   CHARLÉ, EDWIN G.
The demand for coal for power generation in the Tennessee Valley. Ph.D. University of Indiana. 1958.

797.   CHICAGO COAL BOARD
Black Diamond 6: 760 1890/91.

Account of formation.

798.   CHRISTENSON, CARROLL L.
Economic redevelopment in bituminous coal; the special
case of technological advance in United States coal
mines, 1930-1960. Cambridge: Harvard University
Press, 1962. 312p. (Wertheim Publications in Industrial
Relations).

799.   COAL
Fortune Mr 1947 85-99; Ap 1947 99-105.

A series of articles on "our No. 1 national resources, which we
mine inefficiently, transport wastefully and consume foolishly."

800.   COAL: CHALLENGE AND RESPONSE
Forbes My 15, 1963 23-7.

"Now coal may be poised for a real comeback."

801.   COAL: THE DWINDLING DOMAIN
Fortune S 1953 61-2.

"We are a 450-million-ton industry still trying to act like a
750-million-ton industry."

802. COAL COMPANY GETS OFF THE HOOK
Business Week Ap 20, 1957 99-100.

The revitalization of the Philadelphia & Reading Co.

803. A COAL PIPE LINE
Black Diamond 17: 213 1896.

Report of an experiment near Pittsburgh.

804. COAL SHIPPING ON THE GREAT LAKES
Coal Age 4: 374-76, 408-11, 449-51, 531-33 1913.

805. COAL, THE PITT-CONSOL ADVENTURE
Fortune Jl 1947 96-105.

Account of the Pittsburgh-Consolidation Coal Co.

806. COAL TRADE ASSOCIATION OF INDIANA
Coal production in Indiana by rail-shipping mines, 1926-1950, classified by railroads, showing individual mine production, vein of coal, and type of operation. Terre Haute, 1951. 37p.

807. COAL'S COMEBACK AT MOSS NO. 3
Fortune O 1963 130-35.

Moss No. 3 is the giant mine of the Clinchfield Coal Company (Pittston) in southwest Virginia. The mine is an example of the massive investment now being made in coal.

808. CONANT, C. B.
Coal fever: the price and prospects of anthracite coal. *Merchants' Magazine* 52: 349-64 1865.

"Why is coal so high?"

809. CONFERENCE ON ECONOMIC RESEARCH IN THE BITUMINOUS COAL INDUSTRY
Proceedings. Morgantown: West Virginia University, 1953. 15p. (West Virginia University Business & Economic Studies 2: 2).

810. CONFERENCE ON PRICE RESEARCH
Report of the Committee on Prices in the Bituminous Coal Industry. New York: National Bureau of Economics Research, 1938. 144p.

811. CONFERENCE ON THE COMMERCIAL AND ECONOMIC HEALTH OF THE BITUMINOUS COAL INDUSTRY, WEST VIRGINIA UNIVERSITY, 1953
Proceedings. Morgantown, West Virginia University, 1954. 14p. (Business and Economic Studies 3: 1).

812. CONNER, ELI
What is to become of the anthracite coal industry. *Coal Age* 5: 912-17 1914.

"If the railroads must part with their coal holdings, it is suggested that the industry be governed by a board of commissioners."

813. COWAN, DONALD R.
More capital equipment: coal's foremost economic need. Washington: National Coal Association, [1948]. 59p.

814. CREWS, RALPH
Cooperation in the marketing of coal. American Marketing Congress. *Proceedings* 19: 184-92 1916.

815. CRUM, W. L. AND H. B. VANDERBLUE
Coal mining and the business cycle. *Harvard Business Review* 4: 71-77 1925.

816. CUSHING, GEORGE H.
Selling coal. American Economic Association. *Papers & proceedings* 11: 85-93 1921.

817. DADDOW, SAMUEL H.
Coal, iron and oil. Pottsville & Philadelphia, 1866. 808p.

818. DAVIS, BLAINE A.
Marketing problems of bituminous coal. *Harvard Business Review* 11: 97-106 1932.

819. DAY, DAVID T.
The course of the retail coal trade. *National Geographic* 13: 394-98 1902.

820. DEVINE, EDWARD T.
Coal; economic problems of the mining, marketing and consumption of anthracite and soft coal in the United States. Bloomington, Indiana: American Review Service Press, 1925. 448p.

821. DEVINE, EDWARD T.
Fact-finding in the coal industry. Academy of Political Science. *Proceedings* 13: 5-13 1928.

It is in the interest of the public and the industry itself that more information be developed and made available.

822. DILWORTH, JOHN B. (CHAIRMAN)
Report of Committee on Methods of Valuing Coal Properties. AIME. *Transactions* 108: 400-42 1934.

823. DILWORTH, JOHN B.
Valuation of coal properties. AIME. *Transactions* 76: 215-36 1928.

824. DISTRIBUTION AND USE OF BITUMINOUS COAL IN CO-LUMBUS, OHIO
Columbus: Ohio State University, 1933. 43p. (OSU. Bureau of Business Research, Special Report 44).

825. DIXON, HARRY M.
The Illinois coal mining industry. Ph.D. University of Illinois. 1951.

826. DONNEGAN, JOHN J.
Sales promotion activity in the anthracite industry. Thesis. University of Pennsylvania. 1951.

827. DORLAND, JACK A.
The 5½ year cycle in soft coal stocks. *Cycles* 13: 181-3 1962.

828. DULUTH AND WEST SUPERIOR; THEIR PRESENT AND FU-TURE AS GREAT COAL DISTRIBUTING CENTERS
Black Diamond 6: 179-81 1890/91.

829. DUNN, STEPHEN F.
Position paper of United States employer delegate to ILO tripartite technical meeting on the social conse-quences of the crisis in the coal mining industry, Geneva, Switzerland, January 16-26, 1961. Washington: Nation-al Coal Association, 1961. 17p.

830. DURAND, WALTER
Where the consumer's dollar goes. *Ann. Amer. Acad.* 111: 125-44 1924.

Analysis of prices and profits in the anthracite coal industry.

831. EAVENSON, HOWARD N.
Regulation of the coal industry. AIME. *Transactions* 119: 380-91 1936.

832. ECKEL, EDWIN C.
Coal, iron, and war. New York: Holt, 1920. 375p.

833. EGGLESTON, RICHARD C.
Forestry for mining companies. West Virginia Coal Mining Institute. *Proceedings* 1911 270-88.

834. EMERY, JAMES A.
A public policy for the coal industry. American Mining Congress. *Proceedings* 25: 99-105 1922.

835. EVEREST, HERBERT A.
Economics in a small coal mine. **AIME.** *Transactions* 54: 185-87 1916.

836. FEDERAL RESERVE BANK OF CLEVELAND
Changing fortunes of bituminous coal. Cleveland, 1957. 31p.

Appeared first in four issues of its Monthly Review for 1956.

837. FERNOW, B. E.
The mining industry in its relation to forestry. **AIME.** *Transactions* 17: 264-75 1888/89.

838. FIES, MILTON H.
Case of the Alabama coal operators . . . Birmingham, 1934. 16p.

Argument against the threatened competition of the TVA.

839. FISHER, WALDO E.
Economic consequences of the seven-hour day and wage changes in the bituminous coal industry. Philadelphia, 1939. 130p. (Industrial Research Department, Wharton School of Finance & Commerce, University of Pennsylvania. Research Studies XXXII).

840. FISHER, WALDO E. AND CHARLES M. JAMES
Minimum price fixing in the bituminous coal industry. Princeton: Princeton University Press, 1955. 523p.

841. FISHMAN, LEO AND BETTY G.
Bituminous coal production during World War II. *Southern Economic Journal* 18: 391-96 1952.

842. FLEDDERUS, MARY L. AND MARY VAN KLEECK
Technology and livelihood. New York: Russell Sage, 1944. 237p.

Contains data on technological change and increasing labor productivity in the bituminous coal industry.

843. FLEMING, HENRY S.
Report to the Bituminous Coal Trade Association on the present and future of the bituminous coal trade. New York, 1908. 87p.

844. FLYNN, JOHN T.
Bootleg coal. *Colliers* D 5, 1936 12-13.

Account of the "bootleg coal business" in the Pennsylvania anthracite fields.

845. FOHL, W. E.
Division of labor in bituminous coal mining. *Engineering Magazine* 40: 175-80 1910.

"The energies of most coal miners are being inefficiently and dangerously directed." Author blames poor management for many of the difficulties of the coal industry.

846. FOREIGN MARKETS FOR AMERICAN COAL
Washington: GPO, 1900. 312p. (Special Consular Reports XXI, pt. 1).

847. FORSYTHE, J. R.
Coal's comeback; an evaluation. *Analysts Journal* N 1958 33-36.

848. FOSTER, JOHN F. AND RICHARD E. LUND
Economics of fuel gas from coal. New York: McGraw-Hill, 1950. 289p.

849. FRITZ, W. G. AND T. A. VEENSTRA
Regional shifts in the bituminous coal industry. Pittsburgh: University of Pittsburgh, Bureau of Business Research, 1935. 197p. (*Its* Monograph No. 4).

"With special reference to Pennsylvania."

850. GANDY, HARRY L.
A proposal that the coal industry be let alone. *Quarterly Journal of Economics* 39: 484-88 1925.

851. GANDY, HARRY L.
Some trends in the bituminous coal industry. *Ann. Amer. Acad.* 147:84-88 1930.

852. GENERAL POLICIES COMMITTEE OF ANTHRACITE OPERATORS
The anthracite emergency of 1922-1923, and how it was handled. Submitted to the United States Coal Commission April 23, 1923. n.p., 22p.

853. GENERAL POLICIES COMMITTEE OF ANTHRACITE OPERATORS
Competition in the anthracite industry. n.p., 1923. 72p.

"A statement showing unrestricted competition between more than 100 Anthracite Producers, with the largest company producing about 15% of the total."

854. GILBERTSON, H. S.
Introducing the practical man to modern management. *Ann. Amer. Acad.* 119: 115-20 1925.

Discusses efforts to give the mine foreman a broader "company-wide" viewpoint.

855. GINGER, RAY
Managerial employees in anthracite, 1902: a study in occupational mobility. *Journal of Economic History* 14: 146-57 1954.

856. GITLOW, A. L.
Some economic effects of industrial concentration. *Southern Economic Journal* 17: 191-95 1950.

Examination of the effects of concentration in the coal industry.

857. GOLDENWEISER, E. A.
Incomes of bituminous coal producers. *JASA* 17: 203-9 1920.

858. GOLDENWEISER, E. A.
Report of the Bituminous Coal Commission. *American Economic Review* 10: 401-7 1920.

A commentary on the findings of the Commission.

859. GRADY, WILLIAM H.
Cost factors in coal production. AIME. *Transactions* 51: 138-76 1915.

860. GRAYSON, CHARLES
Fresh appraisal of coal industry today. *Magazine of Wall Street* 101: 343-45 1957.

861. GREINER, JOHN E.
Coal docks on the Great Lakes; report of an investigation made for the Baltimore & Ohio Railroad Company. Baltimore, 1914. 317p.

862. GRIESS, P. R. AND G. F. DEASY
Some regional differences in the decline of Pennsylvania's anthracite industry and their implications in area development. Pennsylvania Academy of Science. *Proceedings* 36: 247-54 1962.

863. GUNDLACK, DORIS
Wages, employment, and unionism in the bituminous coal mining industry of the United States from 1929 to 1933. Thesis. University of Illinois. 1934.

864. HAMILTON, WALTER H. AND HELEN R. WRIGHT
The case of bituminous coal. New York: Macmillan, 1925. 310p.

"This inquiry is concerned with the question of how adequately the prevailing form of organization enables the industry to do the things which the community may reasonably expect from it."

865. HAMILTON, WALTER H.
Coal and the economy; a demurrer. *Yale Law Journal* 50: 595-612 1941.

"Joinder in demurrer" by Eugene V. Rostow. *Yale Law Journal* 50: 613-20.

866. HAMILTON, WALTER H.
The problem of bituminous coal. *American Labor Legislation Review* 16: 217-29 1926.

867. HAMILTON, WALTER H. AND HELEN R. WRIGHT
A way of order for bituminous coal. New York: Macmillan, 1928. 365p.

868. HAMMOND, M. B.
The Coal Commission reports and the coal situation. *Quarterly Journal of Economics* 38: 541-81 1924.

869. HAND, ALFRED
Titles to coal land in Pennsylvania and incidental monopolies connected therewith. *Yale Law Journal* 16: 167-75 1907.

870. HARD COAL
Fortune F 1931 72-83.

A general survey of the development and current status of the anthracite industry.

871. HARDING, G. E.
American coal production and use. *Economic Geography* 22: 46-53 1946.

872. HARDY, CARROLL F.
The position of coal—present and future. Kentucky Mining Institute. *Proceedings* 11: 46-58 1952/53.

873. HARING, H. A.
Bootlegging methods in anthracite. *Annalist* 21: 351 1923.

The extreme shortage of coal in the northeast led to bootlegging.

874. HARLINE, OSMOND L.
Economics of the Indiana coal industry. Ph.D. University of Indiana. 1958.

875. HARRIS, GEORGE W.
The Consolidation Coal Company. *Coal Age* 14: 1148-53 1918.
General account of its operations.

876. HAYNES, WILLIAM H.
Present and prospective markets for West Kentucky Coal. Lexington, 1955. 124p. (University of Kentucky. Bureau of Business Research. Bulletin 30).

877. HEDSTROM, ERIC L.
The coal trade of Buffalo. *Black Diamond* S 15, 1888 105-8.

878. HENDERSON, JAMES M.
Efficiency and pricing in the coal industry. *Review of Economics & Statistics* 38: 50-60 1956.

879. HENDERSON, JAMES M.
The efficiency of the coal industry; an application of linear planning. Cambridge: Harvard University Press, 1958. 146p. (Harvard Economic Studies 103).

880. HENDERSON, JAMES M.
A short-run model for the coal industry. *Review of Economics & Statistics* 37: 336-46 1955.

881. HENRY, PATRICIA A.
The attempts of John L. Lewis to stabilize the coal industry. Thesis. University of Wyoming. 1958.

882. HESS, WILLIAM H.
The present and potential uses of sub-bituminous coal. Thesis. University of Pennsylvania. 1948.

883. HESSE, ALFRED W.
The principles of coal property evaluation. New York: J. Wiley, 1930. 183p.

884. HILDEBRANDT COAL COMPANY
Black Diamond N 27, 1954 24.

885. HOFFMAN, JOHN N.
Major economic changes in the mining and distribution of Pennsylvania bituminous coal. Ph.D. Pennsylvania State University. 1961.

886. HOLM, EDWIN E.
Production and marketing of coal in Virginia and the
nation. Richmond: Virginia Department of Conservation
and Development, 1955. 102p. proc.

887. HOLMES, LESLIE A.
Variations in coal tonnage production in Illinois, 1900-
1940. Ph.D. University of Illinois. 1942.

888. HOOPER, WALLACE D.
Operating costs of retailing coal in Columbus. Columbus: Ohio State University, 1932. 43p. (OSU. Bureau
of Business Research. Monograph 20).

889. HOTCHKISS, WILLARD E. AND OTHERS
Mechanization, employment and output per man in bituminous coal mining. Philadelphia: WPA, 1939. 436p.
(National research project on reemployment opportunities and recent changes in industrial techniques . . . Mineral technology and output per man studies . . . Report
E-9).

890. HOWE, R. E.
The coal marketing agency. *Journal of Marketing* 10:
35-41 1945/46.

Account of Appalachian Coals, Inc., a marketing agency in the
southern high volatile fields.

891. HSIANG, T.
Competition of substitute fuels in the anthracite industry. Thesis. University of Pennsylvania. 1947.

892. HULL, AUTHUR M.
Practical plans for getting new business; a book of helpful hints for retail coal merchants. Chicago, 1915. 156p.

893. HUNT, EDWARD EYRE
What the coal commission found; an authoritative summary by the staff. Baltimore: Williams Wilkins, 1925.
416p.

894. HUNT, T. S.
Coal and iron of southern Ohio considered with relation
to the Hocking Valley coal field . . . followed by a view
of the coal trade of the West. Salem, Massachusetts:
Naturalist's Agency, 1874. 78p.

895. HURST, THOMAS E.
Tennessee coal mining and marketing trends. Thesis.
East Tennessee State College. 1951.

896. HUTCHINSON, SPENCER AND A. J. BREITENSTEIN
Competitive position of coal and petroleum in the United States. AIME. *Transactions* 108: 461-75 1934.

897. ILLINOIS COAL OPERATORS ASSOCIATION
Illinois mining machine differential. n.p., 1923. 24p.

"An illustration of arbitrary maintenance . . . of conditions of competitive inequality, to the great prejudice of one of the largest coal producing states." Statement submitted to the U. S. Coal Commission.

898. ILLINOIS MINING QUESTIONS
Black Diamond 6: 812, 844-45 1890/91.

"Reply of the coal miners to the protest and argument of the coal operators of Illinois against adverse legislation."

899. IOWA. STATE PLANNING BOARD
Some aspects of the Iowa coal industry. Des Moines, 1939. 64p. proc.

900. ISLAND CREEK; COAL AT A PROFIT
Fortune Mr 1938 86-94.

Account of the development and operation of the Island Creek Coal Co.

901. JAMES, CHARLES M.
Measuring productivity in coal mining. Philadelphia: University of Pennsylvania. Warton School of Finance and Commerce, 1952. 96p. (Research Report 13).

"A case study of multiple input measurement at the county level in Pennsylvania 1919-1948."

902. JANNEY, JOHN
When public opinion runs out on the law. *American Magazine* F 1937 16-17.

Account of the open bootleg coal industry in the Pennsylvania anthracite fields.

903. JOHNSEN, JULIA E.
Government regulation of the coal industry. New York: H. W. Wilson, 1926. 144p.

904. JOHNSEN, JULIA E.
Selected articles on government ownership of coal mines. New York: H. W. Wilson, 1923. 392p.

905. JOHNSON, ALLEN J.
Anthracite as a domestic fuel. AIME. *Transactions* 108: 360-79 1934.

94

906. JOHNSON, ARTHUR F.
Coal as a source of power for production of aluminum. *Mining Engineering* 7: 358-63 1955.

907. JONES, ELIOT
Anthracite coal combination in the United States; with some account of the early development of the anthracite coal industry. Cambridge: Harvard University Press, 1914. 261p. (Harvard Economic Studies XI).

908. JONES, F. ADDISON
Depletion, depreciation and coal mining. *Taxes* 38: 31-42 1960.

909. KARP, MICHAEL
Why is coal losing its share of the home heating market in Philadelphia. Thesis. University of Pennsylvania. 1960.

910. KELLER, JOSEPH H.
The accounting and tax aspects of depletion in the coal mining industry. Thesis. University of Pennsylvania. 1949.

911. KEMP, JAMES F.
The anthracite situation and problem. New York, 1903. 22p. (Engineering Company of America. Bulletin 1).

912. KIESSLING, O. E.
Coal mining in the south. *Ann. Amer. Acad.* 153: 84-93 1931.

913. KIESSLING, O. E. AND F. G. TYRON
The economics of distribution. *Coal Age* 33: 19-23 1928.

914. KING, CLYDE L., ED.
The price of coal, anthracite and bituminous. *Ann. Amer. Acad.* 111: 1-362 1924.

915. KISH, GABE
A program for coal. *Political Affairs* 26: 1029-39 1947.

916. KOLDE, ENDEL JAKOB
From mine to market; a study of production, marketing, and consumption of coal in the Pacific Northwest. Seattle: University of Washington. Bureau of Business Research, 1956. 64p.

917. LAKE ERIE BITUMINOUS COAL EXCHANGE
Cleveland, [1917]. 29p.

Booklet gives objectives, regulations, membership, etc., of the Exchange.

918. LAMB, GEORGE A.
The bituminous coal rate structure. Thesis. Yale University. 1932.

919. LEBUS, WILLIAM F.
Economic data on Eastern Kentucky coal field. Frankfort: Agricultural & Industrial Development Board, 1956. 32p.

920. LEHIGH COAL AND NAVIGATION COMPANY
Mine management policies, published for the information of executives of the mining department. Lansford, Pa., 1925. 103p.

921. LESHER, C. E.
An introductory survey of the bituminous coal industry. American Economic Association. *Papers & Proceedings* 11: 49-56 1921.

922. LESHER, C. E.
Is the coal shortage real or imaginary? *Coal Age* 18: 429-33 1920.

923. LESHER, C. E.
Prices of coal and coke. Washington: GPO, 1919. 115p.

924. LEWIS, WILLIAM D.
Coal price regulation and the constitution. *Ann. Amer. Acad.* 111: 292-304 1924.

925. LEZIUS, WALTER G.
Geographic aspects of coal cargoes from Toledo. *Economic Geography* 10: 374-81 1934.

926. LILIENTHAL, DAVID E.
Dissolution of coal industry likely if government assistance is rejected. *Annalist* 44: 684-86 1934.

927. LIMITED LIABILITY
Forbes Ap 15, 1958 35-36.

Pittston Company and its financial success.

928. LONG, MILLARD F.
The price of coal; a study of the policies of the National Coal Board. Ph.D. University of Chicago. 1961.

930. LOVE, ROBERT A.
Anthracite distribution; a report on possible adjustments in the existing marketing arrangements. n.p., 1930. 173p.

"Submitted to the Philadelphia & Reading Coal and Iron Company."

931. LUBIN, ISADOR
Miners' wages and the cost of coal. New York: McGraw-Hill, 1924. 316p.

"An inquiry into the wages system in the bituminous coal industry and its effects on coal costs and coal consumption."

932. LUCAS, JOHN W.
Regional sales agencies in the distribution of bituminous coal. Thesis. Ohio State University. 1935.

933. MCAULIFF, EUGENE
Stabilization of the bituminous coal industry. *Coal Age* 17: 486-93 1920.

934. MCCLOUD, LELAND W.
Comparative costs of competitive fuels. Morgantown: West Virginia University, 1951. 89p. (West Virginia University Business & Economic Studies 1: 4).

935. MacDOUGALL, CURTIS
Coal price-fixing in St. Louis. *Nation* 139: 183-84 1934.

936. MCGEE, JOHN F.
Northwestern bituminous coal supply for the season 1920-1921. Minneapolis, 1921. 74p.

937. MCGRAW-HILL DEPARTMENT OF ECONOMICS
The outlook for bituminous coal, 1964-1975. *Coal Age* My 1964 73-80.

938. MCKIE, JAMES W.
The southern industries fuel economy. *Southern Economic Journal* 29: 269-78 1963.

"The shift of industry from other energy sources toward electric power can only react favorably on coal demand."

939. McLEOD, A. A.
The coal supply and the Reading leases. *Forum* 13: 554-60 1892.

940. MANULA, C. B.
Systems simulation—a gaming model for mine management. *Mining Congress Journal* 49: 48-53 1963.

941. MARES, V. E.
Appalachian coal exports and the new fuel policy of the Common Market. *Pennsylvania Business Survey* F 1962 8-12.

942. MARES, V. E.
European market needs U. S. soft coal now. *Pennsylvania Business Survey*. Jl 1963 9.

943. MARKS, AVRUM
The future market for United States exports of coking quality coal to O.E.E.C. Europe. Thesis. University of Pennsylvania. 1958.

944. MEAD, RICHARD R.
An analysis of the decline of the anthracite industry since 1921. Ph.D. University of Pennsylvania. 1933.

945. MECHANIZATION IN THE BITUMINOUS COAL INDUSTRY
Monthly Labor Review 50: 341-44 1940.

946. MERRILL, WILLIAM M.
Economics of the southern smokeless coals. Ph.D. University of Illinois. 1953.
Deals with coal from seven counties of Virginia and West Virginia, 1873-1950.

947. MIHALEK, JOHN A.
An analysis of the changing bituminous coal markets, 1937-1952. Thesis. University of Pittsburgh. 1954.

948. MILLER, E. WILLARD
The southern anthracite region; a problem area. *Economic Geography* 31: 331-50 1955.

949. MISCHAKOW, MICHAEL K.
Post-war variations in the position of German coal and their effect upon importation of United States coal. Ph.D. Indiana University. 1961.

950. MONELL, LOUIS F.
Factors affecting international coal trade. Thesis. West Virginia University. 1962.

951. MOORE, JAMES R.
An inquiry concerning the status of the coal economy in Southern Illinois and the potential benefits which may be derived from canalization of the Big Muddy River and Beaucoup Creek. Thesis. Southern Illinois University. 1962.

952. MORRIS, ISRAEL W.
The duty on coal. Philadelphia: Baird, 1872. 31p.

953. MORROW, J. D. A.
The general coal situation. American Mining Congress. *Proceedings* 23: 436-42 1920.

954. MOSES, H. M.
Out of the wilderness. *Business Week* S 23, 1950 104-10.
Interview with Moses, head of the newly-formed Bituminous Coal Operators Association.

954a. MOYER, REED
Competition in the midwestern coal industry. Cambridge: Harvard University Press, 1964. 226p. (Harvard Economic Studies **CXXII**).

955. MURPHY, RAYMOND E.
Wartime changes in the patterns of United States coal production. Association of American Geographers. *Annals* 37: 185-96 1947.

956. NATHAN (ROBERT R.) ASSOCIATES
The foreign market potential for United States coal. Washington, 1963. 4 vols. proc.

957. NATIONAL COAL ASSOCIATION
Bituminous coal facts. Washington 1948+.
An extremely useful biennial compilation of statistics on all aspects of the coal trade.

958. NATIONAL COAL ASSOCIATION
The facts about the billion dollar water power development of the federal government: the menace to the coal industry of the TVA and similar projects. Washington, 1934. 12p.

959. NATIONAL COAL ASSOCIATION
The regional sales agency plan. Washington, 1931. 53p.

960. NATIONAL COAL ASSOCIATION
Statistical data concerning the bituminous coal industry. [Washington], 1947. 69p.

961. NATIONAL COAL POLICY CONFERENCE
Congress speaks . . . on domestic fuels, oil imports, national security. Washington, 1962. 40p.

962. NATIONAL FUELS AND ENERGY STUDY GROUP
Report on an assessment of available information on energy in the United States. Washington: GPO, 1962. 501p. (87th Cong., 2d Sess. Senate Doc. 159).

963. NATIONAL INDUSTRIAL CONFERENCE BOARD
The competitive position of coal in the United States. New York, 1931. 288p.

964. NAYHOUSE, LUCY
The relocation of the mining of bituminous coal in the United States. Thesis. University of Pittsburgh. 1927.

965. NEARING, SCOTT
Anthracite; an instance of natural resource monopoly. Philadelphia: J. C. Winston, 1915. 251p.

966. NEBRASKA. UNIVERSITY. COMMITTEE ON BUSINESS RESEARCH
Trade practices and costs of the retail coal business in Lincoln, Nebraska, in 1922. Lincoln, 1923. 34p. (Nebraska Studies in Business. Bulletin 7).

966a. NERLOVE, MARC
On the efficiency of the coal industry. *Journal of Business* 32: 271-78 1959.

967. NEW JERSEY. LEGISLATURE. COAL INVESTIGATING COMMITTEE
Intermediate report to the Legislature. Trenton, 1922. 8p.

968. NEW OPPONENT FOR LEWIS
Business Week My 20, 1950 21.

Account of the founding of the Bituminous Coal Operators Association.

969. NEW RIVER AND KANAWHA OPERATORS FORM NEW COMPANY
Coal & Coke Ja 11, 1901 13-14.

The New River & Kanawha Coal Co.

970. NEW RIVER SITUATION
Coal & Coke My 1, 1904 14-15.

Attack on the mismanagement and inactivity of the operators.

971. NEW YORK. LEGISLATURE. ASSEMBLY. RAILROADS COMMITTEE
Report relative to the coal combination. (Albany), 1878. 100p. (Assembly Doc. 128).

972. NEWHOUSE, JOSEPH
Labor cost in the bituminous coal industry. Thesis. West Virginia University. 1951.

973. NICHOLLS, WILLIAM J.
Coal catechism. Philadelphia: Lippincott, 1898. 218p.

974. NOLD, H. E.
Uses of coal in the ceramic industry. AIME. *Transactions* 108: 380-99 1934.

975. NORRIS, R. V.
Anthracite mining costs. AIME. *Transactions* 61: 323-45 1918.

976. NORRIS, R. V.
Anthracite mining costs. *Coal Age* 15: 1124-28 1919.

977. NORRIS, R. V.
The taxation of coal land. American Mining Congress. *Proceedings* 16: 331-38 1913.

978. NORTHERN WEST VIRGINIA COAL OPERATORS ASSOCIATION
The coal industry of the State of West Virginia. Fairmont, W. Va., 1923. 64p.

979. OBERG, HAROLD S.
Attempts at industry stability by control forces in the bituminous coal industry. Thesis. New York University. 1948.

980. OHIO CHAMBER OF COMMERCE
Ohio's coal problem. Columbus, 1926. 19p.

Labor costs are too high.

981. OHIO. COAL MINING COMMISSION
Report to the governor of Ohio. Columbus: F. J. Heer, 1913. 70p.

"To investigate and report an equitable method of weighing coal at the mines when the employees are to be paid for their labor on the basis of weight measure or quantity . . ."

101

982. OHIO. DEPT. OF INDUSTRIAL RELATIONS. DIVISION OF LABOR STATISTICS
Two billion tons of coal; a report of bituminous coal production in Ohio, 1838-1948. Columbus, 1948. 79p.

983. OHIO. MINING COMMISSION, 1871
Report. Columbus: Nevins & Myers, 1872. 199p.

984. OLGA COAL COMPANY.
Black Diamond O 30, 1954 30.

985. OLIN, H. L.
Some aspects of the Iowa coal problem. Iowa Geological Survey. *Technical Paper* 2: 3-8 1930.

Analysis of the decline of Iowa coal production.

986. ORMISTON, THOMAS AND ROGER BROWN
Changing fortunes of bituminous coal. Cleveland: Federal Reserve Bank of Cleveland, 1957. 31p.

987. OUT OF THE DEPTHS
Forbes D 15, 1958 28-29.

The improved financial position of the Peabody Coal Co.

988. PABST, WILLIAM R.
Monopolistic expectations and shifting control in the anthracite industry. *Review of Economic Statistics* 22: 45-52 1940.

989. PARKER, EDWARD W.
Coal supplies and coal production of the United States. *JASA* 13: 139-56 1912.

990. PARKER, EDWARD W.
Conserving our coal deposits. American Mining Congress. *Proceedings* 13: 228-34 1910.

Low profit margins in the industry cause wasteful and unsafe methods of mining.

991. PARKER, EDWARD W.
Cooperation, conservation and competition in coal. American Mining Congress. *Proceedings* 19: 241-49 1916.

992. PARKER, EDWARD W.
The cost of coal mining. American Mining Congress. *Proceedings* 16: 384-90 1913.

993. PARKER, GLEN L.
The coal industry; a study in social control. Washington: American Council on Public Affairs, 1940. 198p.

994. PARRY, V. F.
Trends in the use of energy in the Western states, with particular reference to coal. U. S. Bureau of Mines. Report of Investigations 3680. 1943. 43p.

995. PAXSON, CAROL
Bootleg anthracite. *New Republic* 81: 356-57 1935.

996. PEABODY COAL CASHES IN ON HEIGHTENED EFFICIENCY
Barrons Ja 19, 1959 24-25.

997. PECK, MAYNARD A.
Some economic aspects of the coal industry in Boulder County, Colorado. Ph.D. University of Colorado. 1948.

998. PENNSYLVANIA. ANTHRACITE COAL COMMISSION
Report of the Commission to investigate the increase in the cost of anthracite coal in the Commonwealth of Pennsylvania, to the Governor and Legislature. [Harrisburg, 1915]. 120p.

999. PENNSYLVANIA. ANTHRACITE COAL INDUSTRY COMMISSION
Bootlegging or illegal mining of anthracite coal in Pennsylvania: a census and survey of the facts. Philadelphia, 1937. 84p.

1000. PENNSYLVANIA. ANTHRACITE COAL INDUSTRY COMMISSION
Report [to the Governor of Pennsylvania]. [Harrisburg], 1937. 70p.

1001. PENNSYLVANIA. ANTHRACITE COAL INDUSTRY COMMISSION
Report of the Anthracite Coal Industry Commission. Harrisburg, 1937. 82p.

1002. PENNSYLVANIA. ANTHRACITE COAL INDUSTRY COMMISSION
Report. Sayre, Pennsylvania: Murrelle Printing Co., 1938. 652p.

1003. PENNSYLVANIA. GENERAL ASSEMBLY. JOINT STATE GOVERNMENT COMMISSION
Coal in Pennsylvania: recent developments and prospects. Harrisburg, 1963. 17p.

1004. PENNSYLVANIA. GREATER PENNSYLVANIA COUNCIL
The decline of the bituminous coal industry in Pennsylvania. Harrisburg, 1932. 20p. (*Its* Soft Coal Bulletin No. 1).

1005. PENNSYLVANIA. GREATER PENNSYLVANIA COUNCIL
Freight rates on bituminous coal. Harrisburg, 1933. 28p. (*Its* Soft Coal Bulletin No. 2).

1006. PERNE, ANTON
Effects of a declining coal industry on Illinois mining communities. Thesis. University of Illinois. 1939.

1007. PHILADELPHIA AND READING RAILROAD COMPANY
Argument of Franklin B. Gowen, esq. before the joint committee of the Legislature of Pennsylvania, appointed to inquire into the affairs of the Philadelphia and Reading Coal and Iron Company . . . Philadelphia: Helfenstein, Lewis & Greene, 1875. 114p.

1008. PICKETT, TOM
Coal mining becomes a pushbutton industry. *Manufacturers Record* D 1957 35-38.

Optimistic view of the future of the southern coal industry.

1009. PINCHOT, GIFFORD
Wages, margins and anthracite prices. *Ann. Amer. Acad.* 111: 61-81 1924.

1010. PINCUS, JOHN H.
Soft coal emerges as a solid industry. Thesis. University of Pennsylvania. 1957.

1011. PITTSBURGH. CHAMBER OF COMMERCE
Plight of the coal industry in Western Pennsylvania and what the united business interests are doing to restore it to prosperity. Pittsburgh, 1925. 22p.

1012. PITTSBURGH AND BUFFALO COMPANY
Coal & Coke Mr 15, 1903 7-11.

Account of the company's development and operations.

1013. POPE, HENRY B.
The elements of cost in coal mining in Kentucky. Thesis. University of Kentucky. 1906.

1014. POTTER, CHARLES J.
Forecasting United States coal requirements. *Mining Engineering* Ap 1962 55-59.

1015.   PULTZ, J. L.
        Consolidation of five large coal mines. *Engineering &
        Mining Journal* 82: 640-42 1906.

        Account of the formation of the Pittsburgh and Westmoreland
        Coal Co.

1016.   RAU, OTTO M.
        Preliminary report on stabilization of Illinois coal in-
        dustry. Philadelphia, 1925. 39p.

        Prepared for District 12, UMWA.

1017.   RAUSHENBUSH, HILMAR
        The anthracite question. New York: H. W. Wilson,
        1924. 165p.

        Study of the organization and economic situation of the industry.

1018.   RAUSHENBUSH, HILMAR
        The people's fight for coal and power. New York:
        League for Industrial Democracy, 1926. 36p. (League
        publication 13).

1019.   REED, FRANK H. AND OTHERS
        Trends in coal utilization. Illinois Geological Survey.
        Circular 128, 1947. 25p.

1020.   REED, WILLIAM B.
        Bituminous coal mine accounting. New York: McGraw-
        Hill, 1922. 221p.

1021.   REES, ALBERT
        The economic impact of collective bargaining in the
        steel and coal industries during the post-war period. In-
        dustrial Relations Research Assoc. *Proceedings* 3: 203-
        12 1950.

1022.   REEVES, H. C. AND H. A. SPALDING
        Assessment of coal producing properties in Kentucky.
        National Tax Journal 3: 173-78 1950.

1023.   REITELL, CHARLES
        The shift in soft coal shipments. n.p., 1927. 33p. (Penn-
        sylvania Industrial Survey. Bulletin 1).

1024.   REITH, JOHN W.
        Coal supply of Milwaukee, Wisconsin. *Journal of Geog-
        raphy* 48: 71-77 1949.

1025. REITH, JOHN W.
The decline of coal mining in the Danville district, Illinois; its causes and effects. Ph.D. Northwestern University. 1950.

1026. REYNOLDS, S. C.
The snow-bird mine. *Coal Age* 14: 58-59 1918.

Discussion of the many small "wagon mines" which developed as a result of the high price of coal.

1027. RICE, GEORGE S.
Stabilize industry, conserve coal, and protect miners. *American Labor Legislation Review* 30: 109-13 1940.

1028. RICE, JAMES P.
Taxation and assessment of coal, gas, and oil with special reference to western Pennsylvania, eastern Ohio, and northern West Virginia. Ph.D. University of Pittsburgh. 1957.

1029. RIEDINGER, ROYAL C.
A geographical investigation of the factors affecting profitable mining operations in the bituminous coal industry. Thesis. University of Pennsylvania. 1958.

1030. RISSER, HUBERT E.
Coal in the future energy market. Urbana, 1960. 15p. (Illinois. State Geological Survey. Circular 310).

1031. RISSER, HUBERT E.
Economic trend favoring the use of Illinois coal for metallurgical coke. Urbana, 1962. 15p. (Illinois. State Geological Survey. Circular 338).

1032. RISSER, HUBERT E.
The economics of the coal industry. Laurence, Kansas: University of Kansas, Bureau of Business Research, 1958. 177p.

1033. RISSER, HUBERT E.
Effect of coal inventories on stability of the coal industry. Urbana, 1959. 11p. (Illinois. State Geological Survey. Circular 268).

1034. ROBERTS, PETER
The anthracite coal industry. New York: Macmillan, 1901. 261p.

"A study of the economic conditions and relations of the cooperative forces in the development of the anthracite coal industry in Pennsylvania."

1035.   ROGERS, H. O.
Saving the coal industry. *Survey Graphic* 26: 326-29 1937.

1036.   ROPIEQUET, R. W.
Difficulties I have met in coal litigation. American Mining Congress. *Proceedings* 19: 354-60 1916.

Lack of organization, cooperation, etc., within the industry.

1037.   RORTY, M. C.
Notes on coal consumption. *JASA* 30: 718 1935.

1038.   ROSTOW, EUGENE
Bituminous coal and public interest. *Yale Law Review* 50: 543-94 1941.

An analysis of the history of the Bituminous Coal Act of 1937, "which has failed, and in the nature of the coal industry, had to fall."

1039.   ROTHWELL, RICHARD
Coal production of the United States. AIME. *Transactions* 5: 375-80 1876/77.

1040.   ROWE, J. W. F.
The coal mining industry in Great Britain and the United States. *Economica* (ns) 6: 200-13 1926.

1041.   RUTHERFORD, GEORGE W.
A management analysis of the coal chemical industry. Thesis. University of Pennsylvania. 1960.

1042.   RYAN, JOHN T.
The future of the bituminous coal industry. *Harvard Business Review* 14: 325-336 1936.

1043.   SAALBACH, WILLIAM F.
United States bituminous coal markets; trends since 1920 and prospects to 1975. Pittsburgh: University of Pittsburgh Press, 1960. 44p.

1044.   SALARIES OF MINE OFFICIALS
Coal Age 12: 594-95, 629 1917.

Gives average salaries by state of mine officials—superintendents, foremen, etc.

1045.   SALVATI, RAYMOND E.
Island Creek, a career company devoted to coal. New York: Newcomen Society, 1957. 24p.

1046. SALVATERRA, A. C.
The application of computers in the mining industry.
Thesis. West Virginia University. 1962.

1047. SAWARD, FREDERICK
The coal mines of Pennsylvania. New York: Coal Trade
Journal, 1880. 72p.

Gives names and locations of mines, amount produced, names of
operators, etc.

1048. SAWARD, FREDERICK
The coal trade; a compendium of valuable information
relative to coal production, prices, transportation, etc.
New York, 1874. 73p.

1049. SAWARD, FREDERICK
The growth of American coal exports. *Engineering
Magazine* 22: 321-32 1901/2.

1050. SAWARD, FREDERICK
Large coal consumers of New England. New York,
[1910]. 75p.

List of consumers who use 1,200 tons or more a year.

1051. SAWARD, FREDERICK
Problems of the expansion of the American coal trade.
Engineering Magazine 30: 374-79 1905/6.

1052. SAWARD, FREDERICK
The world's need of coal and the United States' supplies. *Engineering Magazine* 20: 1-8 1901.

1053. SAYE, WILLIAM H.
The development and present status of the bootleg anthracite industry and its influence on legitimate producers. Thesis. Temple University, 1941.

1054. SCOTT, ADDISON
Coal commerce and development in the Great Kanawha
Valley. Charleston: Daily Gazette, 1891. 9p.

A plea for the development of the Great Kanawha River in order to speed the development of the adjacent coal fields.

1055. SEARIGHT, WALTER V.
Coal production, distribution and consumption in Missouri. Rolla, 1949. 52p. (Missouri. Division of Geological Survey & Water Resources. Information Circular 3).

1056. SHOWALTER, W. J.
Coal—ally of American industry. *National Geographic* 34: 407-34 1918.

Useful as a source of excellent contemporary photographs of many aspects of the mining industry.

1057. SHURICK, ADAM
An analysis of the Ohio Mining Commission's report. *Coal Age* 5: 167-70, 196-200 1914.

1058. SHURICK, ADAM
Coal mining costs. New York: McGraw-Hill, 1922. 515p.

1059. SISLER, JAMES D.
The economic aspects of coal losses in Ohio, Pennsylvania, and West Virginia. Morgantown, West Virginia, 1931. 13p. (West Virginia Geological Survey. Mimeograph Series I, Bulletin 4).

1060. SKAGGS, CHARLES P.
Income tax problems of the coal industry. Thesis. West Virginia University. 1963.

1061. SLOSSON, EDWIN E.
The coming of the new coal age. Smithsonian Institution. *Annual Report* 1927: 243-53.

"We stand at the opening of a new era in the utilization of coal."

1062. SMITH, FRANK G.
The attempted stabilization of the bituminous coal industry. *Harvard Business Review* 17: 177-88 1939.

1063. SMITH, GEORGE O. AND C. E. LESHER
The cost of coal. American Mining Congress. *Proceedings* 19: 452-64 1916.

1064. SMITH, GEORGE O.
The 1920 soft coal shortage; underlying reasons for it and how it was overcome. Washington: National Coal Assoc., 1921. 15p.

1065. SMITHERS, F. S. & COMPANY
Bituminous coal; a basic raw material with a new value. New York, 1956. 101p.

1066. SOLOW, HERBERT
Soft coal; how strong a comeback. *Fortune* O 1957 136-37.

1067. SOMERS, GERALD G.
Effects of North-South wage uniformity on southern coal production. *Southern Economic Journal* 20: 121-29 1953.

1068. SOMERS, GERALD G.
Labor supply for manufacturing in a coal area. *Monthly Labor Review* 77: 1327-30 1954.

A newly-established chemical plant found no difficulty in obtaining an adequate labor force in the northern West Virginia coal region.

1069. SOUTH DAKOTA. STATE PLANNING BOARD
South Dakota coal. Brookings, 1936. 47p.

1070. STARR, GEORGE W.
Costs of retailing coal. Bloomington: Indiana University, 1941. 35p. (Indiana Business Reports. Study 23).

1071. "STATEMENT OF FACTS" FROM THE OPERATORS OF THE MIDDLE WEST
Coal Age 7: 498-501 1915.

"The near future contains nothing but disaster unless some relief is extended."

1072. STEEL, ALVIN A.
Coal mining in Arkansas. Little Rock: Democrat Printing, 1910. 632p.

Covers all aspects of the industry, both economic and technical.

1073. STEWART, E.
Analysis of coal mine labor productivity. *MLR* 31: 1333-38 1930.

1074. STEWART, E.
Extent of over-development in the bituminous coal industry. *MLR* 32: 304-11 1931.

1075. STEWART, E.
Tonnage output per pick miner per day in bituminous coal fields. *MLR* 11: 249-59 1921.

1076. STEWART, ETHEL R.
Mechanization of coal mines in West Virginia. Thesis. University of Virginia. 1937.

1077. STEWART, PAUL D.
New small business in a redevelopment coal area in West Virginia. Washington: Small Business Administration, 1962. 192p.

A socio-economic study of Boone, Logan and Raleigh counties.

1078. STOCK, A. R.
The story of 22 coal men who refused to take the count. *Sales Management* Jl 15, 1940 20-22.

Coal operators in Missouri and Kansas establish a cooperative advertising fund.

1079. STRATON, JOHN W.
Some effects of mechanization in the bituminous coal industry. Thesis. University of Pennsylvania. 1949.

1080. SUFFERN, ARTHUR E. AND OTHERS
The bituminous coal industry. American Economic Association. *Papers & Proceedings* 11: 116-22 1921.

1081. SWEET, SYLVANUS H.
Special report on coal: showing its distribution, classification and cost delivered over different routes to various points in the State of New York, and the principal cities on the Atlantic coast. New York: Van Nostrand, 1866. 94p.

1082. TAYLOR, JOHN R.
Study of the financial structures of fifteen selected coal companies operating in the bituminous industry. Thesis. University of Illinois. 1937.

1083. THOMAS, B. B.
The coal monopoly. Correspondence between B. B. Thomas, president of the Thomas Coal Company, and F. B. Gowen, president of the Philadelphia and Reading Railroad Company. New York: Coal Trade Circular Print, [1873]. 13p.

1084. THOMAS, E. H. C.
Coal profits; the truth about the money made in the coal industry. New York, 1920. 15p.

1085. THOMPSON, J. C.
Stabilization of the coal market through storage. American Mining Congress. *Proceedings* 22: 691-98 1919.

1086. THOMPSON, JAMES H.
Markets and marketing methods of the West Virginia coal industry. Morgantown: West Virginia University, 1953. 15p. (Bureau of Business Research, Business and Economic Studies 2: 3).

1087. THOMPSON, JAMES H.
Significant trends in the West Virginia coal industry, 1900-1957. Morgantown: West Virginia University, 1958. 65p. (West Virginia University Business & Economic Studies 6: 1).

Devoted largely to statistics on production, employment, wages, accidents, etc.

1088. THORNLEY, FRED C.
Coal: plan for organized distribution. New York, [1920]. 7p.

1089. THORP, WILLIAM L.
Coal for Europe. *State Dept. Bulletin* 17: 697-702 1947.

1090. TIDEWATER COAL EXCHANGE
n.p. [1917]. 27p.

Booklet gives objectives, regulations, membership, etc., of the Exchange.

1091. TRAER, GLENN W.
Conservation in the coal industry. American Mining Congress. *Proceedings* 11: 152-65 1908.

Author urges greater efficiency and the merging of small units.

1092. TRAPNELL, W. C. AND RALPH ISLEY
The bituminous coal industry, with a survey of competing fuels. Washington: Federal Emergency Relief Administration, 1935. 154p. plus appendix.

1093. TYRON, F. G.
Control statistics of coal production and distribution. *JASA* 17: 314-25 1920.

1094. TYRON, F. G. AND OTHERS
Employment and related statistics of mines and quarries. Philadelphia, 1937. 133p.

1095. TYRON, F. G.
The irregular operation of the bituminous coal industry. American Economic Association. *Papers & Proceedings* 11: 57-73 1921.

1096.   TYRON, F. G.
The underlying facts of the coal situation in the United States. Academy of Political Science. *Proceedings* 10: 685-708 1924.

1097.   TUGENDHAT, GEORGE
A billion dollar coal market? *Fortune* D 1962 102-5.

"Europe is going to need cheap coal, which the U. S. has in plenty."

1098.   TURNER, HARRY
Coal merchandising; a manual for retail coal merchants. Topeka, Kansas, 1933. 76p.

1099.   TWO COUNTIES MINE COAL THE HARD WAY
Business Week S 12, 1953 90-94.

Description of the small non-union mines in Leslie and Clay counties Kentucky.

1100.   U. S. BUREAU OF LABOR STATISTICS
Hours and earnings in bituminous coal, fall and winter of 1921. Washington: GPO, 1922. 37p. (67th Cong., 2d Sess. Senate. Doc. 171).

Running title: Conditions in the Bituminous Coal Fields.

1101.   U. S. BUREAU OF LABOR STATISTICS
Increase of prices of anthracite coal following the wage agreement of May 20, 1912. Washington: GPO, 1913. 128p. (62nd Cong., 3d Sess. House. Doc. 1442).

1102.   U. S. COAL COMMISSION
Report of the United States Coal Commission. Washington: GPO, 1925. 5 volumes. (68th Cong., 2d Sess. Senate. Doc. 195).

1103.   U. S. COMMISSIONER OF LABOR
Bituminous coal, cost of production. *In* Sixth Annual Report (1890) of the Commissioner of Labor, pp195-282.

1104.   U. S. CONGRESS. COMMITTEE ON THE DISTRICT OF CO-LUMBIA
The coal supply of the District of Columbia. Washington: GPO, 1903. 6 vols.

1105.   U. S. CONGRESS. HOUSE
Bituminous coal conservation bill of 1935. Report with majority and minority views. Washington: GPO, 1935. 61p. (74th Cong., 1st Sess. House. Report 1800).

113

1106. U. S. CONGRESS. HOUSE
Bituminous Coal Act of 1936, report submitted by Mr. Doughton from the Committee on Ways and Means. Washington: GPO, 1936. 25p. (74th Cong., 2d Sess. House. Report 2832).

1107. U. S. CONGRESS. HOUSE
Coal Investigation Agency, report submitted by Mr. Bland of Indiana, from the Committee on Labor, to accompany H. R. 11022. Washington: GPO, 1922. 7p. (67th Cong., 2d Sess. House. Report 984).

1108. U. S. CONGRESS. HOUSE
Extension of the Coal Act. Report submitted by Mr. Boland, from the Committee on Ways and Means. Washington: GPO, 1941. 28p. (77th Cong., 1st Sess. House. Report. 324).

1109. U. S. CONGRESS. HOUSE
Increase in prices of anthracite coal following the wage agreement of May 29, 1912, prepared under the direction of the Commissioner of Labor. Washington: GPO, 128p. (62d Cong., 3d Sess. House. Doc. 1442).

1110. U. S. CONGRESS. HOUSE
Preliminary report by the Federal Trade Commission on the production and distribution of bituminous coal; letter from the chairman of the Federal Trade Commission transmitting preliminary report by the Federal Trade Commission on the production and distribution of bituminous coal. Washington: GPO, 1917. 8p. (65th Cong., 1st Sess. House. Doc. 152).

1111. U. S. CONGRESS. HOUSE
United States Coal Commission. Report from Mr. Windslow, of the Committee on Interstate and Foreign Commerce. Washington: GPO, 1922. 3p. (67th Cong., 2d Sess. House. Report 1181).

1112. U. S. CONGRESS. HOUSE. COMMITTEE ON INTERSTATE AND FOREIGN COMMERCE
Coal. Washington: GPO, 1926. 3 vols.

1113. U. S. CONGRESS. HOUSE. COMMITTEE ON INTERSTATE AND FOREIGN COMMERCE
The products of the Ohio Valley, especially coal, considered in reference to the Nicarauga Canal; statement of Governor MacCorkle of West Virginia, May 9, 1896. n.p., 1896. 34p.

1114. U. S. CONGRESS. HOUSE. COMMITTEE ON WAYS AND MEANS
Prohibition upon importation of anthracite coal, hearings, 71st Congress, 2d session, on H. R. 12061, for prohibition upon importation into United States of certain anthracite coal, June 17, 1930. Washington: GPO, 1930. 20p.

1115. U. S. CONGRESS. HOUSE. COMMITTEE ON WAYS AND MEANS
Extension of Bituminous Coal Act of 1937, hearings, 78th Congress, 1st Session, on H. R. 356, H. R. 1454, and H. R. 2296, bills to amend bituminous coal act, as amended, June 21-July 5, 1943. Washington: GPO, 1943. 974p.

1116. U. S. CONGRESS. HOUSE. COMMITTEE ON WAYS AND MEANS
Stabilization of bituminous coal mining industry. Washington: GPO, 1935. 600p.

1117. U. S. CONGRESS. SENATE
Anthracite coal prices; letter from the federal trade commission transmitting, in response to Senate Resolution of June 22, 1916, a report of the Federal Trade Commission to the Senate of the United States on Anthracite coal prices. Washington: GPO, 1917. 4p. (65th Congress, 1st Sess. Senate. Doc. 19).

1118. U. S. CONGRESS. SENATE
Coal industry stabilization bill. Report submitted by Mr. Frelinghuysen, from the Committee on Interstate Commerce. Washington: GPO, 1921. 4p. (67th Cong., 1st Sess. Senate. Report 55).

1119. U. S. CONGRESS. SENATE
Constitutionality of the Bituminous Coal Conservation Act of 1935, argument of Honorable John Dickinson, Assistant Attorney General of the United States before the Supreme Court of the United States in behalf of the government officer defendants in the case of Carter v. Carter Coal Co., Helvering, Et Al., March 12, 1936, in support of the constitutionality of the Bituminous Coal Conservation Act of 1935. Washington: GPO, 1936. 42p. (74th Cong., 2d Sess. Senate. Doc. 197).

1119a. U. S. CONGRESS. SENATE
Distribution and price of coal, conference report on H.
R. 12472, to declare national emergency to exist in production, transportation, and distribution of coal and other fuel, granting additional powers to Interstate Commerce Commission, providing for declaration of car-
service priorities in interstate commerce during present
and any succeeding emergency, and to prevent extortion
in sale of fuel; submitted by Mr. Cummins. Sept. 14,
1922. Washington: GPO, 1922. 4p. (67th Cong., 2d
Sess. Senate. Document 251).

1120. U. S. CONGRESS. SENATE
Effect of strike upon bituminous coal prices. Letter from
the Secretary of Commerce, transmitting in response to
Senate Resolution of June 2, 1922, a statement relative
to the production and prices of bituminous coal and the
action of governmental agencies to end the strike. Washington: GPO, 1922. 7p. (67th Cong., 2d Sess. Senate.
Doc. 209).

1121. U. S. CONGRESS. SENATE
Extension of the Bituminous Coal Act of 1937. Report
submitted by Mr. Bone, from the Committee on Interstate Commerce. Washington: GPO, 1941. 4p. (77th
Cong., 1st Sess. Senate. Report 169).

1122. U. S. CONGRESS. SENATE. COMMITTEE ON EDUCATION
AND LABOR
Regulate interstate and foreign commerce of coal; report to accompany S. 4177 (To regulate interstate and
foreign commerce in coal and to promote general welfare dependent on use of coal). Washington: GPO,
1926. 8p. (69th Cong., 1st Sess. Senate. Report 812).

1123. U. S. CONGRESS. SENATE. COMMITTEE ON EDUCATION
AND LABOR
Report upon the relations between labor and capital,
and testimony taken by the Committee. Washington:
GPO, 1885. 4 volumes.

The "Blair Hearings". References to coal mining are scattered
throughout the testimony. Each volume is indexed.

1124. U. S. CONGRESS. SENATE. COMMITTEE ON INTERIOR AND
INSULAR AFFAIRS
Alaska coal lands. Washington: GPO, 1955. 195p.

Concerns the Secretary of the Interior's "alleged failure to build
the Alaska railroad spur."

1125.   U. S. CONGRESS. SENATE. COMMITTEE ON INTERIOR AND INSULAR AFFAIRS
National fuels study. Hearings before the Committee on Interior and Insular Affairs, United States Senate, Eighty-seventh Congress, First Session, on Senate resolution 105, a resolution to create a Special Committee on a Special National Fuels Study. June 12 and 13, 1961. Washington: GPO, 1961. 239p.

1126.   U. S. CONGRESS. SENATE. COMMITTEE ON INTERSTATE COMMERCE
Bituminous coal commission. Hearings . . . on S. 4490, a bill to regulate interstate and foreign commerce in bituminous coal, provide for consolidations, mergers, and cooperative marketing; regulate the fuel supply of interstate carriers; require the licensing of corporations producing and shipping coal in interstate commerce; and to create a bituminous coal commission, and for other purposes. Washington: GPO, 1929. 352p.

1127.   U. S. CONGRESS. SENATE. COMMITTEE ON INTERSTATE COMMERCE
Extension of Bituminous Coal Act of 1937. Hearings . . . on S. J. Res. 22, S. J. Res. 32, H. J. Res. 101 and H. R. 4146, joint resolutions and an act to extend the provisions of the Bituminous Coal Act of 1937 for a period of two years, and for other purposes. April 2 and 3, 1941. Washington: GPO, 1941. 106p.

1128.   U. S. CONGRESS. SENATE. COMMITTEE ON INTERSTATE COMMERCE
Increased price of coal; hearings before subcommittee pursuant to S. Res. 126, directing Committee on Interstate Commerce to hold hearings in order to make inquiry into causes which have brought about enormous increase in market price of coal and to report its findings and recommendations with view to Congressional or Executive action. Washington: GPO, 1919-20. 483p.

1129.   U. S. CONGRESS. SENATE. COMMITTEE ON INTERSTATE COMMERCE
Price regulation of coal and other commodities. Washington: GPO, 1917. 398p.

1130.   U. S. CONGRESS. SENATE. COMMITTEE ON INTERSTATE COMMERCE
To regulate interstate commerce in bituminous coal, hearings before subcommittee, 75th Congress, 1st Session, on S. 1, Mar. 9, 1937. Washington: GPO, 1937. 260p.

1131. U. S. CONGRESS. SENATE. COMMITTEE ON INTERSTATE COMMERCE
Stabilization of the bituminous coal mining industry. Washington: GPO, 1935. 624p.

Hearings on S. 1417, the bill to establish a National Bituminous Coal Commission.

1132. U. S. CONGRESS. SENATE. COMMITTEE ON INTERSTATE AND FOREIGN COMMERCE
Oil and Coal Shortage. Hearing before a subcommittee of the Committee on Interstate and Foreign Commerce, U. S. Senate, 80th Congress, 1st Session on oil and coal shortage. December 9, 1947. Washington: GPO, 1947. 129p.

1133. U. S. CONGRESS. SENATE. COMMITTEE ON INTERIOR AND INSULAR AFFAIRS
Report of the National fuels and energy study group on an assessment of available information on energy in the United States. Washington: GPO, 1962. 499p. (87th Congress, 2nd Session).

1134. U. S. CONGRESS. SENATE. COMMITTEE ON MANUFACTURE
Publication of production and profits in coal. Washington: GPO, 1921. 3 vols. in 2.

1135. U. S. CONGRESS. SENATE. COMMITTEE ON MANUFACTURERS
Shortage of coal. Washington: GPO, 1918-19. 3 vols.

1136. U. S. CONGRESS. SENATE. COMMITTEE ON MINES AND MINING
Hearings on S. 2935; a bill "to regulate interstate and foreign commerce in bituminous coal . . . and to create a Bituminous Coal Commission." Washington: GPO, 1932. 1351p.

1137. U. S. CONGRESS. SENATE. SPECIAL COMMITTEE TO INVESTIGATE THE FUEL SITUATION ON THE MIDDLE WEST
The fuel situation in the Middle West. Washington: GPO, 1943. 1300p.

1138. U. S. CONGRESS. SENATE. SPECIAL COMMITTEE TO INVESTIGATE INDUSTRIAL CENTRALIZATION
Investigation of industrial centralization. Part 3: Iowa coal resources. Washington: GPO, 1945.

1139. UNITED STATES FEDERAL TRADE COMMISSION
Cost reports of the Federal Trade Commission. Coal. 1919-1921. Washington. 7 volumes. v1. Pennsylvania—bituminous. v2. Pennsylvania—anthracite. v3. Illinois—bituminous. v4. Alabama, Tennessee and Kentucky—bituminous. v5. Ohio, Indiana and Michigan—bituminous. v6. Maryland, West Virginia and Virginia—bituminous. v7. Trans-Mississippi states—bituminous.

1140. U. S. FEDERAL TRADE COMMISSION
Investment and profit in soft coal mining. Washington: GPO, 1922. pt. 1: 10p, pt. 2: 208p. (67th Congress, 2d Session. Senate Document 207).

1141. U. S. FEDERAL TRADE COMMISSION
Preliminary report of the Federal Trade Commission on investment and profit in soft coal mining. Washington: GPO, 1922. 222p.

1142. U. S. TREASURY DEPARTMENT
Taxes of anthracite coal mining companies. Washington: GPO, 1926. 10p. (69th Cong., 1st Sess. Senate. Doc. 48).

1143. UNUSED MANPOWER IN PENNSYLVANIA ANTHRACITE AREA
MLR 54: 1101-6 1942.

1144. UTAH. COMMITTEE TO STUDY OPERATIONS OF STATE GOVERNMENT
An economic study of the development of Utah's coal resources. n.p., 1936. 139p.

1145. VAILE, R. S.
Coal distribution in the twin cities. Minneapolis: University of Minnesota, 1932. 99p. (Minnesota Studies in Economics and Business No. 2).

1146. VAN HISE, CHARLES R.
Relation of big business to mining. *Coal Age* 4: 691-95 1913.

1147. VANCE, STANLEY C.
A critical analysis of the data and methods available for technical capital measurement in bituminous coal mining. Ph.D. University of Pennsylvania. 1951.

1148. VEENSTRA, T. A. AND W. G. FRITZ
Major economic tendencies in the bituminous coal industries. *Quarterly Journal of Economics* 51: 106-130 1936.

1149. VINCENT, MERLE D.
Chaotic coal. *Survey Graphic* 22: 539-45 1933.

Discussion of the role of the "captive" bituminous mines.

1150. VIRGINIA. DIVISION OF PLANNING AND ECONOMIC DEVELOPMENT
Production and marketing of coal in Virginia and the nation. Richmond, 1955. 102p.

1151. VIRTUE, G. O.
The anthracite combinations. *Quarterly Journal of Economics* 10: 296-323 1896.

1152. VOGTLE, A. W.
Coal by wire. *Public Utilities* 63: 433-41 1959.

The increase in transportation costs may force the location of electric utility plants near mines and the utilization of high transmission lines.

1153. VOSKUIL, WALTER H.
Economic and competitive position of Illinois coal. AIME. *Transactions* 119: 392-404 1936.

1154. VOSKUIL, WALTER H.
Potential markets for Illinois coal on the Upper Mississippi Waterway. Illinois Geological Survey. Circular 41, 1938. 19p.

1155. WADLEIGH, F. R.
Hampton Roads coals. *Coal Age* 6: 702-7 1914, 7: 165-69, 331-34, 375-77 1915.

Covers "all phases of marketing and shipping the different coals handled at Hampton Roads."

1156. WADLEIGH, F. R.
International trade in coal. *Ann. Amer. Acad.* 127: 102-11 1926.

1157. WADLEIGH, F. R.
Our future in the trade. *Coal Age* 2: 894-97 1912; 3: 215-17 1913.

1158. WALKER, ALBERT H.
The black elephant of Reading; being a study in coal and finance. New York, 1910. 15p.

Deals largely with the Philadelphia & Reading Coal & Iron Co.

1159. WALKER, FRANCIS
The development of the anthracite combination. *Ann. Amer. Acad.* 111: 234-248 1924.

1160. WARRINER, S. D.
The anthracite industry: wages, prices and regulation. *Ann. Amer. Acad.* 111: 53-60 1924.

1161. WATKINS, HAROLD M.
Coal and men; and economic and social study of the British and American coal fields. London: Allen & Unwin, 1934. 460p.

1162. WEINBERG, EDGAR
Technological change and productivity in the bituminous coal industry. Washington: GPO, 1961. 136p. (U. S. Bureau of Labor Statistics. Bulletin 1305).

1163. WHITE, I. C.
The waste of our fuel resources. [Morgantown, W. Va., 1908]. 31p.

1164. WILLIAMSON, H. A.
The relation of forestry to coal mining. West Virginia Coal Mining Institute. *Proceedings* 1912 302-12.

1165. WING, DAVID L.
Cost, prices, and profits of the bituminous coal industry. American Economic Association. *Papers & Proceedings* 11: 74-84 1921.

1166. WITTELS, DAVID G. AND J. FRANK BEAMAN
Good-by, bootleggers. *Sat. Eve. Post* Mr 20, 1943 p16-17.

The halt in the bootleg coal industry in the Pennsylvania anthracite fields.

1167. WOLFE, CHARLES F.
The marketing of Hocking Valley coal in the Columbus area. Thesis. Ohio State University. 1932.

1168. WOLFE, THOMAS M.
Recent changes in the bituminous coal industry. *Harvard Business Review* 10: 149-160 1931/2.

1169. WOOLRICH, WILLIS R.
The purchase and storage of domestic coal. Knoxville, 1925. 15p. (University of Tennessee. Engineering Experiment Station. Bulletin No. 6).

1170. WOZNIEWICZ, EDWARD J.
Causes and remedies for declining employment in the Pennsylvania anthracite area. Thesis. New York University. 1954.

1171. WYLER, SAMUEL S.
Fundamentals of our coal problem. Columbus, Ohio, 1929. 40p.

1172. YOUNG, C. M.
The coal industry of Illinois. AIME. *Transactions* 57: 560-78 1917.

1173. YOUNG, W. H. AND F. G. TYRON
Distribution statistics in coal market analysis. *JASA* 26, supp.: 20-26 1931.

1174. ZANOLLI, S. W.
The coal miner in a larger scale, highly mechanized, highly integrated, bituminous coal mining plant. Thesis. University of Pittsburgh. 1948.

1,175. ZIERER, CLIFFORD M.
The status of Scranton's mining industry. Geographical Society of Philadelphia. *Bulletin* 26: 11-28 1928.

Life in the Coal Fields

1176. ABBOTT, GRACE
Improvement in rural public relief: the lesson of the coal-mining communities. *Social Service Review* 6: 183-222 1932.

1177. AHRENHOLZ, GLADYS
Factors affecting social participation in coal communities. Thesis. West Virginia University. 1951.

1178. ALLRED, CHARLES E. AND OTHERS
Grundy County, Tennessee; relief in a coal mining community. Tennessee. Agriculture Experiment Station. Report 11. 1936.

1179. AMERICAN CONSTITUTIONAL ASSOCIATION
Life in a West Virginia Coal Field. Charleston, West Virginia, 1923. 58p.

Written to refute "scurrilous articles" which have depicted the coal fields as "an island of barbarity in a sea of civilization."

1180. ARKANSAS. STATE EMERGENCY RELIEF ADMINISTRATION
A study of the Arkansas coal mines and miners. Little Rock, 1934. 97p. proc.

1181. BACH, E. E.
Social and religious organizations as factors in labor problems. AIME. *Transactions* 59: 590-611 1918.

Mr. Bach was "Sociological Director" of the Ellsworth Collieries Co., Ellsworth, Pennsylvania.

1182. BALL, RICHARD A.
The Southern Appalachian coal community; an explorative study. Thesis. West Virginia University. 1960.

1183. BARNES, CLARENCE E.
The pattern and nature of the informal and formal institutional contacts participated in by residents of New Hill. Thesis. West Virginia University. 1952.

New Hill is a small mining community in north-central West Virginia.

1184.   BELL, ISAAC L.
Notes on a visit to coal and iron mines and iron works in the United States. Newcastle-on-Tyne, 1875. 66p.

1185.   BEURY, WILLIAM
The social aspects of coal mines. West Virginia Coal Mining Institute. *Proceedings* 1934 63-77.

A generally cheerful view of life in the West Virginia coal fields by a company executive.

1186.   BRACKER, MILTON
Portrait in black and white. *N. Y. Times Magazine* N 30, 1941. p5.

Life in the southwestern Pennsylvania coal fields (Uniontown area).

1187.   BRANDT, L.
Housing the coal industry. West Virginia Coal Mining Institute. *Proceedings* 1923 51-64.

Author concentrates on the investment required by the operator to supply housing of various standards.

1188.   BROWN, MALCOLM J.
Seven stranded coal towns; a study of an American depressed area. Washington: GPO, 1941. 188p. (WPA. Research Monograph 23).

The Illinois coal fields.

1189.   BROWN, ROLLO W.
The hills are strong. Boston: Beacon Press, 1953 (1952), 244p.

Includes an account of the author's early life in the coal-mining section of southeastern Ohio.

1190.   BROWNELL, BAKER
The other Illinois. New York: Duell, Sloan and Pearce, 1958. 276p.

Southern Illinois is the "other Illinois". Much material on the coal fields.

1191.   BRUERE, ROBERT W.
The coming of coal. New York: Association Press, 1922. 123p.

Prepared for the Federal Council of Churches of Christ in America.

1192.   CABIN CREEK Y.M.C.A. (DECOTA, WEST VIRGINIA)
Coal Age 4: 741-42 1913.

124

1193. COMMONS, JOHN R.
Slavs in the bituminous coal mines of Illinois. *Charities* 13: 227-29 1904.

1194. CONROY, JACK
Boyhood in a coal town. *American Mercury* 23: 83-92 1931.

1195. CRAWFORD, BRUCE
Piney Ridge, Virginia. *Virginia Quarterly Review* 8: 371-84 1932.

Description of life in a coal mining area near the Kentucky border.

1196. CRESSEY, PAUL FREDERICK
Social disorganization and reorganization in Harlan County, Kentucky. *American Sociological Review* 14: 389-94 1949.

1197. DeLAURETIS, FRANK T.
Anthracite coal: a case study of the social problems of a declining industry. Thesis. University of Illinois. 1956.

1198. DENTON, ALMA
Standards of living among bituminous coal miners' families in southern Illinois. Thesis. University of Illinois. 1934.

1199. DOTSON, JOHN A.
The public school in the mining industry. Thesis. University of Kentucky. 1931.

1200. DOWNING, THOMAS F.
Where to build our mining towns and what to build. West Virginia Coal Mining Institute. *Proceedings* 1923 41-51.

The general manager of a large coal company discusses the problems of building towns in the narrow valleys of the coal country.

1201. EAVENSON, HOWARD N.
Building complete thousand-dwelling town for a mine population of 7,000 at Lynch, Kentucky. *Coal Age* 20: 532-36 1921.

1202. EDUCATION IN COLORADO FUEL AND IRON VILLAGES
Coal Age 7: 466-70 1915.

125

1203.   EDWARDS, J. H.
Helping man and family. *Coal Age* D 1944 86-93.

Describes efforts of the Jewell Ridge Coal Company to make the coal towns "better places in which to live" and "to raise the employees esteem of his job." Area located in the coal fields of southern Virginia, near Bluefield, West Virginia.

1204.   THE EDWARDSVILLE IMPROVEMENTS
Coal Age 5: 936-39 1914.

Account of the transformation of Edwardsville, Luzerne County, Pennsylvania into a model coal mining community.

1204a.   ELLIS, MABEL B.
Children of the Kentucky coal fields. *American Child* 1: 285-405 1920.

1205.   ENVIRONMENT AND OPPORTUNITIES FOR WOMEN OF COAL MINERS' FAMILIES
MLR 21: 333-34 1925.

1206.   ERNST, HARRY W. AND CHARLES H. DRAKE
Poor, proud and primitive. *Nation* 188: 490-93 1959.

Deals largely with the depressed coal areas of southern West Virginia. (Reprinted in *ML&W* 35: 3 1959 under the title: Region in Need).

1207.   FAY, C. L.
Liquor problem in mining communities. *Coal Age* 1: 90, 192, 222-24, 258-59 1911/12.

1208.   FRIENDS. SOCIETY OF
Report of the child relief work in the bituminous coal fields by the American Friends Service Committee. Philadelphia: Engle Press, 1932. 67p.

Covers the period S 1, 1931-Ag 31, 1932.

1209.   FRIENDS. SOCIETY OF
A report of the services and relief in the bituminous coal fields by the American Friends Service Committee. Philadelphia: Engle Press, 1933. 32p.

Covers the period S 1, 1932-Ag 31, 1933.

1210.   GILFILLAN, HARRIET W. (LAUREN GILFILLAN, PSEUD.)
I went to pit college. New York: Viking, 1934. 288p.

Account of life in the Pennsylvania coal fields during the early years of the depression.

1211. GLADDEN, JAMES W. AND CHRISTIANSEN, JOHN R.
Emergence of urban values in mining families in eastern
Kentucky. *Rural Sociology* 21: 135-39 1956.

1212. GLEASON, ARTHUR
Company-owned Americans. *Nation* 110: 794-95 1920.

Life in the southern West Virginia coal fields is controlled by
the companies.

1213. GLEASON, ARTHUR
Private ownership of public officials. *Nation* 110: 724-
25 1920.

Control of public officials by coal operators in the southern
West Virginia coal fields.

1214. GORDON, LELAND
Peanut hill. *Nation* 140: 270-71 1935.

Human misery in the Ohio coal fields.

1215. GRIFFIN, GERALD
The truth about eastern Kentucky. *Mountain Life &
Work* 31: 4 1955 17-24 illus.

A discussion of the desperate economic conditions in the coal
fields of eastern Kentucky.

1216. HALL, HELEN
Miners must eat. *Atlantic* 152: 153-62 1933.

Conditions in the West Virginia coal fields.

1217. HALL, R. D.
The industrial clean-up. American Mining Congress.
Proceedings 22: 717-25 1919.

Urges companies to create better housing, recreational facilities,
etc., in the mining towns.

1218. HAMBRIDGE, JAY
An artist's impressions of the colliery region. *Century
Magazine* 55: 822-28 1897/98.

The Pennsylvania anthracite area.

1219. HAMILL, R. H.
Design of buildings in mining towns. *Coal Age* 11:
1045-48 1917.

1220. HOFFMAN, BETTY HANNAH
Meet a soft-coal miner's family of Harlan County, Kentucky. *Ladies Home Journal* 64: 225-32. Mr 1947.

1221. HOLLANDSWORTH, GENEVIEVE
Youth recreation in the coal mining towns of West Virginia. Thesis. West Virginia University. 1948.

1222. HUEBNER, A. F.
Houses for mine villages. *Coal Age* 12: 717-20 1917.

Good housing is not only a profitable investment but has become necessary to keep reliable labor.

1223. HUSBAND, JOSEPH
A year in a coal mine. Boston: Houghton Mifflin, 1911. 171p.

Description, by a young Harvard graduate, of work as an unskilled miner in the Illinois coal fields.

1224. HUSKINSON, FRANK
How a western coal-mining village manages a social club. *Coal Age* 12: 670-71 1917.

Delagua, Colorado.

1225. JOHNSON, ELIZABETH S.
The coal miner and his family in strike times of 1931. *Labor & Industry* N 1931 3-26.

1226. JORDAN, MARGARET W.
A plea for the West Virginia miner. *Coal Age* 6: 914-16 1914.

Experiences of a social worker in the coal fields of southern West Virginia.

1227. JUTELIS, VICTORIA
The effects of a depression upon a mining village. Thesis. University of Illinois. 1934.

1228. KAPLAN, STELLA A.
Recent developments in housing for bituminous coal miners. Thesis. University of Pittsburgh. 1945.

1229. KARSCH, CARL G.
Hardship in the valleys. *Presbyterian Life* S 1, 1960 7-12.

Life in "the declining coal towns of West Virginia."

1230. KEELY, JOSIAH
Successful wives in coal camps. *Coal Age* 11: 591-2 1917.

Author deplores the rivalries of the wives of mine officials and their unsettling effects.

1231.   KELLY, JAMES F. AND THOMAS W. HARRELL
Job satisfaction among coal miners. *Personnel Psychology* 2: 161-70 1949.

Study made among miners in the Illinois coal fields.

1232.   KIRCHWAY, FREDA
Miners' wives in the coal strike. *Century* 105: 83-90 N 1922.

"If the miners are slaves of coal, the women are slaves of slaves." Study made in the West Virginia coal fields.

1233.   KORSON, GEORGE
Black land; the way of life in the coal fields. Evanston, Illinois: Row, Peterson, 1941. 72p.

A popularly-written account of life in the coal fields. Centered largely in West Virginia.

1234.   LANTZ, HERMAN R.
People of Coal Town. New York: Columbia, 1958. 310p.

A study of life in a small mining community in southern Illinois.

1235.   LEE, JENNIE
Kentucky through English eyes. *Living Age* 342: 184-5 1932. (Alternate title: My Old Kentucky Home).

"Of all the God-forsaken spots I have yet visited, American mining camps are certainly the worst."

1236.   LIVING CONDITIONS OF BITUMINOUS MINE WORKERS
MLR 18: 529-35 1924.

1237.   LIVING WITH UNEMPLOYMENT IN A COAL TOWN
Business Week Ja 8, 1955 44-50.

Luzerne County, Pennsylvania.

1238.   LIVINGSTON, WILLIAM J.
Coal miners and religion. Thesis. Union Theological Seminary, Richmond. 1951.

Research was done in Logan County, West Virginia.

1239.   LOHMANN, KARL B.
Improving colliery surroundings in anthracite region. *Coal Age* 6: 739-41 1914.

"There is no good reason why colliery plants should be blots on the surrounding landscape."

1240. MACLEAN, ANNIE M.
Life in the Pennsylvania coal fields with particular reference to women. *American Journal of Sociology* 14: 329-51 1909.

1241. McGILL, NETTIE P.
Welfare of children in the bituminous coal mining communities in West Virginia. Washington: GPO, 1923. 77p. (Children's Bureau Publication 117).

1242. MAGNUSSON, LEIFUR
Company housing in the anthracite region of Pennsylvania. *MLR* 10: 1260-69 1920.

1243. MAGNUSSON, LEIFUR
Company housing in the bituminous coal fields. *MLR* 10: 1045-52 1920.

1244. MALONEY, JOHN
The angel of Happy Hollow. *Saturday Evening Post* 220 F 14, 1948 30-31, 97-99.

Social work of Elizabeth Collins in the Southern Appalachian coal fields.

1245. MARJA, FERN
Forgotten children: the West Virginia Story. Title of a series of six articles appearing in the *New York Post* F 22 to F 28, 1960.

Report on human misery in the coal fields of southern West Virginia.

1246. MARTIN, JOHN B.
Crisis in coaltown. *Saturday Evening Post* S 18, 1954 24-5.

"The case history of dying West Frankfort, Illinois."

1247. MARTIN, JOHN B.
Life and death in coaltown. *New York Times Magazine* Ja 13, 1952 11.

1248. MATTHEWS, ELLEN N.
Work opportunities and school training for the coal miners' children. National Conference of Social Work. *Proceedings* 1921: 287-92.

1249. MAZZEI, FRANK JOSEPH
A study of the factors influencing job satisfaction among factory workers of Clarksburg, West Virginia, and coal miners of Morgantown, West Virginia. Thesis. West Virginia University. 1953.

1250.   MINERS' STORY
         Independent 54: 1407-10 1902.

         The life story of a Pennsylvania miner who started work at the
         age of twelve.

1251.   MORRIS, THOMAS JOHN
         The coal camp; a pattern of limited community life.
         Thesis. West Virginia University. 1950.

1252.   MURPHY, R. E.
         A Southern West Virginia mining community. *Econom-
         ic Geography* 9: 51-59 1933.

1253.   MYERS, JAMES
         Rehabilitation in the coal fields. *Christian Century* 49:
         1053-55 1932.

         Activity of the Quakers in a northern West Virginia coal field.

1254.   NELSON, H. L.
         Life in the coal villages. *Harpers Weekly* 32: 458 1888.

         Reply to the above: *Colliery Engineer* 8: 252-53 1887/88.

1255.   NEUBERT, ANN
         We belong in these hills. *Ladies Home Journal* Jl 1961
         88-91.

         Account of the way of life of the families of unemployed coal
         miners. The Neuberts live in Fayette County, West Virginia.

1256.   NICHOLS, FRANCIS H.
         Children of the coal shadows. *McClures* 20: 435-44
         1902/3.

         Child labor in the anthracite coal fields.

1257.   NOON, W. H.
         The coal camp bootlegger. West Virginia Coal Mining
         Institute. *Proceedings* 1921 78-80.

         The problems created by the bootleggers who cater "to the
         thirst and conviviality" of the mine camps.

1258.   NORTON, HELEN G.
         Feudalism in West Virginia. *Nation* 13: 154-5 1931.

         "Life in West Virginia coal camps is unbelievably feudalistic."

1259.   OBENAUER, MARIE L.
         Living conditions among coal mine workers of the Unit-
         ed States. *Ann. Amer. Acad.* 111: 12-23 1924.

1260. OBENAUER, MARIE L.
Who are the coal mine workers? *North American Review* 219: 609-15 1924.

1261. PARKER, EDWARD W.
Workmen's houses in the anthracite regions. National Planning Association. *Proceedings* 5: 54-66 1916.

1262. PARKER, RUTH L.
With the Friends in the coal fields. *ML&W* O 1932 3-10.

Activities of the American Friends Service Committee in relieving distress in the coal fields.

1263. PARSONS, FLOYD W.
A modern coal mining town. *Engineering and Mining Journal* 82: 830-32 1906.

The glories of Zeigler, Illinois and the Zeigler Coal Co.

1264. PEABODY'S NEW COAL TOWN IN ILLINOIS
Coal Age 5: 133-34 1914.

Account of Kincaid, Illinois.

1265. PEARCE, JOHN E.
The superfluous people of Hazard, Kentucky. *Reporter* Ja 3, 1963. 33-35.

Coal miners are, and will probably remain, superfluous.

1266. POLSKOV, WALTER N.
Sufficient unto himself is the coal digger. *Labor & Nation* My/Je 1947 28-29.

1267. QUARLES, MARY A.
A comparison of some aspects of family life between two areas of Leslie County, Kentucky. Thesis. University of Kentucky. 1952.

1268. RASKIN, A. H.
How miners live. *American Mercury* 64: 421-27 1947.

A generally dismal picture of life in the Pennsylvania and West Virginia coal fields.

1269. RATLIFF, PAUL
Yesterday's coal town. *ML&W* Winter 1960 20-23.

A "photo-essay" depicting conditions in a declining mine village.

1270. RICH, MARK
Some churches of coal mining communities of West Virginia. New York. 1951. 62p.

Survey sponsored by the West Virginia Council of Churches and the Committee for Cooperative Field Research.

1271. RICHARDSON, F. L. W.
Community resettlement in a depressed coal region. *Applied Anthropology* Pt. I 1: 1 O D 1941 24-53; Pt. II 1: 3 Ap/Je 1942 32-61; Pt. III 7: 4 1948 1-27.

1272. RIDENOUR, GEORGE L.
The American coal miner and the social problem. Thesis. Southern Baptist Theological Seminary. 1927.

1273. ROBERTS, PETER
Anthracite coal communities; a study of the demography, the social, educational and moral life of the anthracite regions. New York: Macmillan, 1904. 387p.

1274. ROBERTS, PETER
Slavs in anthracite coal communities. *Charities* 13: 215-22 1904.

1275. ROBINSON, M. B.
Among the coal miners. *Missionary Review* 25: 835-39 1902.

Illinois setting.

1276. ROGERS, JACK
I remember that mining town. *West Virginia Review* 15: 203-5 1938.

Vivid description of life in a West Virginia mine camp during the author's boyhood.

1277. ROLLER, ANNE H.
Wilkes-Barre: an anthracite town. *Survey* 55: 534-38 1926.

1278. ROOD, HENRY E.
A Pennsylvania colliery village. *Century Magazine* 55: 809-21 1897/98.

1279. ROOSEVELT, THEODORE
Coal miner at home. *Outlook* 96: 899-908 1910.

Account of the author's short trip to the Scranton area. TR paints a generally cheerful picture.

1280. ROSS, MALCOLM H.
Machine Age in the hills. New York: Macmillan, 1933.
248p.

"The effects of technology . . . in the coal fields of Kentucky
and West Virginia." A classic report.

1281. ROSS, MALCOLM H.
Permanent part-time. *Survey Graphic* 22: 266-68 1933.

Activity of the Quakers in the West Virginia mine fields.

1282. ROY, ANDREW
Characteristics of miners. *Ohio Mining Journal* 2: 88-
92 1883/84.

Miners are made "quarrelsome and fault-finding" by "the per-
nicious influence of breathing bad air."

1283. RYAN, FREDERICK
The rehabilitation of Oklahoma coal mining communities. Norman: University of Oklahoma Press, 1935.
120p.

1284. THE SALOON EVIL IN THE MINING INDUSTRY
Coal Age 12: 1008-9 1917.

1285. SHANNON, IRWIN V.
Southeastern Ohio in depression and war; the disinte-
gration of an area. Columbus: Ohio State University.
1943. 54p. (Bureau of Educational Research Monograph 24).

1286. SHAW, IRA D.
Welfare work among miners. *Coal Age* 4: 21-22 1913.

1287. SHEPHERD, WILLIAM G.
Big black spot. *Colliers* S 19, 1931 pp. 12-13.

Account of conditions in the West Virginia coal fields, with
special emphasis on the company store.

1288. SHEPPARD, MURIEL
Cloud by day, the story of coal and coke and people.
Chapel Hill: University of North Carolina Press, 1947.
266p.

A description of economic and social conditions in the coal and
coke regions of south-western Pennsylvania.

1289. SHURICK, A. T.
Colliery dwelling construction. *Coal Age* 38-41, 211-14,
1911/12.

Discussion of proper homes for miners and mine officials. Plans
and illustrations are included.
134

1290. SIMPSON, ALEXANDER G.
The life of a miner in two hemispheres. New York: Abby Press, 1903. 300p.

Includes sections on the author's experience as a mine official in Illinois and Alabama.

1291. SMITH, RICHARD C.
Human crisis in the kingdom of coal. New York: Friendship Press, 1952. 113p.

Examines the plight of the coal miner in both Europe and America. Author was for some years director of the Mountaineer Mining Mission in Morgantown, West Virginia.

1292. SOCIOLOGICAL CONDITIONS IN WEST VIRGINIA
Coal Age 2: 733-34 1912.

1293. SOCIOLOGICAL WORK ACCOMPLISHED BY THE CONSOLIDATION COAL COMPANY.
Coal Age 15: 54-58 1919.

Account of social services provided by the Company to its miners—nursing care, education, recreation, etc.

1294. SPAHR, CHARLES B.
The coal miners of Pennsylvania. *Outlook* 62: 805-12 1899.

1295. STOCKTON, RICHARD
Underground in Illinois; how coal miners live, work and struggle for unity. Chicago: National Research League, 1935. 32p.

1296. STRONG, EDNA R.
A sociological analysis of ecology, structure and processes in a Virginia coal mining community. Thesis. Louisiana State University. 1943.

1297. SWADOS, HARVEY
The miners: men without work. *Dissent* 6: 389-401 1959.

Account of life in the coal fields of western Pennsylvania.

1298. TAYLOR, WARREN C.
Father Ligutti's homestead. *Christian Century* 56: 56-8 Ja 11, 1939.

Account of efforts among coal miners in the Granger, Iowa area to combine small farming with mining.

1299. THREE DAYS AMONG THE COAL MINES OF JACKSON COUNTY, OHIO
Black Diamond N 1, 1888 203-5.

1300. TOWSON, CHARLES R.
Replacing the saloon in mining communities. *Coal Age*
8: 264 1915.

With the YMCA.

1301. U. S. WOMEN'S BUREAU
Home environment and employment opportunities of
women in coal-mine workers' families. Washington:
GPO, 1925. 61p. (Women's Bureau. Bulletin 45).

1302. VAN METER, LA RUE
Social organization of an Illinois coal-mining community. Thesis. University of Illinois. 1932.

1303. VENSLAUSKAS, STANLEY C.
Emigration from the Schuylkill County, Pennsylvania
coal fields, 1930-1943. Thesis. University of Pennsylvania. 1944.

1304. WALKER, WILMA
Distress in a southern Illinois county. *Social Service Review* 5: 558-81 1931.

Account of misery in Franklin County, Illinois caused by the
sharp decline in coal mine employment.

1305. WANCE, WILLIAM AND RICHARD BUTLER
Effect of industrial changes on occupational "inheritance" in four Pennsylvania communities. *Social Forces*
27: 158-62 1948.

Study of occupational inheritance in mining families in bituminous coal communities hard hit by technological change.

1306. WARBURTON, AMBER A.
Guidance in a rural-industrial community; Harlan
County, a Kentucky coal mining district, plans with and
for its boys and girls. Washington: National Educational Association, 1954. 249p.

1307. WATTS, A. C.
Utah Fuel Co.'s Somerset Mines prosper under prohibition. *Coal Age* 11: 796-98 1917.

The company's chief engineer claims a vast improvement in conditions since the saloon was turned into a social club (dry).

1308. WETZEL, JOHN A.
Game of black diamonds. *Outlook* 126: 593-97 1920.

General discussion of the industry, especially life of the miners.

1309. WHITE, J. H.
Sanitation in mining towns. *Coal Age* 4: 59-61 1913.

1310. WHITE, J. H.
Houses for mining towns. Washington: GPO, 1914. 64p.
(U. S. Bureau of Mines. Bulletin 87).

Treats of plans for and arrangement of mining towns.

1311. WIECK, AGNES
Ku Kluxing in the miners country. *New Republic* 38:
122-24 1924.

Williamson County, Illinois.

1312. WILLIAMS, L. M.
Transformation of a coal mining town. *Mining Congress
Journal* Ag 1943. 37-40.

Describes the improvement of Wheelwright, Kentucky as the
result of a community improvement program of the Inland Steel
Co.

1313. WILLIAMS, STANLEY B.
Disorganization and delinquency in three coal communities. Thesis. West Virginia University. 1954.

1314. WILSON, EDMUND
Frank Keeney's coal diggers. *New Republic* 67: 195-99,
229-31 1931.

Account of destitution and labor politics in the southern West
Virginia coal fields.

1315. WILSON, JOHN M.
The dark and the damp. New York: Dutton, 1951.
256p.

Autobiography. Includes experiences of the author in the coal
mines of Indiana.

1316. WOODBRIDGE, DWIGHT
Sanitation at mining villages in the Birmingham district, Alabama. Washington: GPO, 1913. 27p. (Bureau
of Mines Technical Paper 33).

1317. ZIMMERMAN, H. O.
Modernization of living conditions in a coal mining
town. Kentucky Mining Institute. *Proceedings* 1: 23-30.
1940.

The town of Wheelwright, Kentucky.

137

Transportation

1318. ACUFF, REECE
The coal rail rate structure and fourth section relief. Thesis. University of Tennessee. 1953.

1319. AMERICAN RAILWAY ASSOCIATION. CONFERENCE COMMITTEE WITH UNITED STATES COAL COMMISSION
Report. Washington, 1923. 104p.

1320. AMERICAN RAILWAY ASSOCIATION. SPECIAL COMMITTEE ON NATIONAL DEFENSE
Bituminous coal in the United States; plan for the distribution of bituminous coal in the United States to secure the minimum of rail transportation. Washington: GPO, 1918. 67p.

1321. ANTHRACITE COAL TRADE, BY RAILWAYS AND CANALS
Merchants Magazine 11: 541-44 1844.

1322. ASSOCIATION OF AMERICAN RAILROADS. RAILROAD COMMITTEE FOR THE STUDY OF TRANSPORTATION
Bituminous coal and lignite. Washington, 1946. 135p.

1323. ASSOCIATION OF AMERICAN RAILROADS. RAILROAD COMMITTEE FOR THE STUDY OF TRANSPORTATION
Report on anthracite and bituminous coal. Washington, 1947. 97p.

1324. BARTLETT, J. H.
Transport of coal on the Ohio and the lower Mississippi. Institute of Civil Engineers. *Proceedings* 134: 334-51 1898.

1325. BEMENT, ALBURTO
The Peabody atlas. Shipping mines and coal railroads in the central commercial district of the United States. Chicago: Peabody Coal Co., 1906. 149p.

1326. BEMENT, ALBURTO
Shipping mines and coal railroads of Illinois and Indiana. Chicago, 1903. 54p.

"Issued with the compliments of the Peabody Coal Company."

138

1327. BLISS, J. A.
What is the role of competition in transporting utility fuel. *Railway Age* N 12, 1962 36-7.

1328. BOGEN, JULES I.
The anthracite railroads; a study in American railroad enterprise. New York: Ronald Press, 1927. 281p.

1329. CAMPBELL, THOMAS C.
The bituminous coal freight-rate structure; an economic appraisal. Morgantown: West Virginia University, 1954. 47p. (*Its* Business and Economic Studies 3: 3).

1330. CARLSON, FRED A. AND FRANK SEAWALL
Coal traffic on the Ohio River system. Columbus: Ohio State University, 1962. 49p. (Ohio State University. Bureau of Business Research. Monograph 107).

1331. CARUSO, JOHN A.
The Coal & Coke Railway Company of West Virginia. *West Virginia History* 11: 62-69 1949.

1332. CHESAPEAKE AND OHIO RAILROAD COMPANY
Notes on the coal trade of the Chesapeake & Ohio Railroad in its bearing upon the commercial interests of Richmond, Virginia. Richmond: Baughman, 1878. 12p.

1333. COAL—ITS COST AND SUPPLY
Scientific American 7: 153 1862.

"Coal which is sold at the mines in Pennsylvania for $1.50 per ton, is sold for no less than $5.50 in New York." A plea for better and cheaper transportation.

1334. COAL ROAD FIFTY YEARS AGO
Colliery Engineer 8: 163 1888.

Brief account of the Danville & Pottsville R.R.

1335. CREDITOR, MORRIS
Rail-river-rail transportation of coal today and days ahead. West Virginia Coal Mining Institute. *Proceedings* 1953 93-100.

1336. CUVELLIER, I. C.
Coal shipping on the Great Lakes. *Coal Age* 4: 338-42 1913.

1337. DAWSON, J. W.
Change of railroad rates in West Virginia. *Coal Age* 8: 973-75 1915.

Writer sees a conspiracy of the Pennsylvania R.R. and the Pittsburgh Coal Co. against the West Virginia operators.

1338. FIRST COAL RAILROAD
Coal 1: 303 1882.

Chesterfield Railroad Company (Virginia, 1828).

1339. FOSTER, JOHN W.
Mineral wealth and railroad development. New York, 1872. 60p.

Series of letters dealing largely with the development of the Indiana coal fields.

1340. GREENBRIER COAL AND COKE CO. VS. NORFOLK AND WESTERN RAILWAY CO.
Coal & Coke Jl 1, 1905 7-10.

Discussion and text of judicial decision concerning discrimination on the part of a railroad in the distribution of coal cars.

1341. GUTHEIM, A. G.
The transportation problem in the bituminous coal industry. American Economic Association. *Papers & Proceedings* 11: 94-105 1921.

1342. HARRISON, FAIRFAX
Hearings before a subcommittee of the Committee on Naval Affairs, United States Senate . . . Statement of Fairfax Harrison on behalf of Southern Railway Company, July 27, 1914. [Washington, 1914]. 49p.

1343. HAUPT, HERMAN
The coal business on the Pennsylvania Railroad. Philadelphia. 1857. 33p.

1344. HEMPHILL, WILLIAM E.
Three-horse team. *Virginia Cavalcade* Autumn 1953 8-9.

Account of two-tongued wagon used to transport coal in Norfolk about 1915.

1345. HOLMES, LESLIE A.
Pre-War truck movement of coal from Illinois mines. *Journal of Geography* 42: 333-38 1943.

1346. HUDSON, JAMES F.
The anthracite coal pool. *North American Review* 144: 43-54 1887.

A denunciation of the railroads for the attempt to control the price of coal.

1347. INDIANA COAL ASSOCIATION
Report of coal production by rail shipping mines in the state of Indiana, during calendar years 1917 to 1953, classified by counties, railroads, veins of coal, and type of operation. Terre Haute, 1954. n.p.

1348. JOHNSTON, RICHARD M.
Coal car distribution and handling in the Pocahontas region. Thesis. University of Pennsylvania. 1959.

1349. JONES, CHESTER L.
The anthracite-tidewater canals. *Ann. Amer. Acad.* 31: 102-16 1908.

1350. JONES, CHESTER L.
The economic history of the anthracite-tidewater canals. Philadelphia: University of Pennsylvania, 1908. 181p. (University of Pennsylvania. Series in Political Economy & Public Law No. 22).

1351. JONES, ELIOT
The commodity clause legislation and the anthracite railroads. *Quarterly Journal of Economics* 27: 579-615 1913.

1352. JOSLIN, FALCON
Government construction of railroads and leasing of coal lands. American Mining Congress. *Proceedings* 15: 167-84 1912.

Attack on government policies in Alaska.

1353. KEITH, JEAN E.
The role of the Louisville and Nashville Railroad in the early development of Alabama coal and iron. Business History Society. *Bulletin* 26: 165-74 1952.

1354. KEITH, HERBERT
Cheap coal; or the Boston & Northwestern, Massachusetts Central and Poughkeepsie railroads. Boston: Rand, 1877. 21p.

1355. KING COAL'S HIGHWAY
Harper 64: 163-77 1882.

Account of the water transportation of coal from the Pittsburgh area to New Orleans.

1356. LAMBIE, JOSEPH T.
From mine to market; the history of coal transportation on the Norfolk and Western Railroad. New York: New York University, 1954. 380p.

A work of the first importance. Vital for an understanding of the history of the great coal fields of southern West Virginia.

1357. LAUCK, W. J.
Freight rates on anthracite coal, 1914-1920. Washington, 1920. 12p.

1358. LAUCK, W. J.
Operating and financial performance of anthracite railroads. Washington, 1920. 29p.

1359. LOWRY, WILLIAM
Comparison of earnings between coal carrying and non-coal carrying railroads. Thesis. West Virginia University. 1950.

1360. McDOWELL, IRA L.
The Lake cargo coal rate controversy. Thesis. West Virginia University. 1932.

1361. MANSFIELD, HARVEY C.
The Lake cargo coal rate controversy; a study in governmental adjustment of a sectional dispute. New York: Columbia, 1932. 273p. (Columbia Studies in History, Economics and Public Law 373).

1362. MARSHALL, L. C.
The commodities clause [of the Hepburn Act]. *Journal of Political Economy* 17: 448-60 1909.

1363. MORAN, E. L.
Coal traffic of the Great Lakes. *Journal of Geography* 15: 150-59 1917.

1364. MORROW, J. D. A.
Transportation factor in the price of coal. Academy of Political Science. *Proceedings* 10: 116-27 1922.

1365. NEW JERSEY. LEGISLATURE. SENATE. COMMITTEE ON HIGHWAYS, TRANSPORTATION AND PUBLIC UTILITIES
Public hearing on Assembly bill 675 (coal slurry pipeline bill) held September 26, 1962. Trenton, 1962. 55p. proc.

1366.   NEW YORK (STATE). PUBLIC WORKS DEPT.
         The New York State canals; the canal as a carrier of
         coal. Albany, 1918. 15p.

1367.   NEWCOMB, HARRY T.
         The anthracite carrying railroads. *Review of Reviews*
         26: 66-69 1902.

1368.   NORFOLK AND WESTERN TURNS COAL TO GOLD
         Business Week N 18, 1950 112-16.

1369.   PAGE, WILLIAM N.
         West Virginia coal. *Engineering & Mining Journal* 81:
         67-68 1906.

         Stresses the importance of transportation in the southern coal
         fields.

1370.   PATTON, NORMAN F.
         The economics of the distribution of anthracite.
         AIME. *Transactions* 119: 405-17 1936.

1371.   PITTSBURGH. CHAMBER OF COMMERCE
         Unjust and discriminatory freight rates of Pittsburgh
         district coal. Columbus, Ohio: Heer Printing Co., 1911.
         44p.

1372.   RAILROAD VS. THE COAL INTEREST
         Black Diamond 5: 170 1889/90.

1373.   REITELL, CHARLES
         Railway rates on bituminous and anthracite coal. *Ann.
         Amer. Acad.* 111: 155-164 1924.

1374.   ROPIEQUET, R. W.
         Coal freight rates—relativity and uniformity. American
         Mining Congress. *Proceedings* 19: 250-60 1916.

1375.   ST. JOHN, ISAAC M.
         Notes on the coal trade of the Chesapeake and Ohio
         Railroad in its bearing upon the commercial interest of
         Richmond, Va. n.p., 1878. 12p.

1376.   SCAMEHORN, HOWARD L.
         Transportation and coal: the development of the coal
         mining industry in Illinois, 1860-1890. Thesis. Univer-
         sity of Illinois. 1952.

1377. SCRANTON. BOARD OF TRADE
Report of the transportation committee of the Scranton Board of Trade on the cheaper transportation of the smaller sizes of anthracite coal, and the value of culm or anthracite waste as a steam producer. Scranton, 1889. 24p.

1378. SHURICK, A.
An analysis of the coal car situation. *Coal Age* 4: 452-55 1913.

1379. SWITCH-BACK RAILROAD
Historical sketch of the switchback railroad, the discovery of anthracite coal, and an account of the rise and growth of the Lehigh Coal & Navigation Company, New York, 1882. 20p.

1380. TAYLOR, GLENN R.
Transportation of Kentucky coal by water. Kentucky Mining Institute. *Proceedings* 1956/57 10-21.

1381. TEXAS EASTERN TRANSMISSION CORPORATION
Coal pipelines; a handbook of facts on a new industry. Houston, 1962. 20p.

1382. TOENGES, ALBERT L. AND FRANK A. JONES
Truck vs. rail haulage in bituminous coal strip mines. Washington: GPO, 1938. 54p. (U. S. Bureau of Mines. *Report of Investigations* 3416).

1383. U. S. CONGRESS. HOUSE
Anthracite and bituminous coal situation. Letter from the chairman of the Federal Trade Commission transmitting report on anthracite and bituminous coal situation and the relation of rail and water transportation to the present fuel problem. Washington: GPO, 1917. 29p. (65th Cong., 1st. Sess. House. Document 193).

1384. U. S. CONGRESS. HOUSE. COMMITTEE ON INTERSTATE AND FOREIGN COMMERCE
The alleged combination of the Philadelphia and Reading Railroad Company and other railroad and canal companies and producers of coal. Washington: GPO, 1892. 261p. (52nd Cong., 2nd Sess. House. Report 2278).

1385. U. S. CONGRESS. SENATE. COMMITTEE ON COMMERCE
Coal slurry pipeline. Washington: GPO, 1962. 246p.

Hearings on S.3044; "a bill to amend the Interstate Commerce Act to grant to any carrier of coal by pipeline . . . the right of eminent domain."

1386. U. S. CONGRESS. SENATE. COMMITTEE ON NAVAL AFFAIRS
Transportation of coal. Washington: GPO, 1915. 901p.

"To investigate the natural and strategic advantages of Charleston, South Carolina, as compared with Norfolk and other Chesapeake Bay ports, as a permanent point for coal distribution."

1387. U. S. FEDERAL TRADE COMMISSION
Anthracite and bituminous coal. Washington: GPO, 1917. 420p. (65th Cong., 1st Sess. Senate. Document 50).

"A report and recommendations on the anthracite and bituminous coal situation and the relation of rail-and-water transportation to the present fuel problem."

1388. U. S. INTERSTATE COMMERCE COMMISSION
Alleged unlawful rates and practices in the transportation of coal and mine supplies by the Atchison, Topeka and Santa Fe Railway Company. Washington: GPO, 1905. 183p. (59th Cong., 1st Sess. Senate. Document 180).

1389. U. S. INTERSTATE COMMERCE COMMISSION
Letter from the Interstate Commerce Commission submitting report of investigation in the matter of the relation of common carriers subject to the act to regulate commerce to coal and oil and the transportation thereof. Washington: GPO, 1914. (63d Cong., 2d Sess. House. Document No. 1124).

1390. U. S. INTERSTATE COMMERCE COMMISSION
Railroad discrimination and monopolies in coal and oil. Washington: GPO, 1909. 21p. (61st Cong., 1st Sess. Senate. Document 39).

1391. U. S. INTERSTATE COMMERCE COMMISSION
Report of investigation by Interstate Commerce Commission into railroad discriminations and monopolies in coal and oil. Washington: GPO, 1908. 23p. (60th Cong., 1st Sess. Senate. Document 450).

1392. U. S. INTERSTATE COMMERCE COMMISSION
Report on discriminations and monopolies in coal and oil. Washington: GPO, 1907. 81p. (59th Cong., 2nd Sess. House. Document 561).

1393. U. S. RAILROAD ADMINISTRATION
Cars for coal shipments. Washington: GPO, 1919. 8p. (66th Cong., 1st Sess. Senate. Document 73).

1394. U. S. RAILROAD ADMINISTRATION
Distribution of coal and coke. Washington: GPO, 1920.
16p. (66th Cong., 2nd Sess. Senate. Document 235).

1395. U. S. TRANSPORTATION INVESTIGATION AND RESEARCH BOARD
The economics of coal traffic flow. Washington: GPO, 1945. 103p. (79th Cong., 1st Sess. Senate. Document 82).

1396. VOSKUIL, WALTER H.
Bituminous coal movements in the United States. *Geographical Review* 32: 117-27 1942.

1397. WALLING, HENRY F.
The Morris and Essex R.R. and the anthracite coal regions of Pennsylvania. New York, 1867. 63p.

"With sketches of cities, villages, stations, scenery, and objects of interest along the route."

1398. WARNER, FAYETTE S.
The future movement of iron ore and coal in relation to the St. Lawrence waterway. Philadelphia: University of Pennsylvania, 1930. 195p. (Wharton School of Finance & Commerce. Research Studies. VIII).

1399. WARNER, LARKIN
The economics of the transportation of Ohio coal. Ph.D. University of Indiana. 1960.

1400. WARNER, LARKIN
Railroad rates and the growth of coal trucking in Ohio. *Land Economics* 38: 231-39 1962.

1401. WHAT'S AHEAD FOR UNIT TRAINS
Railway Age Ap 20, 1964 16-20.

1402. WILLIAMS, WILLIAM H.
Anthracite development and railway progress. American Irish Historical Society. *Journal* 22: 86-96 1923.

Account of the early development of transportation in the Pennsylvania anthracite area.

1403. YERKES, S. L.
Transportation as a factor in irregularity of coal mine operation. *Coal Age* 17: 439-42 1920.

Author advocates a national railroad car pool.

146

Government Regulation

1404. AMERICAN LIBERTY LEAGUE. NATIONAL LAWYERS COMMITTEE
Report on the constitutionality of the Bituminous Coal Conservation Act of 1935. n.p., 1935. 64p.

1405. BAKER, RALPH H.
The National Bituminous Coal Commission: Administration of the Bituminous Coal Act, 1937-1941. Baltimore: Johns Hopkins, 1941. 356p. (Johns Hopkins University. Studies in Historical and Political Science 59: 3).

1406. BITUMINOUS COAL CONSERVATION ACT (GUFFEY ACT) HELD UNCONSTITUTIONAL
MLR 43: 68-74 1936.

1407. CASEY, KATHRYN P.
Bituminous coal handbook; Bituminous coal act of 1937, rules of practice and procedure, rules and regulations for registration, marketing rules and regulations, comptroller general's decisions, general orders and schedules of discounts, statements, opinions and rulings. Albany: M. Bender & Co., 1942. 423p.

1408. CLARK, WALTER
Government ownership the inevitable if not the immediate result of the strike. *American Law Review* 56: 776-83 1922.

1409. CODE FOR COAL
Fortune O 1933 56-63.

Effect of the NRA on the coal industry in general and the Pittsburgh Coal Co. in particular.

1410. COLEMAN, MCALISTER
How to run coal. *Nation* 164: 242-45 1947.

Advocates a federal coal agency.

1411.   COMMITTEE ON PUBLIC ADMINISTRATION CASES
        The consumer's counsel and the National Bituminous
        Coal Commission. Washington: Committee on Public
        Administration Cases, 1949. 87p.

1412.   DEVINE, EDWARD T.
        The outlook for a permanent solution of the coal prob-
        lem in the United States. Academy of Political Science.
        Proceedings 10: 727-42 1924.

        More government regulation is required if the industry is not to
        destroy itself.

1413.   DICK, CHARLES
        Relation of the federal government to mining. American
        Mining Congress. *Proceedings* 11 pt. 2: 18-37 1908.

1414.   GARFIELD, JAMES R.
        The federal government in its relation to the mining in-
        dustry. American Mining Congress. *Proceedings* 11 pt.
        2: 88-97 1908.

1415.   GARNSEY, CYRUS AND OTHERS
        How prices of bituminous coal were fixed by the Fuel
        Administration. *Coal Age* 14: 685-89, 736-39 1918.

1416.   GARNSEY, CYRUS AND OTHERS
        Methods of fixing prices of bituminous coal adopted by
        The U. S. Fuel Administration. AIME. *Transactions* 61:
        346-70 1918.

1417.   GERMAN, RALPH H.
        The Pennsylvania Bituminous Coal Mine Act of 1961.
        Pennsylvania Bar Assoc. Quarterly 33: 229-33 1962.

1418.   GUFFEY COAL CASE
        Harvard Law Review 59: 664-74 1946.

1419.   HARRISON, GEORGE
        Duties of the federal and state governments in relation
        to the mining industry. American Mining Congress. *Pro-
        ceedings* 11 pt. 2: 57-65 1908.

1420.   INTER-UNIVERSITY CASE PROGRAM
        The Consumers' Counsel and the National Bituminous
        Coal Commission, 1937-1938. Rev. Ed. Washington,
        1950. 120p.

1421.   JOHNSON, VIRGINIA B.
        Economic aspects of national regulation of the bitumi-
        nous coal industry, 1933-1943. Thesis. West Virginia
        University. 1950.

1422.   JONES, HAROLD D.
The Bituminous Coal Act of 1937. Thesis. University of
Pennsylvania. 1940.

1423.   KRAVITZ, BIRDIE
Government interest in the bituminous coal industry.
Thesis. New York University. 1943.

1424.   MCADAM, DUNLAP J.
Coal, government ownership or control; government
ownership of navy coal land and control of the coal industry. New York, 1921. 188p.

1425.   MORROW, J. D. A.
Distribution of coal under U. S. Fuel Administration.
AIME. *Transactions* 61: 310-14 1918.

1426.   NEARING, SCOTT
The coal question; some reasons why it is pressing and
some suggestions for solving it. New York: Rand School
of Social Science, 1918. 47p.

1427.   NEW YORK PUBLIC LIBRARY
Nationalization of coal mines; a list of references. New
York, 1920. 11p.

1428.   ORCHARD, JOHN E.
The coal situation and the coal parliament: a rejoinder.
Quarterly Journal of Economics 39: 644-51 1925.

1429.   ORCHARD, JOHN E.
A proposal for regulation of the coal industry. *Quarterly
Journal of Economics* 39: 196-240 1925.

1430.   PHOEBUS, J. W.
Have coal operators any rights. *Black Diamond* 6: 764-
65 1890/91.

1431.   PRATT, JOHN B.
Federal control of coal mines an economic fallacy.
Washington, 1923. 31p.

1432.   ROY, ANDREW
A brief history of mining legislation in the State of Ohio.
Ohio Mining Journal O 1888 21-25.

1433.   RYAN, JOHN A.
Anthracite and ethics. *Catholic World* 122: 297-306
1925.

"The fundamental needs of the industry are unified operation
and pooling of expenses of production, preferably under public
ownership and direction."

1434. SIMPSON, FLOYD R.
Price regulation and the public utility concept: the Sunshine Anthracite Coal Case. *Land Economics* 17: 378-79 1941.

1435. SUTHERLAND, HOWARD
Government controls of the coal industry; speech delivered before the Natural Resources Section of the Chamber of Commerce of the United States, at Washington, D. C., May 16, 1922. Washington: GPO, 1922. 8p.

1436. THOMPSON, CAROL L.
Should the coal mines be nationalized. *Forum* 112: 285-95 1949.

1437. TRISKO, RALPH L.
Bituminous coal industry of the United States, with special reference to Federal regulation. Thesis. Georgetown University. 1943.

1438. UNITED MINE WORKERS OF AMERICA. DISTRICT 2
Why the miners' program? Clearfield, Pennsylvania, [1921]. 12p.

1439. UNITED MINE WORKERS. NATIONALIZATION RESEARCH COMMITTEE
Compulsory information in coal; a fact finding agency. Altoona, Pennsylvania, 1922. 28p.

1440. UNITED MINE WORKERS OF AMERICA. NATIONALIZATION RESEARCH COMMITTEE
How to run coal. n.p., 1922. 39p.

"Suggestions for a plan of public ownership, public control, and democratic management in the coal industry."

1441. U. S. SUPREME COURT
Constitutionality of the Bituminous Coal Conservation Act of 1935. Washington: GPO, 1936. 39p. (74th Cong., 2d Sess. Senate. Document 225).

1442. WORKERS INTERNATIONAL INDUSTRIAL UNION
The mines to the control of the miners. Detroit, 1919. 19p.

Strip Mining

Here are entered titles dealing with the history and the economic and social effects of strip mining. Such matters as the technical aspects of land reclamation are not included. For those interested, a most useful bibliography covering this area has been compiled by David F. Funk. (Revised bibliography of strip-mine reclamation. Columbus: Central States Forest Experiment Station, 1962. 20p.)

1443. BAYKAL, TURAN
Bituminous coal stripping in the United States. Thesis. University of Pittsburgh. 1944.

1444. BERISFORD, FRANK D.
The strip mining of bituminous coal. MBA Thesis. University of Pennsylvania (Wharton School). 1948.

1445. BOTTOMLEY, J. A.
History and development of strip mining in Illinois. Illinois Mining Institute. *Proceedings* 52: 90-100 1944.

1446. CASSIDY, SAMUEL M.
Some economic limits of strip mining. Thesis. University of Kentucky. 1928.

1447. CAUDILL, HARRY M.
The rape of the Appalachians. *Atlantic* Ap 1962 37-42.

A sharp attack on the strip mining industry and the TVA for "the savage destruction of the mountain region by the strip miners."

1447a. COUNCIL OF STATE GOVERNMENTS
Surface mining; extent and economic importance, impact on natural resources and proposals for reclamation of mined land. Chicago, 1964. (*Its* RM 369).

1448. CULVER, HAROLD E.
Preliminary report on coal stripping possibilities in Illinois. Illinois Geological Survey. Cooperative Mining Series. Bulletin 28. 1925. 61p.

1449. DANA, SAMUEL T.
Stearns case; an analysis. *American Forest* S 1955 18-19.

Important decision in which the Stearns Coal & Lumber Co. was denied right to strip mine in the Cumberland National Forest.

1450. FELDMAN, JULIAN
The development of a regulatory policy for the coal stripping industry in Ohio. Thesis. Ohio State University. 1950.

1451. GRAHAM, HERMAN D.
Economics of strip coal mining, with special reference to Knox and Fulton counties, Illinois. Ph.D. University of Illinois. 1948.

Appeared also as Bulletin 66 of the Bureau of Economic and Business Research of the University of Illinois.

1452. GROWTH OF STRIP COAL MINING AND ITS EFFECT ON LABOR
MLR 33: 85-89 1931.

1453. GUERNSEY, JAMES L.
A study of the agriculture and rural settlement pattern of Vigo County, Indiana, with emphasis on the impact of strip coal mining. Ph.D. Northwestern. 1953.

1454. HANNAH, H. W. AND B. VANDERVLIET
Effects of strip mining on agricultural areas in Illinois and suggested remedial measures. *Land Economics* 15: 296-311 1939.

1455. HEBLEY, HENRY F.
Stream pollution by coal mine wastes. *Mining Engineering* 5: 404-12 1953.

1456. HENDRICKSON, JOHN H.
The development of strip coal mining in Indiana. Thesis. Indiana University. 1952.

1457. HOLLISTER, G.
Future of federal programs in strip mining and restoration. Soil Conservation Society of America. *Proceedings* 1962 87-91.

1458. HOLMES, GRANT
Early coal stripping full of heartbreak. *Coal Age* My 29,
Je 5, 1929 797-800; 835-39.

The coal stripping industry is said to have been "born" in Danville, Illinois. The author was a pioneer in the early strip mining
industry.

1459. ILLINOIS COAL STRIPPERS ASSOCIATION
The open cut coal mining industry of Illinois. Chicago,
1939. 37p.

1460. ILLINOIS. STRIP MINE INVESTIGATION COMMISSION
Report of Strip Mine Investigation Commission to the
sixty-third General Assembly of Illinois. Chicago: Illinois Coal Strippers Association, 1943. 40p.

1461. IMPLIED RIGHT TO STRIP MINE COAL
West Virginia Law Review 58: 174-84 1956.

1462. INDIANA COAL PRODUCERS ASSOCIATION
The story of open cut coal mining in Indiana. Terre
Haute, 1940? 26p.

1463. JONES, PAUL M.
Strip coal mining in Western Kentucky. Kentucky Mining Institute. *Proceedings* 4: 39-46 1943/44.

1464. KELLER, ALVIN G.
Bituminous coal strip mines; some financial considerations. Pittsburgh: Mellon National Bank & Trust Company, 1951. 150p.

1465. KENTUCKY. LEGISLATIVE RESEARCH COMMISSION
Strip mining; a 1954 Kentucky Legislative Problem.
Frankfort. 1954. 15p. (Legislative Research Commis-
sion Information Bulletin No. 10).

1466. KIESSLING, O.
The economics of strip coal mining. Washington: GPO,
1931. 32p. (Bureau of Mines. Economic Paper 11).

1467. KOENIG, ROBERT
Economics and techniques of strip coal mining. Colorado School of Mines. *Quarterly* 45, 2B (1950) 29-39.

1468. LANG, R. T.
Bituminous stripping future in Pennsylvania. *Coal Age*
55: 68-69 1950.

1468a. LORENZ, WALTER C.
Progress in controlling acid mine water; a literature review. Washington: GPO, 1962. 40p. (U. S. Bureau of Mines. Information Circular 8080).

207 references are listed. The most comprehensive work in the field.

1469. LORING, ROBERT D.
The growth of strip coal mining in Indiana. Indiana Academy of Science. *Proceedings* 61: 184-86 1951.

1470. LORING, ROBERT D.
Strip coal mining areas of southwestern Indiana: their distribution, growth and restoration. Thesis. Indiana University. 1948.

1470a. MARLEY, HAROLD P.
Coal burden. *Social Science* 39: 102-6 1964.

1470b. MEINERS, ROBERT G.
Strip mining legislation. *Natural Resources Journal* 3: 442-69 1964.

1471. MERZ, ROBERT
Character and extent of land stripped for coal in Kentucky. Kentucky Agricultural Experiment Station. *Circular* 66. 1949. 27p.

1472. MILLER, E. WILLARD
Penn Township—an example of local government control of strip mining in Pennsylvania. *Economic Geography* 28: 256-60 1952.

1473. MILLER, E. WILLARD
Strip mining and land utilization in western Pennsylvania. *Scientific Monthly* 69: 94-103 1949.

1474. MONTGOMERY, HUGH B.
Conscientious coal stripping. *Coal Age* Jl 1962 84-88.

Account of operation "directed to broad land-use benefits to the communities in the area and the economy in general."

1475. MORRISON, VIRGINIA
Butler County, Pennsylvania; an example of a strip mined area. Thesis. University of Pittsburgh. 1950.

1476. MYERS, LEROY O.
Bituminous coal stripping in Pennsylvania. *Western Pennsylvania Historical Magazine* 29: 35-52 1946.

154

1477. OTTO, H. H.
Stripping in the anthracite region. AIME. *Transactions* 94: 181-89 1931.

1478. PARSONS, FLOYD W.
Coal mining by open stripping in Pennsylvania. *Engineering & Mining Journal* 81: 1239-40 1906.

1479. RILEY, CHARLES V.
An ecological and economic study of coal stripped land in eastern Ohio. Thesis. Ohio State University. 1947.

1480. SCOBEE, BARRY
Strip-pit mining in Kansas. *Coal Age* 4: 606-8 1913.

1481. SHAFFNER, M. N.
Bituminous coal strip mining in Pennsylvania. Pennsylvania Dept. of Internal Affairs. *Monthly Bulletin* Ja 1947 16-21.

1482. SHERWOOD, R. H.
Development of strip mining. *Mining Congress Journal* N 1945 31-34.
A brief history.

1483. SIEMS, GEORGE H.
The strip mining of bituminous coal in West Virginia; an analysis of past and present conditions. Thesis. University of Pennsylvania. 1949.

1484. SINKS, ALFRED H.
Battle of the spoil banks. *Harper* 192: 432-38 1946.
Accounting of the conflicts caused by strip mining in Ohio.

1485. SPENCER, K. A.
Strip coal mining in the Southwest. *Mining & Metallurgy* 12: 147-48 1931.

1486. STEWART, CHARLES L.
Strategy in protecting the public's interest in land: with special reference to strip mining. *Land Economics* 15: 312-16 1939.

1487. STRIP MINING; IT'S MORE THAN JUST DIGGING COAL
Business Week Je 26, 1954 166-74.

1488. STRIPPING FOR COAL MINES
Coal 1: 120-21 1882.
Account of stripping operation in the Hazleton, Pennsylvania area.

1489. TENNESSEE. DEPT. OF CONSERVATION AND COMMERCE
Conditions resulting from strip mining for coal in Tennessee. Nashville, 1960. 13p.

1490. VAN WINKLE, PHILIP
Reconnaissance of the strip mining industry of Southern Illinois. Thesis. University of Illinois. 1951.

1491. WALLACE, TOM
Stearns case; coal mining in Cumberland National Forest. *American Forest* Ap 1955 24-27.

Request of a coal company to conduct stripping operations in the Cumberland National Forest caused great controversy.

1492. WALTER, GEORGE H.
Agriculture and strip coal mining. *Agricultural Economics Research* Ja 1949 24-29.

1493. WARRINER, J. B.
Anthracite stripping. AIME. *Transactions* 57: 159-97 1917.

1494. WIENER, FREDERICK B.
Economic interest: rise and fall of a slogan. *Taxes* 37: 777-802 1959.

Study of the depletion allowance permitted the coal stripper. The pertinent court decisions are cited.

Mine Disasters

The "literature of disasters" is both old and voluminous. As might be imagined, much of the writing is sensational in nature. A mine disaster is the journalist's dream, combining as it does horror, drama and pathos. An attempt has been made here to include the best available accounts of the major disasters. Also included, are non-technical articles dealing with safety in general, accident rates, etc.

1495. ANDREWS, JOHN B.
Needless hazards in the coal industry. *Ann. Amer. Acad.* 111: 24-31 1924.

1496. BALLOU, E.
An account of the coal bank disaster at Blue Rock, Ohio. [6th ed.] Malta, Ohio, 1856. 32p.

1497. BEACH, H. D. AND R. A. LUCAS
Individual and group behavior in a coal mine disaster. Washington: National Academy of Sciences, 1960. 160p. (*Its* publication 834; also Disaster Study No. 13).

"This monograph examines individual and group behavior in a coal mine disaster that killed 75 miners and trapped 19 more underground from 6½ to 8½ days."

1498. BIETTO, FRANK J.
A study of the federal government's attempt to promote safety in the bituminous coal mines of the United States. Thesis. Southern Illinois University. 1952.

1499. BONOSKY, PHILLIP
Anatomy of a mine disaster. *Mainstream* Je 1963 8-29.

Account of the disaster and the following investigations at the Robena mine, near Uniontown, Pennsylvania.

1499a. BOYER, R. F.
Coal mine disasters: frequency by month. *Science* 144: 1447-49 1964.

1500. BRAMWELL, J. H. AND OTHERS
The Pocahontas mine explosion. AIME. *Transactions* 13: 237-49 1884/85.

The first great disaster in the newly-opened smokeless coal fields of Virginia/West Virginia.

157

1501. CHANCE, H. M.
An analysis of the casualties in the anthracite coal mines, from 1871-1880. AIME. *Transactions* 10: 67-77 1881/82.

1502. CLUTE, F. P.
The Dayton Mine explosion. Engineering Association of the South. *Publication* 7: 29-41 1896.

In Rhea County, Tennessee.

1503. CORRIGAN, JAMES J.
Death stalks anthracite's "buried valley." Pennsylvania Department of Internal Affairs. *Monthly Bulletin* N 1951 5-10.

Account of mining accidents in Luzerne County, Pennsylvania.

1504. CURRIE, ROBERT D.
Safety in Pennsylvania coal mines. Thesis. Penn State College. 1930.

1505. DARR MINE DISASTER
Mines & Minerals 28: 377-82 1907/8.

1506. DEATH TOOK NO HOLIDAY AT FOURMILE DISASTER
In Kentucky Winter 1949 41-42.

Account of the mine explosion in Bell County, Kentucky, Dec. 26, 1945.

1507. DONNELLY, CLARENCE S.
Notable mine disasters of Fayette County, West Virginia. Oak Hill, 1951. 33p.

1508. DRURY, DORIS
The accident records in coal mines of the United States. Bloomington, Indiana, Indiana University, 1964. 159p.

"A study of the literature with comparisons of the records in other coal-producing countries". A most useful and important contribution.

1509. EAVENSON, HOWARD N.
Safety methods and organization of United States Coal and Coke Co. *AIME. Transactions* 51: 319-64 1915.

In the company's McDowell County, West Virginia mines.

1510. FAIRMONT COAL CO. (FAIRMONT, WEST VIRGINIA)
The explosion at Monongah mines. Fairmont, West Virginia, 1908. 43p. (*Its* Bulletin No. 11).

1511. FAY, A. H.
Coal mine fatalities in the United States 1870-1914.
Washington: GPO, 1916. 370p. (U. S. Bureau of Mines.
Bulletin 115).

Gives fatal accidents described in reports by state mine inspectors by state, cause and year.

1512. FORBES, J. J. AND OTHERS
Federal coal mine inspection—a decade of progress.
Washington: GPO, 1951. 47p. (U. S. Bureau of Mines.
Information Circular 7625).

1513. HALL, CLARENCE AND WALTER O. SNELLING
The waste of life in American coal mining. *Engineering
Magazine* 34: 721-34 1907/8.

1514. HALL, R. D.
The explosion at Eccles, West Virginia. *Coal Age* 5:
846-50 1914.

1515. HARRINGTON, DANIEL AND W. J. FENE
Are new hazards being introduced in coal mines faster
than existing hazards are eliminated. Washington: GPO,
1940. 11p. (U. S. Bureau of Mines. Information Circular 7140).

1516. HARRINGTON, DANIEL
Effects of mechanization of the coal mining industry upon the frequency and severity of accidents, with discussion. U. S. Bureau of Labor Statistics. *Bulletin* 536: 183-93 1931.

1517. HARRINGTON, DANIEL
Safety in the mining industry. Colorado School of
Mines. *Quarterly* 45 No. 2B (1950) 173-279.

A useful review of the history of the efforts to increase mine safety. Includes a discussion of the major problems involved.

1518. HOFFMAN, PHIL
The Lost Creek disaster. *Palimpsest* 26: 21-27 1945.

Account of the mine explosion near Oskaloosa, Iowa. Ja. 24, 1902.

1519. HUMPHRY, HIRAM B.
Historical summary of coal mine explosions in the United States, 1810-1958. Washington: GPO, 1960. 280p.
(U. S. Bureau of Mines. Bulletin 586).

A basic work in the field. Appeared first as Information Circular 7900 in 1959.

1520.   ILLINOIS. BUREAU OF LABOR STATISTICS
        Report on the Cherry mine disaster. Springfield: Illinois
        State Journal Co., 1910. 90p.

1521.   KANSAS MINE DISASTER
        Colliery Engineer 9: 76-77 1888/89.

        Account of the explosion at Frontenac, Kansas which killed 45.

1521a. KEENAN, CHARLES M.
        Historical documentation of major coal-mine disasters in
        the United States not classified as explosions of gas or
        dust, 1846-1962. Washington: GPO, 1963. 90p. (U. S.
        Bureau of Mines. Bulletin 616).

1522.   LAUCK, WILLIAM J.
        Occupational hazards of anthracite miners. Washington,
        1920. 24p.

1523.   LEWIS, JOHN L.
        Testimony of John L. Lewis before the House of Rep-
        resentatives Committee on Education and Labor, April
        3, 1947 . . . Washington: Labor's Non-Partisan League,
        1947. 128p.

1524.   MACHISAK, JOHN C. AND OTHERS
        Injury experience in coal mining, 1960. Washington:
        GPO, 1962. 76p. (U. S. Bureau of Mines. Information
        Circular 8141).

        "Analysis of mine safety factors, related employment, and pro-
        duction data."

1525.   MAGUIRE, DON
        Scofield (Utah) mine disaster. *Mines & Minerals* 20:
        485-86 1899/1900.

1526.   MARTIN, JOHN B.
        The blast in Centralia No. 5; a mine disaster no one
        stopped. *Harpers* 196 Mr 1948 193-220.

1527.   MINE EXPLOSION AT ROYALTON, ILLINOIS
        Coal Age 6: 753-57 1914.

1528.   MISSOURI. BUREAU OF LABOR STATISTICS
        Special report to the governor of an investigation . . . of
        the coal mine explosion at Rich Hill, Missouri, March
        29, 1888. St. Louis: Daly Printing Co., 1888. 63p.

1529.   MONONGAH MINES RELIEF COMMITTEE
History of the Monongah mines relief fund in aid of suffers from the Monongah mine explosion, Monongah, West Virginia, December 6, 1907. Fairmont, West Virginia, 1910. 187p.

1530.   PAGE, WILLIAM N.
The explosion at the Red Ash Colliery, Fayette County, West Virginia. AIME. *Transactions* 30: 854-63 1900.

1531.   PARSONS, FLOYD W.
Disaster at Monongah coal mines Nos. 6 and 8. *Engineering and Mining Journal* 84: 1121-23 1907.

1532.   PAUL, JAMES W.
Red Ash (West Virginia) mine disaster. *Mines & Minerals* 20: 537-39 1899/1900.

1533.   RICE, GEORGE S.
Rescue work at Layland explosion. *Coal Age* 7: 508-9 1915.

See also pp. 633-34, 645 and index of v7. A great dispute about methods of rescue and who should get the credit developed. Layland is in the New River field of West Virginia.

1534.   ROY, ANDREW
The Pocahontas explosion. *Ohio Mining Journal* 3: 3 1885.

Account of the disaster in Tazewell County, Virginia, March 13, 1884.

1535.   ROY, ANDREW AND JOHN POLLOCK
Report of Messrs. Roy and Pollock, Miners' Committee to Columbus, to urge the passage by the Legislature of the Miners' Bill, for the ventilation and inspection of coal mines. Cincinnati, 1872. 22p.

1536.   SOLOMAN, H. J.
Psychological aspects of accident prevention. Washington: GPO, 1948. 10p. (U. S. Bureau of Mines. Information Circular 7460).

1537.   STOEK, H. H.
Monongah mine disaster. *Mines & Minerals* 28: 277-80 1907/8.

1538.   THE TWIN SHAFT DISASTER
Colliery Engineer 17: 17-20 1896/97.

Account of disaster at Pittston, Pennsylvania.

161

1539. U. S. CONGRESS. HOUSE. COMMITTEE ON EDUCATION AND
LABOR
Amendments to Federal Coal Mine Safety Act. Washington: GPO, 1964. 419p.

1540. U. S. CONGRESS. HOUSE. COMMITTEE ON EDUCATION AND
LABOR
To amend the Federal coal mine safety act. Hearings
before the Select Subcommittee on Labor of the Committee on Education and Labor, House of Representatives, Eighty-seventh Congress, First Session, on H. R.
4237 and various bills. Washington: GPO, 1961. 114p.

1541. U. S. CONGRESS. HOUSE. COMMITTEE ON EDUCATION AND
LABOR
Coal mine safety. Hearings before a subcommittee of the
Committee on Education and Labor. Washington: GPO,
1952. 491p.

1542. U. S. CONGRESS. HOUSE. COMMITTEE ON EDUCATION AND
LABOR
Welfare of miners. Hearing before the subcommittee of
the Committee on Education and Welfare. Washington:
GPO, 1947. 167p.

Includes reports of the committee appointed by Gov. Green (Illinois) to investigate the Centralia Mine disaster.

1543. U. S. CONGRESS. HOUSE. COMMITTEE ON MINES AND MINING
Inspections and investigations in coal mines. Washington: GPO, 1940. 566p.

Hearings on S. 2420; a bill "relating to certain inspections and
investigations in coal mines for the purpose of obtaining information relating to health and safety conditions, accidents, and
occupational diseases therein, and for other purposes."

1544. U. S. CONGRESS. SENATE. COMMITTEE ON LABOR AND
PUBLIC WELFARE
Providing for the welfare of coal miners. Hearings before the Sub-committee on Mine Safety. Washington:
GPO, 1952. 443p.

1545. U. S. CONGRESS. SENATE. COMMITTEE ON MINES AND
MINING
Inspections and investigations in coal mines. Washington: GPO, 1939. 151p.

1546. VAN DE WATER, FREDERICK
Eliminating mine slaughter. *Worlds Work* My 1929 74-79.

162

1547. WEST VIRGINIA. MINING COMMISSION
Report of the Mining Commission appointed by the
Governor to revise the mining laws of the state. Charleston: Tribune Printing Co., 1907. 77p.

Published also in West Virginia. Public Documents. 1905-1906
v3. Deals largely with mine safety.

1548. WESTFIELD, JAMES AND OTHERS
Administration of the Federal Coal Mine Safety Act,
1952-61. Washington: GPO, 1962. 56p. (U. S. Bureau
of Mines. Information Circular 8133).

1549. WIECK, EDWARD A.
Gambling with miners' lives. *New Republic* 42: 205-8
1925 (a reply & rejoinder 43: 265-6, 44: 48).

1550. WILSON, H. M. AND A. H. FAY
First National Mine Safety Demonstration, Pittsburgh,
Pennsylvania, October 30 and 31, 1911. Washington:
GPO, 1912. 75p. (U. S. Bureau of Mines. Bulletin 44).

An important "first."

Racial and Minority Groups

1551.   ABBOTT, GRACE
Immigrant and coal mining communities of Illinois.
Springfield: Illinois Department of Registration and
Education, 1920. 43p. (Bulletin 2 of the Immigrants
Commission).

1552.   ALABAMA MINING CAMP
Independent 63: 790-91 1907.

Negroes do about fifty-percent of the unskilled labor. Many
miners are ex-convicts, and the camps are centers of vice and
crime.

1553.   ALLEN, GERALD E.
The Negro coal miner in the Pittsburgh district. Thesis.
University of Pittsburgh. 1927.

1554.   BRAINERD, ALFRED
Colored mining labor. **AIME.** *Transactions* 14: 78-80
1885/86.

1555.   DWYER, KENNETH J.
Immigrant labor in the bituminous coal industry. Thesis. New York University. 1957.

1556.   FRENCH, JACK
Segregation patterns in a coal camp. Thesis. West Virginia University. 1953.

1557.   GUTMAN, HERBERT G.
Reconstruction in Ohio: Negroes in the Hocking Valley
coal mines in 1873 and 1874. *Labor History* 3: 243-64
1962.

1558.   HANDLING THE NEGRO MINER IN THE SOUTH
Coal Age 5: 875 1914.

"This class of labor is naturally shiftless."

164

1559. HARRIS, A. L.
The Negro in the coal mining industry. *Opportunity* F 1926 45-48.

1560. LAING, JAMES T.
Negro miner in West Virginia. *Social Forces* 14: 416-22 1936.

1561. LAING, JAMES T.
Social status among migrant Negroes. *Social Forces* 16: 562-68 1938.

Deals with Negro coal miners in West Virginia.

1562. MATHEWS, P. L.
The Mexican as a coal miner. *Coal Age* 12: 312-15 1917.

Author doubts that the importation of Mexican miners on any large scale would be an answer to the labor shortage.

1563. MINARD, RALPH D.
Race relationships in the Pocahontas Coal Field. *Journal of Social Issues.* 8: 29-44 1952.

Study centered "in that part of the coal field included in McDowell County, West Virginia."

1564. MURRAY, ELLEN P.
Why foreign miners are restless. *Coal Age* 12: 620-21 1917.

Kind words and personal interest are more important than high wages to foreign miners.

1565. NORTHRUP, HERBERT R.
The Negro and the United Mine Workers of America. *Southern Economic Journal* 9: 313-26 1943.

1566. SURFACE, GEORGE T.
The Negro mine laborer: central Appalachian coal field. *Ann. Amer. Acad.* 33: 338-52 1909.

1567. U. S. IMMIGRATION COMMISSION
Immigrants in industries. Washington: GPO, 1911.

Part 1 (2 volumes) is devoted to bituminous coal mining; Part 19 includes a section on Anthracite coal mining.

1568. WALKER, WILLIAM S.
Occupational aspirations of Negro family members in a coal mining community. Thesis. New York University. 1950.

$\mathcal{F}$olklore

1569. ADAMS, JAMES TAYLOR
Death in the dark: a collection of factual ballads of American mine disasters. Big Laurel, Virginia: Adams-Mullins Press, 1941. 119p.

1570. DOMICO, JIM
Mine accidents. *West Virginia Folklore* 11: 38-44 1961.

The folklore of mine accidents.

1571. GREEN, ARCHIE
A discography of American coal miners' songs. *Labor History* 2: 101-115 1961.

1572. GREEN, ARCHIE
The Carter Family's "Coal Miner's Blues." *Southern Folklore Quarterly* 25: 226-37 1961.

1573. GREEN, ARCHIE
The death of Mother Jones. *Labor History* 1: 68-80 1960.

1574. HAMILTON, REX
Stories of the mine. *West Virginia Folklore* 11: 44-49 1961.

Devoted largely to the folklore of mine accidents.

1575. KORSON, GEORGE
Anthracite miners as bards and minstrels. *American Speech* 10: 260-68 1935.

1576. KORSON, GEORGE
Anatomy of a coal mine. *Keystone Folklore* 8: 49-50 1963.

"Traditionally miners describe various parts of a mine in terms of the structure of the human body."

1577. KORSON, GEORGE
Black rock: mining folklore of the Pennsylvania Dutch. Baltimore: Johns Hopkins, 1960. 453p.

166

1578. KORSON, GEORGE
Coal dust on the fiddle; songs and stories of the bituminous industry. Philadelphia: University of Pennsylvania Press, 1943. 460p.

1579. KORSON, GEORGE
Minstrels of the mine patch; songs and stories of the anthracite industry. Philadelphia: University of Pennsylvania Press, 1938. 332p.

1580. KORSON, GEORGE
Pennsylvania songs and legends. Philadelphia: University of Pennsylvania Press, 1949. 474p.

Pp. 354-400 devoted to coal miners.

1581. KORSON, GEORGE
Songs and ballads of the anthracite miner a seam of folklore which once ran through life in the hard coal fields of Pennsylvania. New York: Hitchcock, 1927. 196p.

1582. LOPUSHANSKY, JOSEPH AND MICHAEL
Mining town terms. *American Speech* 4: 368-74 1929.

Terms common in the mining areas near Pittsburgh, Pennsylvania.

1583. MUSICK, RUTH ANN
More stories of the mines. *West Virginia Folklore* 10: 18-36 1960.

1584. MUSICK, RUTH ANN
Stories about mines. *West Virginia Folklore* 8: 54-68 1958.

1585. SMITH, GRACE P.
The miner's chant. *California Folklore Quarterly* 2: 221-23 1943.

A mine ballad from Iowa.

1586. WESTOVER, J. HUTSON
Highland language of the Cumberland coal country. *ML&W* Fall 1960 18-21.

Health

This section is intended as a guide to rather than a complete bibliography of the health problems of the coal industry. An attempt has been made to include the major studies, articles with especially useful bibliographies and very early reports. A complete bibliography of such medical problems as respiratory diseases was felt to be beyond the scope of this work. The literature in this area is voluminous, international in nature and accessible through the medical indexing services.

1587. ANDERSON, WILLIAM H. AND OTHERS
A comparison of coal miners exposed to coal dust and those exposed to silica dust. *AMA Arch. Environ. Health* 1: 540-547 1960.

1588. ANDERSON, WILLIAM H. AND WILLIAM F. SCHMIDT
Evaluation of disability in coal miners with chronic pulmonary disease. *JAMA* 171: 145-50 1959.

1589. BAIER, E. J. AND R. DIAKUN
Pneumoconiosis study in Central Pennsylvania coal mines. II. Environmental Phase. *J. Occup. Med.* 3: 507-521 1961.

1590. BENTLEY, J. G.
Methods of improving mining camp sanitation from standpoint of industrial medicine. *Virginia Medical Monthly* 54: 638-40 1928.

1591. BITTINGER, WILLIAM P.
Syphilis in mining communities. *West Virginia Medical Journal* 34: 506-12 1938.

1592. BOVARD, P. G.
Health and welfare plans (of United Mine Workers Association) from viewpoint of practicing physician. *Pennsylvania Medical Journal* 58: 1329-1330 1955.

1593. BRUNDAGE, D.
Mortality of coal miners. Washington: GPO, 1933. 17p. (Public Health Bulletin 210).

1594. BUREAU OF COOPERATIVE MEDICINE
Conference on medical care in the bituminous coal area.
1st—1952.

First bears the title: Medical-hospital problems in the bituminous coal mining areas. (Published also in the *JAMA* 151: 407-
12 1953).

1595. BUREAU OF COOPERATIVE MEDICINE
Medical care in selected areas of the Appalachian bituminous coal fields. New York: The Bureau, 1939.
55p.

1596. COLLIS, EDGAR L.
The coal miner; his health, diseases and general welfare.
Journal of Industrial Hygiene 7: 221-243 1925.

General survey of physical and psychological disorders of miners. Comparisons of conditions in U. S., Britain and Europe.

1597. DAVENPORT, S. J.
Bibliography of Bureau of Mines publications dealing
with health and safety in the mineral and allied industries, 1910-46. Washington: U. S. Bureau of Mines,
1948. 154p. (Technical Paper 705).

List of 1,684 items; subject and author indexes.

1598. DAVENPORT, S. J. AND G. MORGIS
Physiological aspects of electrical accidents in the coal-
mining industry. Washington: U. S. Bureau of Mines,
1951. 19p. (Information Circular 7620).

1599. DERBY, GEORGE
An inquiry into the influence upon health of anthracite
coal, when used as a fuel for warming dwelling houses
. . . Boston: A. Williams & Co., 1868. 46p.

1600. DOYLE, H. N. AND T. H. NOEHREN
Pulmonary fibrosis in soft coal miners: an annotated
bibliography on the entity recently described as soft
coal pneumoconiosis. Washington: GPO, 1954. 59p.
(Public Health Service Publication 352 & Public
Health Bibliography Series 11).

1601. DRAPER, WARREN F.
Conference on medical care in bituminous coal mine
area: views and suggestions. *JAMA* 151: 848-849 1953.

1602. DRAPER, WARREN F.
A hospital network for coal miners and their families.
West Virginia Medical Journal 56: 70-73 F 1960.

Description of some of the medical problems encountered in the
West Virginia-Tennessee-Kentucky coal fields.

1603. DRAPER, WARREN F.
UMWA Welfare and Retirement Fund medical care program. *American Journal of Public Health* 43: 757-62 1953.

1604. DRAPER, WARREN F.
Problems encountered in operation of United Mine Workers of America welfare and retirement fund. *Pennsylvania Medical Journal* 58: 1334-1339 1955.

1605. DRAPER, WARREN F.
Voluntary health insurance on national scene: United Mine Workers health program. *American Journal of Public Health* 40: 595-601 1950.

A brief survey of the health problems existing when the UMWA's Welfare and Retirement Fund went into effect (1948) and the plans and progress evolving from the Fund's program.

1606. DRENCKHAHN, C. K.
Vasospastic disease of the hands of miners due to vibration. *Illinois Medical Journal* 70: 354-357 1936.

1607. DYER, N. H.
Cancer as related to mining industry in West Virginia. *West Virginia Medical Journal* 48: 187-189. 1952.

1608. ENTERLINE, PHILIP E.
Mortality rates among coal miners. *American Journal of Public Health* 54: 758-68 1964.

"Death rates for miners are nearly twice those for all working men in the United States."

1609. FALK, LESLIE A.
Group health plans in coal mining communities. *Journal of Health & Human Behavior* 4: 4-13 1963.

1610. FERRIS, B. G., JR. AND N. R. FRANK
Pulmonary function in coal miners. *J. Occup. Med.* 4: 274-281 1962.

1611. FIELD, LEWIS AND OTHERS
Observations on the relation of psychological factors to psychiatric illness among coal miners. *International Journal of Social Psychiatry* 3: 133-45 1957.

The authors are staff members of the Bluefield, (West Virginia) Mental Health Center. Discussion of the "trapped, hopeless life situation" of the miner.

1612. FLINN, R. H. AND OTHERS
Anthraco-Silicosis among bituminous coal miners. *Industrial Medicine* 11: 470-73 1942.

1613. FLINN, R. H. AND OTHERS
Soft coal miners health and working environment. Washington: GPO, 1941. 118p. (Public Health Bulletin 270).

1614. FRIEDMAN, LOUIS L.
Significant case of pneumoconiosis in a soft-coal worker, *A.M.A. Archives of Internal Medicine* 95: 328-332 1955.

1615. GAGE, E. LYLE
Mining community health. West Virginia Coal Mining Institute. *Proceedings* 1947 76-86.

Discussion of medical service in the coal area of southern West Virginia.

1616. HAYHURST, E. R.
Health hazards and mortality statistics of soft coal mining in Illinois and Ohio. *Journal of Industrial Hygiene* 1: 360-67 1919.

1617. HIGH MORTALITY RATES OF COAL MINERS
MLR 40: 88-91 1935.

1618. HOTCHKISS, S. C.
Occupational diseases in the mining industry. *American Labor Legislation Review* 2: 131-39 1912.

1619. HYATT, R. E. AND OTHERS
Respiratory disease in southern West Virginia coal mines. *American Review of Respiratory Diseases* 89: 387-401 1964.

Study of the relationship between respiratory diseases and the number of years spent in mines.

1620. KAMMER, ADOLPH G.
Occupational health problems of the bituminous coal miner. *AMA Archives of Industrial Health* 15: 466-67 1957.

1621. KERR, LOREN E.
Coal workers' pneumoconiosis. *Industrial Medicine & Surgery* 25: 355-62 1956.

Includes an extensive review of the literature.

171

1622. KING, JAMES B., JAMES K. MORROW AND OTHERS
The bituminous coal country: a psychiatric frontier.
Mental Health in Virginia 10: 38-40 1959.

Essentially the same information was presented by the same
authors in the *West Virginia Medical Journal* 55: 164-67 1959.

1623. KRAFFT, FRED A.
Conserving health of employees in the coal industry.
AIME. *Transactions* 119: 433-42 1936.

1624. KRATZ, RACHEL E.
The possibility of medical social work in the welfare and
retirement fund of the United Mine Workers of America. Thesis. University of Pittsburgh. 1951.

1625. LEVINE, MILTON D. AND MURRAY B. HUNTER
Clinical study of pneumoconiosis of coal workers in Ohio
River Valley. *JAMA* 163: 1-4 1957.

1626. LIEBEN, JAN AND W. W. McBRIDE
Pneumoconiosis in Pennsylvania's bituminous mining
industry. *JAMA* 183: 176-179 1963.

A study of 16,000 miners. A high incidence—34 percent in central Pennsylvania—of pneumoconiosis was discovered.

1627. LIEBEN, JAN AND OTHERS
Pneumoconiosis study in central Pennsylvania coal
mines. I. Medical phase. *Journal of Occupational Medicine* 3: 493-506 1961.

1628. McBRIDE, W. W. AND OTHERS
Pneumoconiosis study of Western Pennsylvania bituminous coal miners. *Journal of Occupational Medicine* 5: 376-388 1963.

1629. MARTIN, JOSEPH E.
Breathless coal workers as seen at the Golden Clinic.
AMA Archives of Industrial Health 15: 494-98 1947.

1630. MARTIN, JOSEPH E.
Coal miners' pneumoconiosis. *American Journal of Public Health* 44: 581-91 1954.

1631. MASSIE, WILLIAM A.
Medical services for rural areas. Cambridge: Harvard,
1957. 68p.

Results of a study conducted by the Tennessee Medical Foundation. The area studied most intensively was Pruden Valley, which lies in the northwestern part of Claiborne County. It also includes portions of Campbell County, Tennessee, and Bell County, Kentucky. The area has a population of 6,000, mostly coal miners and their families.

172

1632.   MEDICAL-HOSPITAL PROBLEMS IN BITUMINOUS COAL
MINING AREA
JAMA 151: 407-412 Jan 1953.

Reports of survey teams studying medical and hospital facilities
in Kentucky, Tennessee and West Virginia mining areas.

1633.   MEISER, E. W.
What U.M.W.A. Welfare and Retirement Fund agree-
ment means to county medical societies. *Pennsylvania
Medical Journal* 59: 465-69 1956.

1634.   MERIWETHER, F. V.
Sanitary survey of the coal mines of Alabama. Washington: GPO, 1926. 20p. (U. S. Bureau of Mines. Report
of Investigations 2746).

1635.   MILLER, HAROLD W.
Characteristics of mining and non-mining psychiatric
patients. Thesis. West Virginia University. 1960.

1636.   MILLER, IVA A.
Child health in mining camp and village. *ML&W* 8:
5-8 Ja 1933.

1637.   MILLER, LEE H.
Disability appraisal of miners. Thesis (Doctor of Industrial Medicine). University of Cincinnati. 1954.

1638.   MORGIS, GENEVIEVE G.
Bibliography of Bureau of Mines health and safety publications, July 1, 1955 through June 30, 1961. Washington: GPO, 1962. 46p. (U. S. Bureau of Mines. Information Circular 8121).

1639.   MORTALITY RATES OF COAL MINERS
U. S. Bureau of Labor. *Bulletin* 616: 771-74 1936.

1640.   NESTMANN, RALPH H.
Incidence of emotional illness in coal miners in West
Virginia (preliminary report). *West Virginia Medical
Journal* 52: 149-52 1956.

1641.   OHIO. STATE DEPARTMENT OF HEALTH
Health of Ohio coal miners. Columbus, 1919. 24p.

1642.   PEMBERTON, JOHN
Chronic bronchitis, emphysema and bronchial spasm in
bituminous coal workers; epidemiologic study. *AMA Archives of Industrial Health* 13: 529-544 1956.

1643. POHLMANN, KENNETH E.
Rehabilitation of disabled miners. *American Journal of Public Health* 42: 791-794 1952.

Work of the UMWA's Welfare and Retirement Fund.

1644. POHLMANN, KENNETH E.
Rehabilitation of severely disabled: UMWA Welfare and Retirement Fund experience. *American Journal of Public Health* 43: 445-451 1953.

A follow-up report detailing specific results of a program of rehabilitation of the severely disabled coal miner.

1645. PREVALENCE OF ANTHRACO-SILICOSIS IN PENNSYLVANIA
MLR 41: 974-78 1935.

1646. PREVENTION OF DISEASE AMONG SOFT-COAL MINERS OF OHIO AND ILLINOIS
MLR 9: 899-902 1919.

1647. RAYMOND, R. W.
The hygiene of mines. *Transactions of the American Institute of Mining Engineers* 8: 97-120 1879.

1648. REYNOLDS, JAMES E.
Anxiety in coal miners. Thesis. West Virginia University. 1959.

"Some relevant characteristics of miners whose conditions were diagnosed as 'Anxiety Reaction' in McDowell County, West Virginia during the years 1955 through 1957."

1649. ROSEN, GEORGE
The history of miners' diseases, a medical and social interpretation. New York: Schuman, 1943. 490p.

A general history of miners' health from earliest times through the 19th century. References are primarily to British and European mines.

1650. ROSS, W. D. AND OTHERS
Emotional aspects of respiratory disorders among coal miners. *JAMA* 156: 484-87 1954.

1651. ROY, ANDREW
Miners' hospitals. *Ohio Mining Journal* F 1889 23-27.

Author suggests establishment of state-supported hospitals in the mining regions. Report of Committee on Miners' Hospitals appears N 1890 29-31.

1652. SCHNEIDER, EDWARD AND ROBERT E. HYATT
Peptic ulcer and pulmonary disease in coal miners. *JAMA* 186: 1061-64 1963.

1653. STACY, CHARLES B.
Medical service in coal fields. *Industrial Medicine* 18: 253-256 1949.

Pineville, Kentucky mine surgeon discusses aspects of serving a mining community and advantages of a contract or pre-paid medical plan.

1654. STEELE, H. E.
Negro and White miners under Alabama's pneumoconiosis law. *Industrial Medicine & Surgery* 31: 383-91 1962.

1655. STOECKLE, J. D. AND OTHERS
Respiratory disease in U. S. soft coal miners. *Journal of Chronic Diseases* 15: 887-905 1962.

1656. STOEK, H. H.
First aid movement in the anthracite region of Pennsylvania. *Engineering Magazine* 37: 321-36 1909.

1657. TELEKY, LUDWIG
History of factory and mine hygiene. New York: Columbia, 1948. 342p.

1658. TRASKO, VICTORIA M.
Silicosis, a continuing problem. *Public Health Reports* 73: 839-46 1958.

1659. TRASKO, VICTORIA M.
Some facts of the prevalence of silicosis in the United States. *AMA Archives of Industrial Health* 44: 379-86 1956.

1660. U. S. CHILDREN'S BUREAU
Occupational hazards to young workers. Report No. 3: The coal-mining industry. Washington: GPO, 1942. 55p. (*Its* Publication 275).

1661. U. S. COAL MINES ADMINISTRATION
A medical survey of the bituminous coal industry. Washington: GPO, 1947. 244p.

Includes a *Supplement to the Report* entitled "The Coal Miner and His Family." A study of first importance.

1662. WAINWRIGHT, J. M. AND H. D. NICHOLS
Evidence that the miner resists tuberculosis. *Coal Age* 2: 269-70, 303-4, 1912.

1663.   WATERMAN, DAVID H.
Pulmonary disease problems in 2140 hospital admissions of soft coal workers. *AMA Archives of Industrial Health* 15: 477-86 1957.

The Knoxville Chest Group experience.

1664.   WIESEL, CARL AND ARNY, MALCOLM
Psychiatric study of coal miners in eastern Kentucky area. *American Journal of Psychiatry* 108: 617-24 1952.

1665.   WILKERSON, W. V.
Co-operative community medical service. West Virginia Coal Mining Institute. *Proceedings* 1947 70-75.

A general defense of the contract medical service in the coal areas of southern West Virginia.

1666.   WILSON, ISABELLA C.
Sickness and medical care among a rural bituminous coal-mining population of Arkansas. Fayetteville: University of Arkansas, 1940. 44p. (Agricultural Experiment Station Bulletin 394).

A study to determine amount and kinds of sickness prevalent, availability, type and cost of medical services and the effect of income, location and occupational status on the use of medical service. Summary in *Monthly Labor Review* 51: 1421-1424 1940.

1667.   WYATT, JOHN P.
Morphogenesis of pneumoconiosis occurring in southern Illinois bituminous workers. *Archives of Industrial Health* 21: 445-57 1960.

General Descriptive
Accounts of Coal Regions

In this section emphasis has been placed on early descriptions of each of the major coal fields. Publication of these accounts attracted the attention of capitalists and contributed significantly to the development of new fields.

1668. ALLEN, JOSEPH H.
Coals and cokes of eastern Kentucky. AIME. *Transactions* 21: 53-60 1892/93.

1669. ALLEN, JOSEPH H.
Western Kentucky coals and cokes. AIME. *Transactions* 16: 581-93 1887/88.

1670. ANDREWS, EBENEZER B.
The lower Sunday Creek Valley (Ohio), its coal and iron ores; its shipping and manufacturing facilities. With a view of the markets for the Hocking coals. Columbus: Ohio State Journal, 1875. 67p.

1671. ANDROS, STEPHEN O.
Coal mining in Illinois. Urbana: University of Illinois. 1915. 250p. (Illinois Coal Mining Investigations . . . Bulletin 13).

1672. ASHBURNER, CHARLES A.
The anthracite coal beds of Pennsylvania. AIME. *Transactions* 11: 136-59 1882/83.

1673. ASHBURNER, CHARLES A.
Brazos coal field, Texas. AIME. *Transactions* 9: 495-506 1880/81.

1674. ASHBURNER, CHARLES A.
Brief description of the anthracite coal fields of Pennsylvania. Philadelphia, 1884. 32p.

"Paper read before the Engineers' Club of Philadelphia."

1675. ASHBURNER, CHARLES A.
Coal production in Utah, 1886. AIME. *Transactions* 16: 356-59 1887/88.

1676. ASHBURNER, CHARLES A.
The development and statistics of the Alabama coal fields for 1887. AIME. *Transactions* 17: 206-226 1888/89.

1677. ASHLEY, GEORGE H.
Cannel coal in the United States. Washington: GPO, 1918. 127p. (USGS. Bulletin 659).

1678. ASHLEY, GEORGE H.
The Cumberland Gap coal field. *Mining Magazine* 10: 94-100 1904.

1679. ASHLEY, GEORGE H.
The eastern interior coal field. *In* USGS. 22nd Annual Report pt. 3 pp265-305 1902.

1680. ASHLEY, GEORGE H.
Rhode Island coal. Washington, 1915. 62p. (USGS. Bulletin 615).

1681. ASHLEY, GEORGE H.
The valuation of public coal lands. Washington: GPO, 1910. 75p. (USGS. Bulletin 424).

1682. BACHE, FRANKLIN
The Arkansas-Indian Territory coal fields. *Engineering & Mining Journal* 76: 390-92 1902.

1683. BAIN, H. F.
The western interior coal field. *In* USGS. 22nd Annual Report pt. 3 pp333-66 1902.

1684. BEMENT, A.
Illinois coal: a non-technical account of its occurrence, production and preparation. Urbana, 1929. 112p. (Illinois Geological Survey. Bulletin 56).

1685. BOTT, MATTHIAS W.
Some aspects of the coal mining industry in Monongalia County, West Virginia. Thesis. West Virginia University. 1949.

1686. BRADY, S. DUNLAP
A new West Virginia coal field. *Mining Congress Journal* Mr 1944 24-28.

1687. BREWER, W. M.
The Coosa coal field in Alabama. *Engineering & Mining Journal* 56: 7-8 1893.

1688. BRINSMADE, R. B.
Mining coal at Morgantown, West Virginia. *Engineering & Mining Journal* 92: 414-16 1911.

1689. BROOKS, ALFRED H.
The coal resources of Alaska. *In* USGS. *22nd Annual Report* pt. 3 pp515-71 1902.

1690. BROOKS, ALFRED H.
Geography in the development of Alaska coal deposits. Association of American Geographers. *Annals* 1: 85-94 1911.

1691. BROOKS, ALFRED H.
The outlook for coal mining in Alaska. AIME. *Transactions* 26: 489-507 1905.

1692. BROWN, GEORGE M.
The McAlester coal field in Oklahoma. *Coal Age* 4: 153-55 1913.

1693. BROWN, ROBERT
On the geographical distribution and physical characteristics of the coal fields of the north Pacific coast. Edinburgh Geological Society. *Transactions* 1: 305-25 1870.

1694. BUCK, STUART M.
Coal mining in the Kanawha Valley of West Virginia. *In* Mineral Resources of the United States, 1883-84. Washington: GPO, 1885. pp131-43.

1695. BURKE, J. W.
Mobile—the great coal port of the future: the coal fields of Alabama and the Great Warrior Basin. n.p., [1885]. 32p.

1696. BUSH, B. F.
The coal fields of Missouri. AIME. *Transactions* 25: 903-17 1904.

1697. CAMPBELL, M. R. AND K. W. KEMBALL
The Deep River coal field of North Carolina. Chapel Hill, 1923. 95p. (North Carolina Geological & Economic Survey No. 33).

1698. CARDIFF COAL AND IRON COMPANY (CARDIFF, TENN.)
The town of Cardiff, and lands and mines of the company in Roane, Cumberland and Morgan counties. Boston, 1890. 23p.

1699. CARMIN, ROBERT L.
Coal mining industry of Guernsey County, Ohio. *Economic Geography* 19: 292-300 1943.

1700. CHANCE, HENRY M.
Appraisement of Michigan coal lands. *Coal Age* 2: 13-14, 51-53 1912.

1701. CHANCE, HENRY M.
The available tonnage of the bituminous coal fields of Pennsylvania. AIME. *Transactions* 10: 144-62 1881/-82.

1702. CHANCE, HENRY M.
Report on an exploration of the coal fields of North Carolina. Raleigh: P. M. Hale, 1885. 66p.

1703. CLAGHORN, CLARENCE R.
Notes on the Bernice anthracite coal basin, Sullivan County, Pennsylvania. AIME. *Transactions* 17: 606-16 1888/89.

1704. CLEARFIELD (PENNSYLVANIA) COAL REGION
Black Diamond 6: 60-61 1890/91.

Includes an account of the coal companies active in the area.

1705. COAL MINES OF UTAH AND WYOMING
Coal 2: 19-20 1883.

1706. COLLIER, ARTHUR J.
The Arkansas coal field. Washington: GPO, 1907. 158p. (USGS. Bulletin 326).

1707. COLLIER, ARTHUR J.
Coal resources of the Yukon. Washington: GPO, 1903. 71p. (USGS. Bulletin 218).

1708. COLLIER, ARTHUR J.
Geology and coal resources of the Cape Lisburn region, Alaska. Washington: GPO, 1906. 54p. (USGS. Bulletin 278).

1709. COLTON, HENRY
The Upper Measure coal field of Tennessee. AIME. *Transactions* 14: 292-305 1885/86.

1710. CRANE, W. R.
Coal mining in Arkansas. *Engineering & Mining Journal* 80: 774-77 1905.

1711. CRANE, W. R.
Coal mining in the Indian Territory. *Engineering & Mining Journal* 81: 658-60 1906.

1712. CRANE, W. R.
Coal mining in the Indian Territory—the southwestern field. *Engineering & Mining Journal* 76: 577-81 1903.

1713. CRANE, W. R.
Coal resources of Alaska. American Mining Congress. *Proceedings* 16: 192-205 1913.

1714. CRANE, W. R.
The Kansas coal mines of the Mississippi Valley. *Engineering & Mining Journal* 74: 514-16 1902.

1715. CRANE, W. R.
Kansas coal mining. *Engineering & Mining Journal* 72: 748-52 1901.

1716. CRANE, W. R.
The Pratt coal mines in Alabama. *Engineering & Mining Journal* 79: 177-80 1905.

1717. CULBERT, JAMES L.
New developments in New Mexico coal mining (abstract). Association of American Geographers. *Annals* 50: 312-13 1960.

1718. DEASY, GEORGE F. AND PHYLLIS R. GRIESS
Geographical significance of recent changes in mining in the bituminous coal fields of Pennsylvania. *Economic Geography* 33: 283-98 1957.

1719. DILWORTH, J. B.
The Black Mountain coal district, Kentucky. AIME. *Transactions* 43: 129-56 1912.

1720. D'INVILLIERS, E. V.
Report on the property of the Coal River Land Company (Logan & Boone counties, West Virginia). n.p., 1910. 20p.

Includes information on mining costs, markets, etc.

1721.   DOERR, ARTHUR
Chicago's coal; its origin, movement to market and use.
Journal of Geography 49: 261-69 1950.

1722.   DOERR, ARTHUR
Coal mining and changing land patterns in Oklahoma.
Land Economics. 38: 51-56 1962.

1723.   DOERR, ARTHUR
Coal mining and landscape modification in Oklahoma.
Norman: University of Oklahoma, 1961. 48p. (Oklahoma Geological Survey. Circular 54).

1724.   DOERR, ARTHUR
Geography of the coal industry of Williamson and Franklin counties, Illinois. Thesis. Indiana University. 1948.

1725.   DOERR, ARTHUR
Williamson and Franklin counties: coal counties of southern Illinois. *Journal of Geography* 49: 193-200 1950.

1726.   EASTON, H. D.
The cannel coal fields in Kentucky. *Coal Age* 2: 454-56 1912.

1727.   EDWARDS, WILLIAM S.
Coal and coke in West Virginia. Cincinnati: R. Clarke, 1892. 162p.

Covers the southern West Virginia fields only.

1728.   EVANS, GEORGE W.
Alaskan coal fields. AIME. *Transactions* 66: 286-98 1921.

1729.   EVANS, GEORGE W.
Coal mining problems in the State of Washington. Washington: GPO, 1924. 19p. (U. S. Bureau of Mines. Bulletin 190).

1730.   FENNEMAN, N. M. AND HOYT S. GALE
The Yampa coal field, Routt County, Colorado. Washington: GPO, 1906. 96p. (USGS. Bulletin 297).

1731.   FISHER, HOWELL
Report on the agricultural and mineral resources of Virginia and West Virginia, and more particularly on the extent, quality, and value of the coal and iron deposits situated along the line of the Chesapeake and Ohio Railroad, showing the advantage of that region for successful mining and manufacturing industry. New York: Wyndkoop & Hollenbeck, 1870. 24p.

1732.   FISHER, WALTER L.
Alaska coal problems. Washington: GPO, 1912. 32p. (U. S. Bureau of Mines. Bulletin 36).

1733.   FLORANCE, J. E.
Alaskan coal fields; their possibilities and their plight. *Engineering Magazine* 46: 881-90 1913/14.

1734.   FOWLER, GEORGE L.
Coals and coal mining methods of the Pocahontas field. *Engineering Magazine* 27: 217-32 1904.

1735.   FOWLER, GEORGE L.
Social and industrial conditions in the Pocahontas coal fields. *Engineering Magazine* 27: 383-96 1904.

1736.   FULTON, JOHN
Coal mining in the Connellsville coke region of Pennsylvania. AIME. *Transactions* 13: 330-41 1884/85.

1737.   GALE, HOYT S.
Coal fields of northeastern Utah. Washington: GPO, 1910. 265p. (USGS. Bulletin 265).

1738.   GASPER, DONALD
A geographic analysis of bituminous coal mining in Jefferson County, Pennsylvania. Thesis. Penn State College. 1951.

1739.   GIBSON, A. M.
The Coosa coal field (Alabama). Montgomery: Roemer Printing Co., 1895, 143p. (Alabama Geological Survey. Special Report No. 7).

"The Geological Survey is, at this time, the only agency at work for the development of this coal field."

1740.   GIBSON, A. M.
The coal measures of Blount Mountain (Alabama). Montgomery: Brown Printing Co., 1893. 80p. (Alabama Geological Survey. Special Report No. 5).

"More coal had been developed in one season by the Geological Survey than had been done by all preceding prospectors."

1741. GLENN, L. C.
Coal resources of the south. Southern Commercial Congress. *Proceedings* 1908 256-65.

1742. GOODYEAR, WATSON A.
Coal mines of the western coast of the United States. San Francisco: A. L. Bancroft, 1877. 153p.

1743. GREEN, STEPHEN H.
Coal and coal mining in Washington. Olympia, 1947. 41p. (Washington. Dept. of Conservation & Development. Division of Mines & Geology. Report of Investigations 4R).

1744. GRIFFITH, W. T.
Big Sandy coal fields, Kentucky. *Engineering & Mining Journal* 92: 508-10 1911.

1745. HALE, PETER M.
In the coal and iron counties of North Carolina. Raleigh, 1883. 425p.

1746. HALL, R. D.
The Fairmont, West Virginia coal region. *Coal Age* 1: 138-43 1911/12.

1747. HALL, R. D.
Georges Creek coalfield, Maryland. *Coal Age* 1: 10-14 1911/12.

1748. HANES, J. E. AND FLOYD W. PARSONS
Coal mining in Colorado. *Engineering & Mining Journal* 82: 793-95 1906.

1749. HAUGHT, OSCAR L.
Coal and coal mining in West Virginia. Morgantown: West Virginia Geological Survey, 1964. 38p.
Comprised largely of statistical tables.

1750. HAYES, CHARLES W.
The coal fields of the United States. *In* USGS. 22nd Annual Report pt. 3: 7-24 1902.

1751. HAYES, CHARLES W.
The Southern Appalachian coal field. *In* USGS. 22nd Annual Report pt. 3: 227-63 1902.

1752. HEWETT, G. C.
The northwestern Colorado coal region. AIME. *Transactions* 17: 375-80 1888/89.

184

1753. HILL, F. A.
Coal mining in Washington. AIME. *Transactions* 61: 371-74 1918.

1754. HODGE, JAMES M.
The Big Stone Gap coal field. AIME. *Transactions* 21: 922-38 1892/93.

1755. HOLMES, CHARLES
Coal mining in Michigan. *Mines & Minerals* 20: 59-62 1899/1900.

1756. HOSEA, R. M.
Anthracite coal mining in Colorado. *Engineering & Mining Journal* 82: 399-401 1906.

1757. HUDSON COAL COMPANY
The story of anthracite. New York, 1932. 425p.

1758. HUNT, THOMAS S.
Coal and iron in Alabama. *Coal* 2: 66-68 1883.

1759. HUNT, THOMAS S.
Coal and iron in southern Ohio. Boston: Cassino, 1881. 152p.

1760. JACKSON COUNTY, OHIO COAL FIELD
Black Diamond 6: 17-18 1890/91.

1761. JARRETT, F. G.
Coal mining in Carbonado, Washington. *Coal Age* 14: 308-12 1918.

1762. JOHNSON, JASPER
The Wilmington, Illinois coal field. AIME. *Transactions* 3: 188-202 1874/75.

1763. JOHNSON, WALTER J.
The coal industry in northern Wyoming and the State of Montana. *Mining Engineering* 5: 1262-71 1953.

1764. KEIGHLEY, F. C.
The Connellsville Coke region. *Engineering Magazine* 20: 17-40 1901.

1765. KILLEBREW, JOSEPH
Iron and coal of Tennessee. Nashville, 1881. 220p.

1766.   KILLEBREW, JOSEPH
         Special report on the coalfield of Little Sequatchee, with
         a general description of the Cumberland table-land.
         Nashville, 1876. 40p.

1767.   KIMBALL, JAMES P.
         The Quemahoning coalfields of Somerset County, Penn-
         sylvania. AIME. *Transactions* 12: 468-96 1883/84.

1768.   KOENIG, GEORGE A. AND OTHERS
         Expert reports on the mineral properties of the East
         Tennessee Land Company. New York: South Publish-
         ing Co., 1891. 44p.

1769.   KUHN, H. A.
         The Pittsburgh coal fields in Western Pennsylvania.
         AIME. *Transactions* 50: 640-57 1914.

1770.   LANE, ALFRED C.
         Coal in lower Michigan. Saginaw, 1899. 36p.

1771.   LANE, ALFRED C.
         The northern interior coal fields. *In* USGS. 22nd An-
         nual Report pt. 3 pp307-31 1902.

1772.   LEWIS, ROBERT S.
         The Book Cliffs coal field, Utah. AIME. *Transactions*
         50: 658-78 1914.

         Includes account of companies active in the field.

1773.   LUTHER, EDWARD T.
         The coal industry of Tennessee. Nashville: State De-
         partment of Conservation & Commerce. Division of Ge-
         ology, 1960. 58p. (*Its* Information Circular No. 10).

1774.   LUTHER, EDWARD T.
         The coal reserves of Tennessee. Nashville: State De-
         partment of Conservation and Commerce. Division of
         Geology. 1959. 294p. (*Its* Bulletin 63).

1775.   McCALLEY, HENRY
         Coal measures of the Plateau Region of Alabama; in-
         cluding a report on the coal measures of Blount County,
         by A. M. Gibson. Montgomery: Smith, Alfred & Co.,
         1891. 238p. (Alabama Geological Survey. Special Re-
         port No. 3).

1776. McCALLEY, HENRY
The Warrior coal field (Alabama). Montgomery: Barrett & Co., 1886. 571p. (Alabama Geological Survey. Special Report No. 1).

1777. MACFARLANE, GRAHAM
The eastern coal regions of Kentucky. AIME. *Transactions* 25: 518-32 1895.

1778. MACFARLANE, GRAHAM
Notes on American cannel coal. AIME. *Transactions* 18: 436-38 1889/90.

1779. MACFARLANE, JAMES
The coal regions of America; their topography, geology and development. New York: Appleton, 1873. 679p.

1780. M'KILLOP, JAMES
Coal and American coal mining. Airdrie: Baird & Hamilton, 1876. 91p.

"The result of observations made by me during a visit to America in 1869."

1781. MARSHALL, J. J.
Method of mining in southern West Virginia. *Coal Age* 1: 302-6 1911/12.

1782. MARTIN, G. C.
A reconnaissance of the Matanuska coal field, Alaska. Washington: GPO, 1906. 36p. (USGS. Bulletin 289).

1783. MAURY, MATTHEW F.
The resources of the coal field of the Upper Kanawha, with a sketch of the iron belt of Virginia, setting forth some of their markets and means of development. Baltimore: Sherwood, 1873. 44p.

1784. MELL, P. H.
The coal and iron interests of Alabama. *Coal* 1: 389-91 1882.

1785. MILLER, B. L.
The tertiary coal fields of the Rio Grande. *Coal Age* 4: 260-63 1913.

1786. MURPHY, RAYMOND AND MARION
Anthracite region of Pennsylvania. *Economic Geography* 14: 338-48 1938.

1787. MURPHY, RAYMOND AND HUGH E. SPITTAL
Movements of the center of coal mining in the Appalachian Plateaus. *Geographical Review* 35: 624-33 1945.

1788. MURPHY, RAYMOND AND HUGH E. SPITTAL
A new production map of the Appalachian bituminous coal region. Association of American Geographers. *Annals* 34: 164-72 1944.

1789. NELSON, WILBUR A.
The southern Tennessee coal field. Nashville: Tennessee. Division of Geology, 1925. 239p. (*Its* Bulletin 33-A).

1790. NORTON, R. HENRY
Notes on coal mining in Oregon. AIME. *Transactions* 19: 23-28 1890/91.

1791. PARSONS, FLOYD W.
Coal mining in southern West Virginia. *Engineering and Mining Journal* 84: 881-85 1907.

1792. PARSONS, FLOYD W.
Mining in the George's Creek coal field. *Engineering & Mining Journal* 82: 687-91 1906.

1793. PARSONS, FLOYD W.
Coal mining in the Fairmont Field, West Virginia. *Engineering & Mining Journal* 82: 1018-20, 1070-74 1906.

1794. PARSONS, FLOYD W.
The coal mines of southern Wyoming. *Engineering & Mining Journal* 85: 118-20 1908.

1795. PARSONS, FLOYD W.
The coal mining situation in northern Wyoming. *Engineering and Mining Journal* 84: 930-35 1907.

1796. PARSONS, FLOYD W.
Mining coal on the Virginian Railroad. *Coal Age* 1: 1039-43 1911/12.

1797. PARSONS, FLOYD W.
Montana's great coal fields and its collieries. *Engineering and Mining Journal* 84: 978-81 1907.

1798. PAYNE, HENRY M.
Future of the Williamson and the Tug River coal field. *Illustrated Monthly West Virginian* Ag 1908 45-49.

1799. PAYNE, HENRY M.
Mining coal in Texas. *Engineering & Mining Journal* 91: 626-27 1911.

1800. PECK, W. R.
The pocket coal field of Lee County, Virginia. *Coal Age* 5: 761-3 1914.

1801. PECK, W. R. AND R. J. SAMPSON
The Harlan coal field in Kentucky. *Coal Age* 3: 796-800 1913.

1802. PELTIER, M. F.
Coal mining in northern Wyoming. *Coal Age* 10: 832-34 1916.

1803. PIERCE, R. A.
The lignite fields of Colorado. *Coal Age* 1: 534-38 1911/12.

1804. PULTZ, JOHN L.
The Big Stone Gap coal field of Virginia and Kentucky. *Engineering Magazine* 28: 71-85 1904/5.

1805. RAMSAY, E.
The Pratt mines of the Tennessee Coal, Iron and Railroad Company, Alabama. AIME. *Transactions* 19: 296-313 1890/91.

1806. RANDOLPH, BEVERLEY S.
Seaboard coal regions along the Baltimore & Ohio Railroad. *Mining Magazine* 11: 229-32 1905.

The area about Fairmont, West Virginia.

1807. RAY, FRANK A.
The Ohio coal supply and its exhaustion. Columbus, 1914. 46p. (Ohio State University. College of Engineering. Bulletin 12).

1808. REYNOLDS, W. C.
Report on the Coal River coal field (West Virginia). Charleston, 1897. 11p.

Made for the proposed Coal River Railroad Co.

1809. RICHARDSON, G. B.
Reconnaissance of the Book Cliffs coal field, between Grand River, Colorado and Sunnyside, Utah. Washington: GPO, 1909. 54p. (USGS. Bulletin 371).

Pp47-51 on market and development.
189

1810.   ROBINSON, NEIL
        The Kanawha and New River coal fields of West Virginia. Charleston, 1904. 23p.

1811.   ROCKWELL, CLEVELAND
        The Coos Bay coal fields (Oregon). *Engineering & Mining Journal* 73: 238-40, 270-71 1902.

1812.   ROWE, J. P.
        The Montana coal fields: their commercial value. *Mining Magazine* 11: 241-50 1905.

1813.   ROWE, J. P.
        The coal industry of Montana. *Engineering & Mining Journal* 85: 1055-58 1908.

1814.   ROY, ANDREW
        The Thacker coal field of West Virginia. *Mines & Minerals* 19: 472 1898/99.

        Early notice of the opening of the Williamson Field.

1815.   SCHAEFER, CHARLES B.
        The coal fields of Saginaw, Mich. Saginaw, 1898. 88p.

1816.   SHAW, A. H.
        The Arkansas semi-anthracite field. *Coal Age* 2: 486-88 1912.

1817.   SHERIDAN, J. E.
        The coal mines and plant of the Stag Canon Fuel Co., Dawson, N. M. AIME. *Transactions* 40: 354-81 1909.

1818.   SHURICK, A. T.
        The Diamondville coal field, Wyoming. *Engineering & Mining Journal* 85: 118-20 1908.

1819.   SHURICK, A. T.
        The Federal Valley field in Ohio. *Coal Age* 1: 1236-38 1911/12.

1820.   SIMMONS, JESSE
        The Cambria coal fields in Wyoming. *Coal Age* 1: 766-68 1911/12.

1821.   SIMMONS, JESSE
        The Sheridan, Wyoming coal field. *Coal Age* 1: 866-68, 932-34 1911/12.

1822. SMITH, GEORGE O.
The coal fields of the Pacific coast. *In* USGS. 22nd Annual Report pt. 3 pp473-513 1902.

1823. SMURTHWAITE, WILLIAM
Coal mining at Steubenville, Ohio. *Ohio Mining Journal* 1: 53-59 1882/83.

1824. SNOW SHOE COAL FIELD.
Coal 1: 366 1882.
Glowing account of the economic future of the area (Centre County, Pennsylvania).

1825. SQUIRE, JOSEPH
The Cahaba coal field (Alabama). Montgomery: Brown Printing Co., 1890. 189p. (Alabama Geological Survey. Special Report No. 2).

1826. STEBINGER, EUGENE
The coal fields of Montana. AIME. *Transactions* 46: 889-919 1913.

1827. STOEK, H. H.
The Pennsylvania anthracite coal field. *In* USGS. 22nd Annual Report pt. 3 pp55-117 1902.

1828. STONE, RALPH W.
Coal resources of the Russell Fork Basin in Kentucky and Virginia. Washington: GPO, 1908. 127p. (USGS. Bulletin 348).

1829. STORRS, ARTHUR H.
The anthracite coal fields of Pennsylvania. *Mining Magazine* 11: 211-21 1905.

1830. STORRS, L. S.
The Rocky Mountain coal field. *In* USGS. 22nd Annual Report pt. 3 pp415-71 1902.

1831. STOW, AUDLEY H.
Mining in the Pocahontas field. *Coal Age* 3: 594-600 1913.

1832. TAFF, JOSEPH A.
The southwestern coal field. *In* USGS. 22nd Annual Report pt. 3 pp367-413 1902.

1833. TENNESSEE. BUREAU OF AGRICULTURE, STATISTICS AND MINES
Coal. Report of Henry E. Colton . . . Nashville: A. B. Tavel, 1883. 128p.

1834. TENNESSEE COAL, IRON AND RAILROAD CO.
Descriptions of plants and mines, with illustrations. Birmingham, Alabama, 1900. 174p.

1835. TOENGES, ALBERT L.
Coal development in Alaska. *Mining Engineering* 1: 361-64 1949.

1836. TRINIDAD, COLORADO: THE CENTER OF THE GREAT LAS ANIMAS COAL FIELD
Black Diamond Mr 1888 7-10.

1837. UNITED STATES BUREAU OF MINES
Mining industry of the United States of America. Washington, 1922. 62p.

1838. VAUGHAN, THOMAS W.
Reconnaissance on the Rio Grande coal fields of Texas. Washington: GPO, 1900. 100p. (USGS. Bulletin 164).

1839. WATTS, ALFRED C.
Coal mining in Carbon County, Utah. *Coal Age* 3: 400-4 1913.

1840. WEEKS, JOSEPH D.
The Elk Garden and Upper Potomac coal fields of West Virginia. AIME. *Transactions* 24: 351-64 1894.

1841. WETHERILL, J. PRICE
An outline of anthracite coal mining in Schuylkill County, Pennsylvania. AIME. *Transactions* 5: 402-22 1876/77.

1842. WHITE, DAVID AND OTHERS
The Northern Appalachian coal field. *In* USGS. 22nd Annual Report pt. 3 pp119-225 1902.

1843. WHITE, I. C.
The barren zone of the Northern Appalachian coal field and its relation to Pittsburgh's industries. American Mining Congress. *Proceedings* 11: 166-76 1908.

"If this waste continues, some of you in this audience will see the finish in the northern Appalachian field of all cheap and easily won coal."

1844. WHITE, I. C. AND OTHERS
The Pittsburgh coal bed. AIME. *Transactions* 74: 481-506 1926.

192

1845.   WHITESIDE, F. W.
        Central coal fields in Colorado. *Coal Age* 2: 2-5 1912.

1846.   WHITESIDE, F. W.
        The Trinidad district in Colorado. *Coal Age* 1: 632-35,
        664-67 1911/12.

1847.   WHITESIDE, F. W.
        The Yampa coal field of Colorado. *Coal Age* 11: 654-57
        1917.

1848.   WOLFE, MARSHALL L.
        Coal mining in Bates County, Missouri. *Coal* 2: 412-13
        1883.

1849.   WOODWORTH, JAY B.
        The Atlantic Coast triassic coal field. *In* USGS. Annual
        Report 22 pt. 3 pp25-53 1902.

Miscellaneous

1850. BAILEY, CAROL
Training for coal miners in cooperation with the public schools of Tennessee. Thesis. University of Tennessee. 1952.

1851. BEEBE, GILBERT W.
Differential fertility by color for coal miners in Logan County, West Virginia. *Milbank Memorial Fund Quarterly* 19: 189-95 1941.

1852. BENDALL, JOHN WENTWORTH
A study of the Minnesota multiphasic personality inventory and its use in identification of acceptable mine foremen. Thesis. West Virginia University. 1955.

1853. CLEGG, HERMAN D.
The evaluation of a psychological test battery as a selective device for foremen in the mining industry. Thesis. West Virginia University. 1962.

1854. COAL PRODUCERS COMMITTEE FOR SMOKE ABATEMENT
Smoke and air pollution, a study. Cincinnati, Ohio, 195? 4 vols.

1855. DAVIES, MATTHEW J.
The care of mine mules. *Coal Age* 1: 1021-22 1911/12.

1856. DURRETT, HAROLD L.
A validation study of a psychological test battery for selection of Joy ripper-type continuous miner operators. Thesis. West Virginia University. 1960.

1857. ESFANDIARY, MARY S.
Coal research organizations; their activities and publications. Washington: GPO, 1961. 64p. (U. S. Bureau of Mines. Information Circular 8008).

194

1858. FORBES, R. D.
Anthracite region discovers its "surface." *American Forests* 50: 424-27 1944.

Development of scientific forestry in the Pennsylvania anthracite region.

1859. FOSTER, J. S.
Taxpayers' associations; their origin and how they have been operated in the anthracite coal region. *Mines & Minerals* 20: 345-47 1899/1900.

1860. GAUGER, A. W.
Coal and research—two great national resources. *Coal Utilization* D 1952 23-33.

1861. GRAVITY COAL PIERS AT HOBOKEN
Scientific American 46: 226-27 1882.

Contains a number of illustrations of the methods used in handling "the enormous traffic in coal."

1862. GREENE, HOMER
Coal and the coal mines. Boston: Houghton Mifflin, 1889. 246p.

On cover: The Riverside Library for Young People.

1863. HAAS, FRANK
Conservation in West Virginia. *Coal Age* 2: 872-74 1912.

The coal producers operate far more efficiently and with less waste than the coal consumers.

1864. HALL, BETTY S.
The role of rhetoric in the northern West Virginia activities of the United Mine Workers, 1897-1927. Thesis. West Virginia University. 1955.

1865. HAUGHEE, J. W.
The dog mines of Muskingum County (Ohio). *Ohio Mining Journal* N 1890 93-95.

Dogs were used to haul coal in the mines.

1866. HEINRICH, OSWALD J.
The industrial school for miners and mechanics at Drifton, Luzerne County, Pennsylvania. AIME. *Transactions* 9: 390-95 1880/81.

1867. HIBBS, WILLIAM
The mining foreman and his duties. *Ohio Mining Journal* 1894 45-54.

195

1868. HIGGINS, WALLACE W.
Mine dogs and dog miners. Chillicothe, Ohio: Ross
County Historical Society, 1958. 5p.

Working conditions in small Ohio coal mines during 1870's 1880.
Dogs were used to help pull cars.

1869. HOGG, E.
Care of the mine mule. *Mines & Minerals* 26: 149-51
1905/6.

1870. HOLBROOK, E. A.
Research in the coal mining industry. AIME. *Transactions* 63: 747-67 1920.

1871. HUMAN PRICE OF COAL: A STUDY OF CERTAIN ASPECTS
OF THE BITUMINOUS COAL INDUSTRY
New York: Association Press, 1932. 67p.

1872. ILLINOIS. GEOLOGICAL SURVEY
Research needs of Illinois' coal industry. Urbana, 1930.
89p. (Cooperative Research Series. Bulletin 33).

1873. IMBACH, THEODORE F.
Raising mushrooms in a coal mine. *Coal Age* 8: 168-70
1915.

1874. KARASKA, GERALD J.
The pattern of settlements in the southern and middle
anthracite region of Pennsylvania. Ph.D. Penn State
University. 1962.

1875. KENWORTHY, WILMER E.
First aid to soft coal—then a major operation. *ML&W*
Ap 1933 1-6.

1876. LORD, N. W.
The Department of Mining of the State University.
Ohio Mining Journal O 1888 13-17.

Account of mining education at OSU.

1877. LORD, N. W.
Education of mining engineers. *Ohio Mining Journal* 6:
3 1888 13-18.

1878. MacCORKLE, WILLIAM A.
Relation of West Virginia coals to the Panama Canal address before the West Virginia Coal Mining Institute on the relation of West Virginia coals to the Panama Canal. Delivered at Charleston, West Virginia on Dec. 8, 1913, by William A. MacCorkle, ex-governor of the state of West Virginia. Washington: GPO, 1914. 16p. (63d Cong., 2d Sess. Senate. Document 484).

1879. MARKLE, DONALD
Anthracoal: a new domestic and metallurgical fuel. AIME. *Transactions* 66: 535-49 1921.

1880. MASON, ARTHUR J.
Comments of an ore engineer [on the bituminous coal industry]. American Economic Association. *Papers & Proceedings* 11: 106-16 1921.

1881. METROPOLITAN PRESS AND THE COAL COMBINE
Colliery Engineer 12: 228 1891/92.

Editorial complaint about the "amazing stupidity" of newspapers in dealing with coal news.

1882. MITCHELL, JOHN
Conservation in the coal industry. American Mining Congress. *Proceedings* 11 pt. 2: 185-95 1908.

1883. MONNETT, OSBORN AND OTHERS
Smoke-abatement investigations at Salt Lake City, Utah. Washington: GPO, 1926. 98p. (U. S. Bureau of Mines. Bulletin 254).

1884. MUMFORD, JOHN KIMBERLY
Anthracite. New York: Industries Publishing Co. 1925. 150p.

(Romance of Industry Series)

1885. MUNROE, HENRY S.
A summer school of practical mining. AIME. *Transactions* 9: 664-71 1880/81.

For students at the School of Mines, Columbia University.

1886. NATIONAL COAL ASSOCIATION
The story of bituminous coal. Washington, 1937. 23p.

1887. NATIONAL COAL POLICY CONFERENCE
Coal today; a basic memorandum about America's essential fuel. Washington, [1959]. 9p.

1888. NATIONAL INDUSTRIAL CONFERENCE BOARD
Foreman training in the anthracite industry. New York,
1944. 24p. (Studies in personnel policy 66).

1889. NEW USES FOR COAL: RESEARCH PROGRAM BACKED BY
OPERATORS AND CARRIED OUT BY BATTELLE INSTITUTE
Business Week D 28, 1940 39-40.

1890. NEWHARD, I. C.
Care of mine mules. *Mines & Minerals* 28: 56-58
1907/8.

1891. OUTLOOK AND RESEARCH POSSIBILITIES FOR BITUMI-
NOUS COAL
Washington, 1956. 52p. (U. S. Bureau of Mines. Infor-
mation Circular 7754).

1892. PARKER, EDWARD W.
Coal briquetting in the United States. AIME. *Transactions* 38: 581-620 1907.

Appeared also in slightly different form in Bulletin 316 of the
USGS, pp460-85.

1893. PATTON, JAMES L.
Vocational education in coal mining. Kentucky Mining
Institute. *Proceedings* 6: 9-35 1945/46.

Selected high schools in the coal regions should include vocational training in mining.

1894. PAUL, J. W.
State mine inspection in coal mining states. American
Mining Congress. *Proceedings* 12: 239-57 1909.

A state-by-state survey.

1895. PITTSBURGH CONSOLIDATION COAL COMPANY
Coal evolution, not revolution; a discussion of the fuel
situation and research project for the making of synthetic fuel from coal. Library, Pennsylvania, 1947. 10p.

1896. POPE, GEORGE S.
The purchase of coal by the Government under specifications. Washington: GPO, 1910. 80p. (USGS. Bulletin
428).

1897. RANDALL, D. T.
The purchase of coal under government and commer-
cial specifications on the basis of its heating value.
Washington: GPO, 1908. 27p. (USGS. Bulletin 339).

1898. RHODES, BEN
Appalachian coal companies grow timber as a crop.
Mining Congress Journal Ja 1953 27-30.

1899. RICE, GEORGE S.
Standardization of coals for the trade. American Mining
Congress. *Proceedings* 22: 699-710 1919.

1900. ROBERTS, ELLIS W.
A history of land subsidence and its consequences
caused by the mining of anthracite coal in Luzerne
County, Pennsylvania. Ph.D. New York University.
1948.

1901. RODEN, B. F.
The commissary: its indispensability and purposes. *Coal
Age* 4: 240-42 1913.

1902. RYAN, FREDERICK
The development of coal operators' associations in the
Southwest. *Southwestern Social Science Quarterly* 14:
133-44 1933.

1903. RUTLEDGE, J. J.
Demonstration coal mines. AIME. *Transactions* 63:
945-52 1920.

1904. SANBORN COMPANY, J. B., CHICAGO
Line yards; comprising a list of lumber yards, elevators,
coal dealers, etc., operating two or more branch yards
at which coal is sold at retail in the states of Colorado,
Idaho, Illinois, Indiana, Iowa, Kansas, Minnesota, Missouri, North Dakota, Montana, Wisconsin, Nebraska,
Oregon, South Dakota & Washington, also the Canadian
provinces; indicating main offices, branch yards, lines
handled, and purchasing offices with a comprehensive
index. Chicago: The J. B. Sanborn Company, 1917. 84p.

1905. SENSATIONAL JOURNALISM AND THE COAL MINING IN-
TERESTS
Colliery Engineer 12: 13 1891/92.

Editorial complaint that many papers "frequently convey the
idea to general readers that colliery owners and colliery officials
are as a rule a set of inhuman fools."

1906. SPEARE, MORRIS E.
The coal industry. Cambridge, Massachusetts: Bellman,
1957. 32p. (Vocational and professional monographs,
No. 89).

199

1907. SPENCER, HAROLD H.
The accounting treatment of large repair items in the strip coal industry. Thesis. University of Pennsylvania. 1958.

1908. STEELMAN, JAMES
The English Language in the coal mining regions. *Coal Age* 6: 834-36 1914.

The problem of teaching English to foreign born miners.

1909. STEVENSON, GEORGE E.
Reflections of an anthracite engineer. New York, 1931. 238p.

1910. STORE CHECKS VS. THRIFT
Coal Age 8: 619 1915.

Editorial on the role of the company store. It triggered a number of letters on the subject on pp. 812-13, 852-54, 895-97.

1911. SUTHERLAND, HOWARD
The bituminous coal industry; debate in the Senate of the United States, June 8, 1922. Washington: GPO, 1922. 31p.

1912. TAYLOR, SAMUEL A.
The purchase of coal by the B.T.U. method, and some practical questions connected therewith. American Mining Congress. *Proceedings* 12: 335-49 1909.

1913. TENNESSEE. STATE PLANNING COMMISSION
Problems surrounding the distribution of convict-mined coal in Tennessee. Nashville, 1938. 14p.

1914. TOWNS BUILT OVER A FURNACE
Business Week My 4, 1963 98-100.

Towns in eastern Pennsylvania are being endangered from fires burning in old coal mines.

1915. TRAER, GLENN W.
Conservation in the coal industry, protection of life and prevention of waste. American Mining Congress. *Proceedings* 11 pt. 2: 152-65 1908.

1916. U. S. CONGRESS. HOUSE. COMMITTEE ON INTERIOR AND INSULAR AFFAIRS
Coal. Hearings before the Special Subcommittee on Coal Research pursuant to H. Res. 400, to authorize a study leading to the establishment of a research and development program for the coal industry. Washington: GPO, 1956. 164p.

1917.   U. S. CONGRESS. HOUSE. COMMITTEE ON INTERIOR AND
INSULAR AFFAIRS
Coal Hearings before the Special Subcommittee on Coal
Research, on the establishment of a research and devel-
opment program for the coal industry. Washington:
GPO, 1957. 579p.

1918.   U. S. CONGRESS. SENATE. COMMITTEE ON INDIAN AFFAIRS
Leasing of the segregated coal deposits of the Choctaw
and Chickasaw Nations in Oklahoma. Washington:
GPO, 1942. 101p.

This is the "basic" hearing on this subject. There were also hearings during 1943 on S. 314 and H. R. 1859, both dealing with
essentially the same matter.

1919.   U. S. CONGRESS. SENATE. COMMITTEE ON INTERIOR AND
INSULAR AFFAIRS
Coal research. Hearings before the Sub-committee on
Minerals, Materials, and Fuels . . . on S. 49 and S. 1362,
bills to encourage and stimulate the production and
conservation of coal in the United States. Washington:
GPO, 1959. 70p.

1920.   U. S. CONGRESS. SENATE. COMMITTEE ON THE DISTRICT
OF COLUMBIA
Coal situation in the District of Columbia. Washington:
GPO, 1926. 224p.

1921.   U. S. DEPARTMENT OF THE INTERIOR
Regulations governing coal land leases in the Territory
of Alaska . . . with information regarding coal lands.
Washington: GPO, 1916. 86p.

1922.   U. S. FEDERAL FUEL DISTRIBUTOR
Final report. Washington: GPO, 1923. 51p.

Final report of Federal Fuel Distributor to President of United
States, Sept. 21, 1923.

1923.   U. S. LIBRARY OF CONGRESS. DIVISION OF BIBLIOGRAPHY
List of references on the coal situation in the United
States, 1921-1922. Washington, 1922. 16p.

1924.   USE FOR OLD COAL MINES
Black Diamond 16: 819 1896.

Abandoned coal mines are ideal for raising mushrooms.

1925. WADLEIGH, FRANCIS R.
A list of books and other sources of information regarding coal and coal products. Washington: W. F. Roberts, 1935. 63p.

1926. WILDER, HENRY J.
Agriculture in the coal regions of southwestern Pennsylvania. *In* U. S. Dept. of Agriculture. Yearbook, 1909. 321-32.

1927. WILFONG, HARRY DEAN
A cross-validation study of a mining foreman selection key, devised from the Minnesota Multiphasic Personality Inventory. Thesis. West Virginia University. 1957.

1928. WILLIAMS, DORCAS A.
Food habits of the pupils in Monongahela & Dunbar (West Virginia) High School whose parents are engaged in coal mining. Thesis. West Virginia University. 1952.

Biography

Biographies of even quite important figures in the coal industry are often almost impossible to locate. This is especially true with regard to the early operators. They lived before the days of "public relations" and had little interest in—indeed they often avoided—personal publicity. As Tams notes (p76), "we have books and articles galore about minor political and literary figures, yet it is often difficult to find even the birth and death dates of men of vastly greater importance to the history of West Virginia." The same situation prevails throughout the nation.

The only major "who's who" of the coal industry was compiled by Arthur M. Hull. His *Coal Men of America* (Chicago: Retail Coalman, 1918. 506p.) contains several hundred short professional biographies of leading operators and officials. Photographs of most of the biographees are included. The only other major sources of biographical material are the trade journals in the field, especially *Black Diamond* and *Coal Age*. Special emphasis has been placed on the period before 1930, for the conventional biographical sources are more adequate after that date.

Adams, K. C. *Black Diamond* Jl 7, 1956 p13.
Adams, Thomas K. *Coal Age* 4: 55 1913.
Albright, Joseph J. *Black Diamond* F 1888 p10.
Alderson, J. Cary. In *Thurmond* pp85-6.
Alexander, O. L. *Black Diamond* Ja 28, 1950 p13.
Allen, Wm. L. *Black Diamond* F 23, 1924 p202.
Andrews, Chauncey H. *Ohio Mining Journal* 1894: 135-39.
Atwater, A. J. *Black Diamond* 5: 492 1889/90.
Atwater, John J. *Black Diamond* Ja 13, 1962 p9.
Baker, Robert B. *Black Diamond* Mr 30, 1957 p7.
Bardin, Ernest. *Black Diamond* Ag 22, 1931 p5.
Barger, D. H. *Black Diamond* My 2, 1931 p8.
Barnard, I. P. *Black Diamond* D 28, 1929 p7.
Battin, Joseph. *Pennsylvania Magazine of History & Biography* 73: 337-48 1949.
Bausewine, George. *Black Diamond* F 19, 1944 p14.
Baylor, James M. *Black Diamond* Mr 24, 1962 p9.
Bellis, Enoch. *Coal Age* 37: 256 1932.
Bement, A. *Coal Age* 2: 402 1912.
Bennett, Ensign. *Black Diamond* Mr 1888 p10.
Bennett, S. P. *Black Diamond* 6: 58 1890/91.
Berwind, Charles P. *Engineering & Mining Journal* 50: 687 1890; In *Tams* pp77-79.
Beury, Joseph L. In *Tams* pp79-80.
Bird, Eugene H. *Black Diamond* Jl 30, 1960 p6.
Bischoff, J. W. *Coal Age* 11: 478 1917.
Blakely, Abraham G. *Coal Age* 10: 29 1916.
Boileau, John W. *Coal Age* 6: 636 1914.
Botsch, Roch P. *Black Diamond* Je 11, 1955 p13.
Bowditch, Richard L. *Black Diamond* Ja 3, 1948 p14.
Bowen, J. P. In *Tams* p80.

Bradley, Joseph G. *Coal Age* 14: 404 1918.
Brady, Samuel D. *Coal Age* 36: 343 1931.
Bramwell, J. H. AIME. *Transactions* 24: 749-51 1894.
Brashears, George W. *Ohio Mining Journal* 1894: 141-42.
Bretz, C. L. *Coal & Coke* Ag 15, 1903 p12.
Britley, Joseph V. *Coal Age* 12: 899 1917.
Broughton, Thomas A. *Black Diamond* 17: 308 1896.
Brown, Robert L. *Black Diamond* Jl 30, 1927 p10.
Bryden, Alexander. *Coal Age* 12: 684 1917.
Buchanan, D. W. *Black Diamond* Je 18, 1960 pp10-11.
Buchtel, John R. *Ohio Mining Journal* 1894: 135.
Burr, William E. *Black Diamond* 21: 185 1898.
Burrell, George A. *Coal Age* 10: 917 1916.
Burrows, Lemuel. *Black Diamond* Ja 9, 1926 p36.
Bush, Benjamin. *Black Diamond* Ag 6, 1927 p10.
Bush, Morris W. *Coal Age* 10: 917 1916.
Butler, J. G. *Black Diamond* Ap 13, 1957 p7.
Butler, John E. *Coal Age* 11: 996-7 1917.
Button, Steward E. *Coal Age* 13: 342 1918.

Cake, Joseph L. *Coal Age* 2: 54 1912.
Callahan, John. *Coal Age* 18: 222 1920.
Calloway, Alfred W. *Coal Age* 5: 1016 1914, *Black Diamond* S 18, 1926 p291.
Campbell, Herbert C. *Coal Age* 6: 512 1914.
Campbell, John C. *Black Diamond* 5: 660-C 1889/90.
Caperton, George & W. G. In *Tams* p81.
Capps, George A. *Black Diamond* Mr 29, 1958 p9.
Carney, William J. *Black Diamond* Jl 2, 1927 p57.
Cartlidge, Oscar. *Coal Age* 5: 652 1914.
Chafin, Don. In *Thurmond* pp88-7.
Chance, H. M. *Coal Age* 1: 1082 1911/12.
Charles, J. Lundy. *Black Diamond* Je 6, 1931 p13.
Chase, F. M. *Coal Age* 2: 578 1912.
Chase, W. M. *Coal Age* 13: 683 1918.
Cheyney, Jessee S. *Coal Age* 5: 1056 1914.
Chilson, Ernest. *Black Diamond* Ja 10, 1931 p9.
Christy, Joseph M. *Coal Age* 11: 704 1917.
Clark, John A. *Coal & Coke* Ap 19, 1901 p12.
Clingerman, Walter H. *Coal Age* 7: 211 1915.
Clothier, W. J. *Black Diamond* S 22, 1962 p7.
Coen, P. A. *Coal Age* 13: 669 1918.
Colley, James W. In *Thurmond* pp87-88.
Collins, Justice. In *Tams* pp81-82.
Connell, William L. *Coal Age* 2: 540 1912.
Connor, Eli T. *Mines & Minerals* 27: 463 1906/7. *Coal Age* 1: 104 1911/12.
Constans, J. F. *Coal & Coke* O 1, 1902 p16.
Cooper, John. In *Tams* pp82-83.
Corcoran, Thomas. *Ohio Mining Journal* 1894: 139-41.
Coxe, Eckley B. *Colliery Engineer* 15: 244 1894/95.
Crankshaw, Hugh M. *Coal Age* 9: 591 1916.
Crawford, James L. *Mines & Minerals* 25: 444 1904/5.
Crowe, Carl C. *Black Diamond* Ja 18, 1958 p9.
Cunningham, Walter H. *Coal Age* 15: 275 1919, *Black Diamond* F 19, 1944 p14.
Curran, Henry B. *Engineering & Mining Journal* 50: 743 1890.
Curran, John J. American Catholic Historical Society. *Records* 63: 67-84 1952.
Curtin, Norman C. *Black Diamond* Ag 25, 1962 p9.

Davis, Edwin H. *Black Diamond* D 17, 1960 p9.
Davis, Joseph E. *Black Diamond* My 28, 1955 p7.
204

Dean, John. *Engineering & Mining Journal* 50: 717 1890.
DeArmit, William P. *Colliery Engineer* 13: 280 1892/93.
Deegans, W. E. *Coal Age* 14: 1075 1918.
Denari, Andrew. *Black Diamond* My 24, 1958 p7.
Dering, Charles L. *Black Diamond* N 1, 1930 p7.
De Venny, Thomas. *Black Diamond* F 26, 1927 p17.
Deyerle, Oscar M. *Black Diamond* Je 3, 1950 p24.
Disque, Brice P. *Black Diamond* Mr 12, 1960 p7.
Dixon, Samuel L. In *Tams* pp83-85.
Dodson, Charles M. *Coal Age* 11: 427 1917.
Dodson, Truman M. *Coal Age* 8: 935 1915.
Donovan, Frank J. *Black Diamond* Ap 13, 1957 p9.
Dougherty, C. B. *Coal Age* 8: 1068 1915.
Drennen, Everett. *Coal Age* 6: 911 1914.
Duncan, David. *Coal* 2: 233 1883.
Dunlop, John. *Coal Age* 6: 150 1914.

Ebbert, Charles B. *Black Diamond* N 20, 1929 p7.
Effinger, J. Fred. In *Tams* p85.
Ellison, Richard. *Black Diamond* D 13, 1930 p7.
Elmore, R. P. *Black Diamond* 20: 17 1898.
Enzian, Charles. *Coal Age* 5: 972 1914.
Evans, Cadwallader. *Coal Age* 11: 1029 1917.
Evans, George W. *Coal Age* 6: 430 1914.
Evans, W. H. *Black Diamond* Je 21, 1947 p15.

Fisher, H. G. *Black Diamond* 5: 820 1889/90.
Fleming, Robert. *Black Diamond* F 23, 1924 p202.
Fox, Edward G. *Fortune* N 1956 p231.
Francis, James D. *Black Diamond* Ja 18, 1958 p8; In *Tams* pp86-87; In *Thurmond* pp88-90.
Freeman, John. In *Tams* p87.
Frick, Charles. *Coal & Coke* Ja 25, 1901 p15.
Fulton, John A. *Coal Age* 2: 89 1912; 9: 200 1916.

Gandy, Harry A. *Black Diamond* Ag 31, 1957 p8.
Garcia, John A. *Coal Age* 14: 360 1918.
Gardiner, James T. *Mining Magazine* 11: 207-10 1905.
Garland, Frank. *Black Diamond* Jl 14, 1962 p7.
Garrison, Oliver L. *Black Diamond* Ap 11, 1925 p427.
Gay, Harry S. In *Thurmond* pp90-91.
Gay, Samuel. *Colliery Engineer* 14: 155 1893/94.
Geismer, Henry S. *Coal Age* 6: 28-29 1914.
Gilman, S. W. *Black Diamond* 5: 492 1889/90.
Glover, H. A. *Black Diamond* Ag 24, 1929 p14.
Gluck, Leo. *Coal Age* 6: 991 1914.
Goodman, Herbert E. *Coal Age* 12: 629 1917.
Gowen, Franklin B. *Black Diamond* 5: 413 1889/90; *Coal* 1: 183 1882.
Grady, Edward L. *Black Diamond* N 3, 1962 p7.
Grant, Richard F. *Black Diamond* Je 8, 1957 p11.
Grant, Robert. *Black Diamond* F 12, 1927 p9.
Griffith, William. *Coal Age* 3: 304 1913.
Gutheim, A. G. *Coal Age* 18: 274 1920.

Haas, Frank. *Coal Age* 1: 1146 1910/11.
Haddock, John C. *Coal Age* 5: 932-33 1914.
Haislip, Fred. In *Thurmond* pp91-92.
Halliday, W. P. *Black Diamond* 20: 409 1898.
Hamilton, Robert. *Coal Age* 6: 106 1914.
Harrington, George B. *Black Diamond* My 21, 1960 p7.
Hart, Brent. *Black Diamond* Jl 30, 1960 p6.
Hartley, Roger. *Colliery Engineer* 17: 444 1896/97.
Hathaway, J. L. *Black Diamond* 21: 464 1898.
Haven, William. *Coal Age* 5: 694 1914.
Hawthorne, Hugh R. *Black Diamond* Ja 27, 1962 p9.

Hayatt, D. P. *Black Diamond* 20: 298 1898.
Hayes, Frank J. *Coal Age* 13: 876-77 1918.
Hazard, Erskine. *Coal* 1: 3 1882.
Healy, John F. *Coal Age* 6: 675 1914.
Heaps, George. *Black Diamond* Ag 24, 1929 p15.
Heatherman, W. J. *Coal Age* 13: 1008-9 1918.
Heilner, Marcus G. *Engineering & Mining Journal* 51: 207 1891; *Colliery Engineer* 13: 107 1892/93.
Heitzman, Fred A. *Black Diamond* Ja 18, 1958 p9.
Herriman, F. E. *Coal Age* 14: 20 1918.
Hesse, Herman V. *Coal Age* 2: 262 1912.
Hewett, George C. *Mines & Minerals* 28: 160 1907/8.
Hewitt, John. *Coal & Coke* O 15, 1903 p13; *Coal Age* 5: 735 1914.
Hill, Frank A. *Coal Age* 8: 221 1915.
Hill, John A. *Coal Age* 9: 215-16 1916.
Hill, Robert C. *Black Diamond* Mr 15, 1947 p15.
Hinten, Oscar M. *Black Diamond* Ap 12, 1947 p21.
Hobart, Robert E. *Coal Age* 13: 680 1918.
Hodgson, Thomas. *Black Diamond* 17: 710 1896.
Holden, Albert F. In *Thurmond* pp92-93.
Holland, Horace B. *Black Diamond* F 13, 1960 p9.
Holmes, Joseph A. *Coal Age* 2: 124 1912.
Honnold, Fred C. *Black Diamond* D 20, 1930 11.
Hood, Kuper. *Black Diamond* O 6, 1923 p410.
Hosler, Rush N. *Coal Age* 11: 318 1917.
Housman, B. B. *Black Diamond* Ag 27, 1960 p7.
Houston, H. H. *Black Diamond* S 7, 1929 p16.
Howard, G. Turner. *Black Diamond* Ja 18, 1947.
Hoyt, George A. *Coal* 1: 47 1882.
Huber, Charles F. *Coal Age* 1: 846 1911/12.
Hughes, Benjamin. *Mines & Minerals* 20: 458 1899/1900.
Hughes, William S. *Coal Age* 11: 363 1917.
Ingersoll, I. Frederick. *Black Diamond* 20: 296 1898.
Inglis, W. W. *Coal Age* 9: 420 1916.
Invilliers, Edward d'. *Coal Age* 5: 694 1914.
Irving, Robert M. *Coal Age* 6: 471 1914.
Jenks, William J. *Black Diamond* Ja 30, 1960 p8.
Jennings, J. T. *Coal Age* 2: 800 1912.
Jermyn, Joseph J. *Coal Age* 1: 1249 1911/12.
Jervis, Frank I. *Black Diamond* S 1885 p5.
Jessup, Albert B. *Coal Age* 2: 11-12 1912.
John, Evan D. *Coal Age* 12: 204 1917.
Johnston, Jesse K. *Coal Age* 6: 194 1914.
Jones, Charles T. & George W. In *Tams* pp87-88.
Jones, Edward. *Colliery Engineer* 13: 15 1892/93.
Jones, Edward S. *Black Diamond* F 1, 1947 p18.
Jones, George M. In *Thurmond* 94-5.
Jones, Herbert E. In *Thurmond* pp95-96.
Jones, Homer T. *Black Diamond* N 8, 1958 p9.
Jones, James F. *Mines & Minerals* 28: 283 1907/8.
Jones, Jenkin. In *Tams* pp88-89.
Jones, John H. *Coal & Coke* Mr 15, 1903 7-11; *Coal Age* 1: 682 1911/12.
Jones, Lewis M. *Coal Age* 10: 845 1916.
Jones, Mary H. Mother Jones. *Coal Age* 3: 887-88 1913. SEE ALSO entries in Index.
Jones, Mary H. Autobiography of Mother Jones. Chicago: C. H. Kerr, 1925. 242p.
Jones, Mary H. The miners called her mother. *Masses & Mainstream* Mr 1950 pp38-50.
Joy, Joseph F. *Black Diamond* Mr 2, 1957 p9.
Joy, Wilbur R. *Black Diamond* Jl 2, 1960 p8.

Kanarr, Harry M. *Coal Age* 5: 615 1914.
Keely, Josiah. *Coal Age* 6: 344 1914.
Keighley, F. C. *Coal Age* 7: 717 1915.
Keith, Charles S. *Coal Age* 6: 553 1914.
Kelce, L. R. *Black Diamond* Jl 6, 1957 p9.
Keller, Theodore C. *Black Diamond* S 13, 1930 p8.
Kelly, James J. *Black Diamond* 16: 304 1896.
Kelly, John A. In *Thurmond* pp96-98.
Kemmerer, John L. *Black Diamond* Mr 18, 1944 p19.
Kilpatrick, Worth. *Black Diamond* O 24, 1931 p9.
Kline, Roy F. *Black Diamond* D 8, 1956 p13.
Koepler, W. E. E. *Coal Age* 13: 834 1918.
Kooi, Peter. *Coal Age* 6: 234 1914.
Kuecken, William. *Black Diamond* 20: 634 1898.

Laing, James & John. In *Tams* pp89-90.
Laing, John. *Coal Age* 1: 976 1911/12.
Lambie, R. M. *Coal Age* 17: 459 1920.
LaMonte, Arthur C. *Coal Age* 8: 1022 1915.
Lathrop, William A. *Coal Age* 1: 926 1911/12.
Law, Robert. *Black Diamond* 20: 240 1898.
Lawson, John R. Out of the depths; the story of John R. Lawson by B. B. Beshoar. Denver: Denver Trades & Labor Assembly, 1942 372p.
Leckie, George W. *Black Diamond* Ja 26, 1924 p95.
Leckie, William. *Coal Age* 18: 1134 1920; In *Tams* p91.
Lee, A. R. *Black Diamond* 16: 336 1896.
Lee, Robert. *Coal Age* 6: 796 1914.
Lesher, Carl E. *Black Diamond* D 31, 1960 p6.
Lewis, John L. SEE ALSO entries in Index.

Alinsky, Saul. John L. Lewis, an unauthorized biography. New York: Putnams, 1949. 387p.

Brophy, John. President Lewis and the coal miners. *New Republic* 61: 145-6 1929.

Carnes, Cecil. John L. Lewis; leader of labor. New York: Robert Speller, 1936 331p.

Chamberlain, John. The special case of John L. Lewis. *Fortune* S 1943 106-9.

Gallagher, Mary B. John L. Lewis; the oratory of pity and indignation. *Today's Speech* S 1961 pp15-16.

Garrett, G. Labor and Napoleonism. *Sat. Eve. Post* S 4, 1937 pp12-13.

Given, Ivan A. Lewis era . . . 1920-1960. *Coal Age* Ja 1960 pp66-71.

Haas, Eric. John L. Lewis exposed. New York: Labor News Co., 1937. 69p.

Hardman, J. B. S. John L. Lewis, labor leader and man: an interpretation. *Labor History* 2: 3-29 1961.

Hutchinson, John. Captain of a mighty host; a note on the retirement of John L. Lewis. *Yale Review* 50: 42-52 1960.

Myerscough, Tom. The name is Lewis—John L. n.p., nd. 40p. Subtitle reads: "Czar of the U.M.W.A./Servant of the Big Coal Interests/An Example of an A.F. of L. leader. (Myerscough was president of the National Miners Union).

Pearse, Ben. The indestructible John L. *Sat. Eve. Post* Ja 17, 1959 pp19, 83-4.

Pretshold, Karl. Labor leader. North American Review 237: 142-50 1934.

Raskin, A. H. John L. Lewis; god of coal. *American Mercury* 70: 523-33 1950.

Rothman, Richard. On the speaking of John L. Lewis. *Central States Speech Journal* 14: 177-185 1963.

Stolberg, Benjamin. Education of John L. Lewis. *Nation* 143: 149-51; 177-79 1936.

Stolberg, Benjamin. John L. Lewis; portrait of a realist. *Nation* 143: 121-24 1936.
Stolberg, Benjamin. King Coal's boss. *Independent* 115: 45-47 1925.
Sulzberger, C. L. Sit down with John L. Lewis. New York: Random, 1938. 163p.
United Mine Workers of America. John L. Lewis and the International Union. Washington 1952. 255p.
Wechsler, James A. Labor baron; a portrait of John L. Lewis. New York: William Morrow, 1944. 278p.
Weckesser, Ernest. The radio rhetoric of John L. Lewis. Ph.D. Michigan State University. 1963.

Leyner, John G. *Coal Age* 18: 589 1920.
Lilly, William. *Colliery Engineer* 14: 160 1893/94.
Lincoln, John J. In *Tams* p91. *Black Diamond* Ja 31, 1948 p21.
Lister, Alfred E. *Coal Age* 9: 259 1916.
Lloyd, John. *Coal Age* 8: 759 1915.
Loomis, Edward E. *Mines & Minerals* 19: 551 1898/99.
Love, George H. *Fortune* S 1962 102-7.
Love, Hooper. *Black Diamond* D 6, 1958 p7.
Loveridge, Henry. *Engineering & Mining Journal* 50: 687 1890.
Lucas, Ward. *Black Diamond* My 6, 1961 p5.
Ludlow, Edwin. *Black Diamond* F 16, 1924 p174.
Lukins, Frederick W. *Coal Age* 13: 688-89 1918; *Black Diamond* Ja 23, 1926 p82.
Lumaghi, Louis F. *Black Diamond* Ag 29, 1931 p7.
Lunch, Thomas. *Coal Age* 7: 130 1915.
Luther, E. C. *Coal Age* 12: 974 1917.
Luther, Roland. *Black Diamond* My 19, 1962 p8.

McAuliffe, Eugene. *Coal Age* 11: 523 1917.
McAvity, Malcolm. *Black Diamond* My 13, 1944 p28.
McDonald, Bruce. In *Thurmond* pp98-99.
McElroy, Dennis L. *Black Diamond* Mr 1, 1947 p15.
McGeorge, Donald H. *Black Diamond* S 13, 1958 p18.
McKell, Thomas G. & William. In *Tams* pp91-93.
McQuail, E. J. *Black Diamond* Mr 29, 1924 p372.
McVann, E. J. *Coal Age* 18: 886 1920.
Magraw, Robert M. *Coal Age* 12: 248 1917.
Mahan, Thomas B. *Black Diamond* N 29, 1930 p6.
Maher, N. D. *Coal & Coke* Jl 1, 1901 p18.
Mancourt, Edward M. *Black Diamond* D 7, 1929 p15.
Manley, Frank A. *Coal Age* 2: 762 1912.
Mann, Isaac T. In *Tams* pp93-94.
Markle, John. *Coal Age* 6: 391 1914.
Marshall, W. A. *Black Diamond* Ap 22, 1961 p9.
Martin, David W. *Black Diamond* Je 3, 1950 p24.
Masse, Peter F. *Black Diamond* Mr 10, 1962 p8.
Massey, Evan. *Black Diamond* F 24, 1962 p9.
Massey, William E. *Black Diamond* Mr 10, 1962 p9.
Matthews, Armstrong R. *Black Diamond* Ap 9, 1960 p8.
Mauthe, James L. *Black Diamond* O 30, 1954 p24.
May, W. A. *Coal Age* 1: 1214 1911/12.
Mead, Edwin H. *Engineering & Mining Journal* 50: 648 1890.
Meagher, John F. *Coal Age* 7: 574 1915.
Means, C. M. *Coal Age* 9: 996 1916.
Megeath, G. W. *Black Diamond* Ap 4, 1931 p7.
Mercur, Frederick. *Colliery Engineer* 8: 133 1887.
Merryweather, George H. *Black Diamond* O 11, 1930 p6.
Miller, Alexander W. *Black Diamond* Ap 26, 1958 p6.
Miller, Erskine. In *Tams* pp94-95.
Miller, J. Mason. *Coal & Coke* D 1901 p11.
Mitchell, John. SEE ALSO Entries in Index.

Gluck, Elsie. John Mitchell. New York: Day, 1929. 270p.
Montavon, Paul A. The economic and social thought of John Mitchell. Washington, 1950. 4 microcards. (Catholic University. School of Social Studies. Studies in Economics: Microcard Series v1).
Randall, Robert. John Mitchell exposed. New York: Labor News Co., 1905. 32p.
Steffens, Lincoln. John Mitchell and what he stands for. *McClures* 19: 355-57 1902.
Warne, Frank F. John Mitchell; the labor leader and the man. *Review of Reviews* 26: 556-60 1902.
Weyl, Walter. John Mitchell; the man the miners trust. *Outlook* 82: 657-62 1906.
Moderwell, C. M. *Coal Age* 1: 948 1911/12.
Moffat, James D. *Black Diamond* Mr 26, 1960 p11.
Monser, Edward L. *Black Diamond* Ap 23, 1960 p11.
Moore, J. W. *Black Diamond* 10: 95 1893.
Morgan, Dwight C. *Coal Age* 6: 74 1914.
Morgan, James W. *Black Diamond* F 16, 1957 p7.
Morrow, J. D. A. *Coal Age* 13: 290 1918.
Morton, Quin. *Black Diamond* Mr 14, 1925 p303.
Moses, Thomas. *Black Diamond* F 28, 1948 p18.
Moss, W. L. *Coal Age* 5: 895 1914.
Mouser, Otis. *Black Diamond* N 9, 1929 p7.
Mullins, Thomas C. *Black Diamond* Ag 7, 1954 p11.
Murray, W. J. *Coal Age* 14: 643 1918.

Neale, James B. *Coal Age* 14: 897 1918.
Needham, Jesse. *Coal Age* 10: 1011 1916.
Newsam, Richard. *Coal Age* 4: 243 1913.
Newton, John B. *Black Diamond* O 3, 1931 p9.
Nibleck, James G. *Black Diamond* 10: 193 1893.
Nixon, William J. *Black Diamond* My 16, 1925 p575.
Norris, R. V. *Coal Age* 2: 464 1912; 18: 326 1920.

Ogle, Alfred M. *Black Diamond* My 13, 1944 p28.
Orr, James M. *Black Diamond* S 10, 1927 p9.
Owen, Charles A. *Black Diamond* Ag 3, 1957 p9.
Owens, William D. *Coal Age* 11: 749 1917.

Packer, Asa. *Coal* 1: 25 1882.
Pape, Delbert H. *Black Diamond* Ja 3, 1948 p14.
Parker, Edward W. *Coal Age* 7: 853 1915; *Black Diamond* Ja 8, 1944 p20.
Parsons, Floyd W. *Coal Age* 2: 542 1912.
Patterson, Robert. *Coal Age* 5: 735 1914.
Patterson, Samuel W. *Coal Age* 37: 420 1932.
Pauley, James B. *Black Diamond* N 30, 1929 p15.
Payne, Henry W. *Black Diamond* Jl 24, 1954 p12.
Peabody, Francis S. *Coal Age* 3: 691-92 1913.
Pearson, James. *Coal Age* 6: 29 1914.
Peltier, M. F. *Coal Age* 10: 309 1916.
Perrin, Howard W. *Black Diamond* Ag 17, 1929 p6.
Perry, Herman. *Black Diamond* Ap 18, 1931 p6.
Pettebone, E. R. *Coal Age* 9: 18 1916.
Pfahler, Fred S. *Coal Age* 11: 281 1917.
Phillips, Henry. *Coal Age* 11: 428 1917.
Phillips, R. A. *Coal Age* 2: 226 1912.
Poindexter, William B. *Black Diamond* Je 7, 1958 p11.
Potter, A. A. *Black Diamond* Jl 2, 1960 p10.
Potter, Charles J. *Black Diamond* My 24, 1958 p11.
Potts, William R. *Black Diamond* F 25, 1922 p172.
Pratt, Horatio. *Black Diamond* F 1888 p7.
Price, C. W. *Coal Age* 16: 605 1919.
Pursglave, Joseph Jr. *Black Diamond* Mr 1, 1947 p15.
Pursglave, Samuel. *Black Diamond* Je 21, 1947 p15.

Puterbaugh, Jay G. *Coal Age* 10: 795 1916.
Quealy, P. J. *Black Diamond* N 22, 1930 p7.
Quin, R. A. *Coal Age* 1: 714 1911/12.

Ramsay, Erskine. *Coal Age* 2: 193 1912.
Ramsay, Richard. *Black Diamond* 20: 102 1898.
Rash, Frank D. *Coal Age* 6: 272 1914.
Read, Thomas T. *Black Diamond* Je 7, 1947 p23.
Reed, Benjamin F. *Black Diamond* F 27, 1960 p8.
Reed, George W. *Black Diamond* S 14, 1957 p7.
Reese, John P. *Coal Age* 5: 18-19 1914.
Reid, John C. *Coal Age* 5: 895 1914.
Relf, Richard. *Black Diamond* O 27, 1956 p9.
Rhodes, John H. *Black Diamond* Ag 16, 1958 p7.
Rice, George S. *Coal Age* 2: 155 1912.
Richards, John S. *Black Diamond* 18: 491 1897.
Richards, Thomas M. *Engineering & Mining Journal* 50: 625 1890.
Richards, W. J. *Coal Age* 2: 726 1912; In *Tams* pp95-96.
Riley, L. A. *Black Diamond* My 2, 1925 p509.
Roach, Michael T. *Coal & Coke* D 15, 1904 p12.
Robinson, Carel. *Black Diamond* O 8, 1960 p8.
Robinson, Clarence D. *Black Diamond* O 26, 1929 p17.
Robinson, Neil. *Coal Age* 10: 878-9 1916.
Roby, Isaac G. *Coal Age* 10: 679 1916.
Rogers, P. J. *Coal Age* 7: 595 1915, 12: 1015 1917.
Rogers, R. Earl. *Black Diamond* Ag 11, 1962 p9.
Rose, C. C. *Coal Age* 2: 432 1912, 8: 131 1915.
Ross, David. *Coal Age* 10: 877-8 1916.
Ross, J. J. In *Thurmond* pp99-100.
Rothenhoefer, Walter. *Black Diamond* My 20, 1961 p9.
Rothermel, Samuel H. *Black Diamond* 18: 130 1897.
Routh, John S. Jr. *Black Diamond* D 29, 1962 p8.
Roy, Andrew. *Black Diamond* 5: 823 1889/90.
Ryan, C. J. *Black Diamond* N 2, 1929 p6.

Salm, Casper F. *Black Diamond* Ap 22, 1961 p9.
Salvati, Raymond E. In *Thurmond* p100.
Saunders, Harry W. *Black Diamond* N 5, 1960 p17.
Saward, Frederick E. *Coal Age* 12: 1057 1917.
Sayre, Robert H. *Mines & Minerals* 27: 310 1906/7.
Schluederberg, George W. *Coal Age* 11: 704 1917.
Schmick, William L. *Black Diamond* Ap 18, 1925 p456.
Scott, William L. *Colliery Engineer* 12: 83 1891/92.
Seal, George H. *Black Diamond* Ap 7, 1962 p7.
Sharp, William G. *Coal Age* 16: 232-33 1919.
Sheridan, John. *Coal & Coke* F 15, 1902 p11.
Shirkie, Edward. *Black Diamond* Je 13, 1925 p688.
Shoemaker, George M. *Coal Age* 12: 285 1917.
Sholz, Carl. *Coal Age* 1: 814 1911/12.
Shomo, O. G. *Coal Age* 11: 20 1917.
Sigfried, Joshua K. *Colliery Engineer* 17: 22 1896/97.
Simpson, S. L. *Coal & Coke* F 8, 1901 p10.
Sloan, Samuel. *Coal* 1: 55 1882.
Smith, Howard M. *Coal Age* 5: 660-C 1889/90.
Smith, John B. *Colliery Engineer* 15: 148 1894/95.
Smith, P. B. C. *Black Diamond* Ap 12, 1947 p19.
Snyder, DeWitt C. *Black Diamond* Ap 7, 1962 p7.
Snyder, P. M. *Black Diamond* S 15, 1956 p9.
Speer, Clyde E. *Black Diamond* Ap 9, 1960 p8.
Spencer, Kenneth A. *Black Diamond* F 27, 1960 p8.
Stauffer, Harry K. *Black Diamond* Mr 22, 1924 p331.
Stearns, Irving A. *Coal Age* 2: 650 1912; 18: 897-98 1920.
Stoek, H. H. *Coal Age* 1: 1112 1911/12.

Strother, John C. *Black Diamond* F 13, 1960 p9.
Stuart, Charles E. *Coal Age* 14: 861 1918.

Taggart, J. K. *Black Diamond* Ag 11, 1962 p9.
Taylor, Harry N. *Coal Age* 37: 451 1932.
Taylor, James. *Coal Age* 16: 236 1919.
Taylor, Samuel A. *Coal Age* 1: 914 1911/12.
Taylor, Wm. H. *Coal Age* 5: 1056 1914.
Tetlow, Percy W. *Black Diamond* D 3, 1960 p18.
Thedford, Thomas. *Black Diamond* 5: 535 1889/90.
Thomas, David. *Coal* 1: 18 1882.
Thomas, David H. *Colliery Engineer* 15: 175 1894/95.
Thomas, Thomas. *Coal Age* 3: 107-8 1913.
Thompson, James S. *Coal Age* 7: 983 1915; 15: 183 1919.
Thurmond, W. D. In *Tams* p97.
Thurmond, Walter R. *Black Diamond* N 22, 1958 p5.
Tierney, John & Laurence. In *Tams* pp97-98.
Traer, Glenn W. *Coal Age* 2: 688 1912.
Tryon, F. G. *Coal Age* 17: 829 1920.
Tucker, W. C. *Coal Age* 3: 534 1913.
Tully, John M. *Black Diamond* N 3, 1962 p7.
Turner, Harry. *Black Diamond* O 12, 1929 p11.

Van Dusen, Joseph B. *Black Diamond* 18: 521 1897.
Van Horn, Ezra. *Black Diamond* N 13, 1954 p10.

Walter, T. Frank. *Colliery Engineer* 8: 176 1887/88.
Ward, George S. *Black Diamond* S 28, 1957 p9.
Warner, W. H. *Black Diamond* N 7, 1931 p13.
Warren, Harry M. *Coal Age* 1: 1014 1911/12.
Warriner, Samuel D. *Coal Age* 1: 748 1911/12.
Watson, Clarence W. *Coal Age* Je 1940 p112.
Watson, James E. *Black Diamond* Ag 14, 1926 p158.
Watts, Alfred C. *Coal Age* 10: 230 1916.
Webb, Lewis M. *Black Diamond* F 1, 1947 p18.
Weitzel, E. H. *Coal Age* 2: 368 1912.
Wentz, Daniel B. *Black Diamond* F 13, 1926 p172.
Wheelwright, Jere H. *Coal Age* 17: 232 1920.
White, E. E. In *Tams* pp98-99; *Black Diamond* N 22, 1930 p7.
White, John P. *Coal Age* 1: 782 1911/12.
White, Robert V. *Black Diamond* Jl 2, 1960 p8.
Whiteside, F. W. *Coal Age* 5: 615 1914.
Whitfield, A. F. *Black Diamond* Mr 15, 1947 p15.
Whittlesey, Charles. *Ohio Mining Journal* 5: 2 1887 pp95-97.
Wiley, William M. *Black Diamond* Jl 4, 1931 p7; In *Thurmond* pp101-3.
Williams, H. G. *Coal Age* 12: 495 1917; 20: 796 1921.
Williams, Morris. *Coal Age* 1: 880 1911/12.
Wilshire, William W. *Black Diamond* Ag 25, 1962 p9.
Wilson, Herbert M. *Coal Age* 5: 204-5 1914.
Wilson, Hugh T. *Black Diamond* Ap 16, 1955 p12.
Wilson, John F. *Engineering & Mining Journal* 51: 91 1891.
Wilson, P. J. *Black Diamond* S 24, 1927 p9.
Wittenberg, C. J. *Engineering & Mining Journal* 51: 141 1891.
Wood, George R. *Coal Age* 5: 652 1914.

Young, Hiram M. *Black Diamond* Ja 15, 1927 p35.
Young, Willard B. *Black Diamond* Ja 8, 1944 p17.

Subject & Author Index

(Numbers refer to items.)

212

Breitenstein, A. J. 896
Brewer, W. M. 1687
Bridges, Leonard H. 19a
Brinsmade, R. B. 1688
Briquetting 1892
British Coal Mining Productivity Team 781
Broehl, Wayne G. 294a
Brooks, Alfred H. 1689, 1690, 1691
Brooks, John G. 295, 296
Brophy, John 297, 297a
Brotherhood of Locomotive Engineers 493, 657, 661
Brown, George M. 1692
Brown, Malcolm J. 1188
Brown, P. 298
Brown, Robert 1693
Brown, Roger 986
Brown, Rollo W. 1189
Brownell, Baker 1190
Bruere, Robert W. 299, 1191
Brundage, D. 1593
Buch, John W. 20
Buchanan, John A. 300
Buck, Stuart M. 1694
Buck, William J. 21
Buffalo 227, 877
Bureau of Cooperative Medicine 1594, 1595
Burke, J. W. 1695
Burke, Stephen P. 782
Burlingame, M. G. 132a
Burrows, John S. 783
Bush, B. F. 1696
Business cycles 815, 827
Butler, Richard 1305
Butler County, Pennsylvania 1476
Byers, W. L. 784

Cabin Creek, West Virginia 1192
Caldwell, Nat 785
California 76
Campbell, M. R. 1697
Campbell, Roy E. 23
Campbell, Thomas C. 786, 1329
Campbell County, Tennessee 1631
Canals 1321, 1349, 1350, 1366
Cancer SEE Health Problems
Cannel coal 787, 1677, 1726, 1778
"Captive mines" 1149
Carbon County Historical Society 24
Carbon County, Pennsylvania 241
Carbon County, Utah 149, 1839
Carbonado, Colorado 1761
Carbondale, Pennsylvania 168
Cardiff Coal & Iron Co. 1698
Carlson, Fred A. 1330
Carlson, Oliver 788
Carmin, Robert L. 1699
Carpenter, Samuel 25
Carter, Charles F. 302, 303

Carter, Edward W. 789
Carter Family 1572
Cartlidge, Oscar 26
Caruso, John A. 1331
Casey, K. P. 1407
Cashman, Joseph T. 304
Cassano, James 790
Cassidy, Samuel M. 1446
Castner, Curran & Bullitt 22
Caudill, Harry M. 27, 1447
Central Competitive Field 272
Central Pennsylvania Coal Producers' Assoc. 306
Centralia Mine disaster 1526, 1542
Centre County, Pennsylvania 1824
Ceramic industry 974
Chafin, Don 641
Chamberlain, J. G. 307, 308
Chamberlain, Neil W. 309
Chamberlin, J. W. 791
Chance, H. M. 792, 793, 794, 1501, 1700, 1701, 1702
Chaplin, Herman W. 311
Chaplin, Ronald L. 795
Chapman, Mary L. 28
Charle, E. G. 796
Charleston, South Carolina 1386
Chatham County, North Carolina 111
Check-off 387, 464
Cherry Mine disaster 1520
Chesapeake & Ohio Railroad 1332, 1375, 1731
Chesterfield Railroad Co. 1338
Chicago Coal Board 797
Chicago, Illinois 1721
Chicago, Wilmington & Franklin Coal Co. 86
Child labor 502, 503, 504, 520, 672, 732, 1256
Children & youth SEE ALSO Child labor 1204a, 1208, 1209, 1221, 1241, 1245, 1248, 1306, 1313, 1636, 1928
Childs, C. G. 29
Childs, Marquis W. 312
Christenson, Carroll L. 313, 314, 798
Christiansen, John R. 1211
Christy, David 30
Cincinnati 39
Cist, Jacob 31, 138
Claghorn, Clarence R. 1703
Claiborne County, Tennessee 1631
Clark, J. M. 315
Clark, Stanley 31a
Clark, Walter 1408
Clay County, Kentucky 1099
Clayton, E. E. 316
Clearfield, Pennsylvania 1704
Clegg, Herman H. 1853

214

Cleveland 234
Clifford, Albert J. 32
Clinchfield Coal Co. 807
Clute, F. P. 1502
Coal & Coke Railway Co. 1331
Coal chemical industry 1041
Coal Commission SEE U. S. Coal Commission
Coal Producers Committee for Smoke Abatement 1854
Coal River Collieries 661
Coal River Land Co. 1720
Coal River Railroad Company 1808
Coal schooners 150
Coal Trade Association of Indiana 806
Coates, Harold W. 39
Cobb, William H. 40
Coke 784, 923, 1031, 1394, 1668, 1669, 1727, 1764
Cole, E. L. 319
Coleman, James W. 320, 321
Coleman, McAlister 322, 323, 1410
Collective bargaining 363, 368, 370, 376, 406, 492, 545, 574, 642, 643, 1021
Collier, Arthur J. 1706, 1707, 1708
Collins, Elizabeth 1244
Collis, Edgar L. 1596
Colorado 246, 269, 271, 274, 291, 293, 324-32, 339, 342, 347, 348, 368, 372, 373, 380, 413, 423, 430, 474, 510, 517, 519, 570, 571, 587, 600, 605, 618, 674, 675, 679, 680, 691, 719, 997, 1202, 1224, 1730, 1748, 1752, 1756, 1803, 1809, 1836, 1845, 1846, 1847
Colorado Coal Commission SEE U. S. Colorado Coal Commission
Colorado Fuel & Iron Co. 325, 605, 618
Colorado Industrial Commission 325, 326
Colorado Mine Operators Assoc. 327
Colorado National Guard 328
Colorado Special Board of Officers 329
Colorado State Federation of Labor 330
Colton, Henry 1709, 1833
Columbus, Ohio 824, 888, 1167
Committee of Coal Mine Managers 332
Committee on Public Administration Cases 1411
Common Market SEE Export trade
Commons, John R. 1193
Company stores 106, 1901, 1910

Compensation SEE Workmen's compensation
Competition 786, 869, 897, 954a, 965, 971, 979, 988, 991, 1083, 1138, 1151, 1159
Competitive fuels 625, 891, 896, 934, 961, 962, 963
Computers 1046
Conant, C. B. 808
Conference on Economic Research 809
Conference on Price Research 810
Conference on the Commercial & Economic Health of the Bituminous Coal Industry 811
Conley, Phil 41, 42
Connellsville, Pennsylvania 69, 1736, 1764
Connellsville scale (wages) 334
Conner, Eli 812
Conroy, Jack 1194
Conservation 990, 1091, 1863, 1882, 1915
Consolidation Coal Company 9, 126, 505, 805, 875, 1293
Convicts as miners 436, 437, 1913
Coolidge, William H. 335
Cornell, Robert J. 336
Coronada Coal Co. 530
Corrigan, James J. 43, 1503
Corruption of public officials 1213
Cort, John C. 337
Costello, E. J. 338
Cost of production 975, 976, 992, 1013, 1058, 1103, 1165
Costigan, Edward P. 339
Council of State Governments 1447a
Cowan, Donald R. 813
Cowley, Malcolm 340
Craford, Charles B. 341
Crane, W. R. 1710-16
Crawford, Bruce 1195
Creditor, Morris 1335
Creel, George 342
Cressey, P. F. 1196
Cresson & Clearfield Coal & Coke Co. 620
Crews, Ralph 814
Crum, W. L. 815
Cubby, Edwin A. 44
Culbert, James L. 1717
Culin, Stewart 343
Culver, Harold E. 1448
Cumberland, Maryland 45
Cumberland County, Tennessee 1698
Cumberland National Forest 1449, 1491
Cummings, John 344
Currie, Robert D. 1504
Cushing, George H. 816

216

Fink, Walter H. 368
Firmstone, William 62
Fisher, Cassius A. 65
Fisher, Howell 1731
Fisher, Waldo E. 369, 370, 371, 839, 840
Fisher, Walter L. 1732
Fishman, Betty 841
Fishman, Leo 841
Fitch, John A. 372, 373
Fledderus, Mary L. 842
Fleming, A. B. 66
Fleming, Henry S. 843
Flinn, R. H. 1612, 1613
Florance, J. E. 1733
Floyd, W. M. 67
Flynn, Elizabeth G. 374
Flynn, John T. 844
Fohl, W. E. 845
Folklore 1569-86
Forbes, J. J. 1512
Forbes, R. D. 1858
Foremen SEE ALSO Management 1867, 1888
Forestry SEE Forests
Forests 767, 833, 837, 1164, 1858, 1898
Forsythe, J. R. 847
Foster, J. S. 1859
Foster, John F. 848
Foster, John W. 1339
Foster, William Z. 375
Fourmile Mine disaster 1506
Fowler, Charles B. 376
Fowler, George L. 1734, 1735
Frank, B. 377
Frank, N. R. 1610
Franklin County, Illinois 1304, 1724, 1725
Frazier, Edward K. 379
French, Jack 1556
Freytag, R. C. 68
Frick Coke Co. 69, 229
Friedman, Louis L. 1614
Friedman, Morris 380
Friends, Society of 1208, 1209, 1253, 1262
Frisch, Isadore 70
Fritz, W. G. 849, 1148
Frontenac disaster 1521
Fulton, G. 71
Fulton, John 1736
Fulton County, Illinois 1451
Gage, E. L. 1615
Gagliardo, Domenico 381
Gale, Hoyt S. 1730, 1737
Gallup, New Mexico 383, 384, 525
Gandy, Harry L. 850
Gannes, Harry 382
Garfield, James R. 1414
Garnsey, Cyrus 1415, 1416
Gasification 848

Gasper, Donald 1738
Gauger, A. W. 1860
Gay, Katherine 383, 384
Geauga County, Ohio 201
Gebbart, John G. 385
Geiner, John E. 861
General Policies Committee (Anthracite Operators) 386, 387, 852, 853
George, Henry 388
George, John E. 390
George's Creek Coal & Iron Co. 72
Georgia 207
German, Ralph H. 1417
Germans 505
Germany 949
Gibson, A. M. 73, 1379, 1740
Gilbertson, H. S. 854
Gilfillan, Harriet W. 1210
Gilfillan, Lauren 1210
Ginger, Ray 74, 855
Girard, Stephen 226
Gitlow, A. L. 856
Gladden, James W. 1211
Glasser, Carie 391
Gleason, Arthur 1212, 1213
Glenn, L. C. 75, 1741
Goldenweiser, E. A. 857, 858
Gompers, Samuel 392, 393, 394
Goodrich, Carter 395, 396, 397
Goodspeed, Allen W. 767
Goodyear, Watson A. 1742
Gordon, Leland 1214
Gordon, Z. H. 207
Government contracts 1896, 1897
Government Regulation 217, 381, 742, 764, 812, 831, 903, 904, 924, 1160, 1404-42, 1498, 1894
Gowen, Franklin B. 1007, 1083
Grady, William H. 859
Graham, Gene S. 785
Graham, Herman D. 1451
Granger, Iowa 1299
Grauman, Lawrence 398
Gray, George 399
Grayson, Charles 860
Great Lakes 762, 763, 791, 804, 861, 1336, 1360, 1361, 1363
Greeks 149
Green, Archie 1571, 1572, 1573
Green, Stephen H. 1743
Green, William 403, 404
Greenbaum, Fred 405
Greenbrier Coal & Coke Co. 1340
Greene, Charles S. 76
Greene, Homer 1862
Greene, Victor R. 401, 402
Greenslade, Rush V. 406
Greenwood Slope Colliery 84
Gregg, Robert 77
Griess, P. R. 862, 1718
Griffin, Gerald 1215

217

Griffith, W. T. 1744
Griffith, William 78, 79, 80
Groner, Isaac N. 407
Grundy County, Tennessee 132, 1178
Guernsey, James L. 1453
Guernsey County, Ohio 1699
Guffey Act SEE Bituminous Coal Conservation Act
Gundlack, Doris 863
Gutheim, A. G. 1341
Gutman, Herbert G. 408, 409, 410, 1557
Guyandotte Land Co. 81
Guyer, John P. 411
Haas, Frank 1863
Hack, John T. 82
Hackamack, Lawrence C. 412
Hager, Charles J. 83
Halberstadt, B. 84
Hale, Peter M. 1745
Hall, Betty S. 1864
Hall, Clarence 1513
Hall, Helen 1216
Hall, R. D. 1217, 1514, 1746, 1747
Hambridge, Jay 1218
Hamill, R. H. 1219
Hamill, W. S. 60
Hamilton, Rex 1574
Hamilton, Walter H. 864, 865, 866, 867
Hammond, M. B. 868
Hampshire County, West Virginia 220
Hampton Roads 1155
Hand, Alfred 869
Hanes, J. E. 1748
Hanford, Ben 413
Hannah, H. W. 1454
Hapgood, Powers 414
Hard, William 415, 416
Harding, G. E. 871
Hardt, Anton 85
Hardy, Carroll F. 872
Harger, Charles M. 417
Haring, H. A. 873
Harlan County, Kentucky 338, 398, 556, 644, 688, 1196, 1220, 1306, 1636, 1801
Harline, O. L. 874
Harrell, Thomas W. 1231
Harrington, Daniel 1515, 1516, 1517
Harrington, George B. 86
Harris, A. L. 1559
Harris, George W. 875
Harris, Herbert 418
Harrison, Fairfax 1342
Harrison, George 1419
Harrison, S. M. 419
Harvey, Helen B. 87
Harvey, Katherine A. 88, 420

Haugee, J. W. 1865
Haught, O. L. 1749
Haupt, Herman 1343
Hayes, Charles W. 1750, 1751
Hayhurst, E. R. 1616
Haynes, William H. 876
Haynes, W. W. 779
Hazard, Erskine 89, 90
Hazard, Kentucky 1265
Health & welfare plans SEE ALSO UMW. Welfare & Retirement Fund 1609, 1665
Health problems 1587-1667
Hebley, Henry F. 1455
Hedstrom, Eric L. 877
Heinrich, O. J. 91, 1866
Hemphill, William E. 1344
Henderson, James M. 878, 879, 880
Henderson, Kentucky 114
Hendrickson, John 1456
Henry, Patricia A. 881
Herlihy, Ann 421
Herling, John 422
Hermelin, Samuel G. 92
Herrin Massacre 249, 281, 554
Herrington, Fred 423
Hess, William H. 882
Hesse, Alfred W. 883
Hester, Patrick 433
Hewett, G. C. 1752
Hibbs, William 1867
Hicken, Victor 424
Higgins, Wallace W. 1868
Hildebrandt Coal Co. 884
Hildreth, S. P. 93
Hill, F. A. 1753
Hinds, Roy W. 426
Hinrichs, Albert F. 427
Hoboken, New Jersey 1861
Hockhocking Valley 25, 273, 564, 611, 894, 1557
Hodge, James M. 1754
Hoffman, Betty H. 1220
Hoffman, John N. 885
Hoffman, Phil 1518
Hogg, E. 1869
Holbrook, E. A. 1870
Holbrook, Stewart H. 428
Hollandsworth, G. 1221
Hollister, G. 1457
Holloway, Richard B. 429
Holm, Edwin E. 886
Holmes, Charles 430, 1755
Holmes, Grant 1458
Holmes, Leslie A. 887, 1345
Holt, Homer A. 431
Home heating market 905, 909
Hooper, Wallace D. 888
Horsley, Albert 428
Hosea, R. M. 1756

218

220

222

Pinkowski, Edward 584, 584a
Pipelines 803, 1365, 1381, 1385
Pittsburgh 479, 1553
Pittsburgh & Buffalo Co. 1012
Pittsburgh & Westmoreland Coal Co. 1015
Pittsburgh. Chamber of Commerce 1011, 1371
Pittsburgh Coal Co. 1337, 1409
Pittsburgh Consolidation Coal Co. 1895
Pittston Company 927
Pneumoconiosis SEE Health problems
Pocahontas Mine disaster 1500, 1534
Pocahontas Operators Assoc. 162
Pohlmann, Kenneth E. 1643, 1644
Police 243, 343, 411, 578, 621, 736
Pollak, Katherine E. 585
Pollard, Spencer D. 586
Pollock, John 1535
Pollution 1455, 1468a
Polskov, Walter N. 1266
Pomeroy, Samuel W. 163
Pope, George S. 1896
Pope, Henry B. 1013
Portal-to-portal pay 596
Porter, Eugene O. 587
Posey, Thomas E. 588, 589
Potter, Charles J. 1014
Pottsville, Pennsylvania 84
Pratt, John B. 1431
Price fixing SEE ALSO Competition 782, 789, 840, 935
Price of coal 759, 778, 808, 830, 878, 914, 923, 924, 928, 998, 1063, 1101, 1109, 1117, 1119a, 1128, 1129, 1139, 1160, 1364, 1415, 1416
Pritchard, Paul W. 589a, 589b
Productivity 745, 760, 781, 842, 992
Profits 760, 830, 857, 1084, 1140, 1141, 1165
Progressive Miners of America 289, 422, 432, 695, 740, 741
Pryde, George B. 165
Psychological studies SEE ALSO Mental Health 1852, 1853, 1856
Public assistance 1176, 1178, 1286
Public health SEE Health problems
Public relations SEE Journalism
Pultz, J. L. 1015, 1804
Purcell, William J. 590
Quakers SEE Friends, Society of
Quarles, Mary A. 1267
Raccoon Coal & Iron Co. 30
Racial & minority groups SEE ALSO Negroes 1551-67
Railroads SEE ALSO Names of

individual railroads 1318-23, 1325-29, 1331-35, 1337-43, 1346-49, 1351-55, 1356-59, 1367-76, 1378, 1379, 1382-84, 1387-97, 1399-1403
Raleigh County, West Virginia 206
Ramsay, E. 1805
Randall, D. T. 1897
Randall, James G. 591
Randolph, B. S. 166, 1806
Randolph, L. S. 167
Randolph County, West Virginia 40
Rashleigh, Alice V. 168
Raskin, A. H. 592, 1268
Ratliff, Paul 1269
Rau, Otto M. 1016
Raushenbush, Hilmar 1017, 1018
Raushenbush, Stephen 593
Ray, Frank A. 1807
Raymond, R. W. 1647
Read, Thomas L. 594
Reading Railroad 678, 939
Recreation 1221
Red Ash Colliery disaster 1530, 1532
Redevelopment 1077
Reed, Frank H. 1019
Reed, William B. 1020
Rees, Albert 1021
Reeves, H. C. 1022
Regulation SEE Government Regulation
Rehabilitation 1643, 1644
Reitell, Charles 1023, 1373
Reith, John W. 1024, 1025
Relief SEE Public assistance
Religion 1181, 1238, 1270
Rescue work SEE Accidents
Research 1857, 1860, 1870, 1872, 1889, 1891, 1895, 1916, 1917, 1919
Respiratory diseases SEE Health problems
Retail coal trade 819, 892, 966, 1070, 1098
Retraining of miners 461
Reynolds, James E. 1648
Reynolds, Robert J. 597
Reynolds, S. C. 598, 1026
Reynolds, W. C. 1808
Rhea County, Tennessee 1502
Rhetoric SEE ALSO John L. Lewis 1864
Rhode Island 1, 174, 192, 1680
Rhodes, Ben 1898
Rhodes, James F. 599
Rice, George S. 1027, 1533, 1899
Rice, James P. 1028
Rice, M. M. 600
Rich, Mark 1270
Rich, Paul 169
Rich Hill disaster 1528

Sisler, James D. 1059
Skaggs, Charles P. 1060
Skinner, B. F. 623
Slab Fork Coal Co. 194
Slavs 401, 402, 707, 1193, 1274
Slocum, William J. 625
Slosson, Edwin E. 1061
Smith, Eugene 195
Smith, Frank G. 626, 1062
Smith, George O. 627, 1063, 1064, 1822
Smith, Grace P. 1585
Smith, Hamilton 196
Smith, Richard C. 1291
Smith, Samuel R. 197
Smithers, F. S. & Co. 1065
Smoke control SEE Air Pollution
Smurthwaite, William 198, 1823
Snelling, Walter O. 1513
"Snow bird" mines 1026
Social disorganization SEE ALSO
  Life in the coal fields 1196
Soloman, H. J. 1536
Solow, Herbert 1066
Somers, Gerald G. 628, 1067, 1068
Somerset County, Pennsylvania 1767
Songs SEE Folklore
South Carolina 1386
South Dakota 1069
South Dakota. State Planning Board 1069
Southern Appalachian Coal Operators' Assoc. 629
Spahr, Charles B. 1294
Spalding, H. A. 1022
Spaulding, Bishop 523
Speare, Morris E. 1906
Spencer, Harold H. 1907
Spencer, K. A. 1485
Spero, S. D. 630
Spittal, Hugh E. 1787, 1788
Squire, Joseph 1825
Stabilization SEE Bituminous Coal
  Stabilization Legislation
Stacy, Charles B. 1653
Stag Canon Fuel Co. 1817
Standard of living SEE ALSO
  Wages 1198, 1236
Stanley, Louis 631
Starr, George W. 1070
Stearns Coal & Lumber Co. 1449, 1491
Stebinger, Eugene 1826
Steel, Alvin A. 1072
Steele, H. E. 1654
Steelman, James 1908
Stern, Elizabeth SEE Eleanor Morton
Steubenville, Ohio 198, 1823
Stevenson, George E. 1909
Stewart, Charles L. 1486

Stewart, E. 1073, 1074, 1075
Stewart, Ethel R. 1076
Stewart, Paul D. 1077
Stock, A. R. 1078
Stocking, George W. 632
Stocks & bonds 827
Stockton, Richard 633, 1295
Stoddard, C. E. 634
Stoeckle, J. D. 1655
Stoek, H. H. 1537, 1656, 1827
Stone, Ralph W. 1828
Stone, Warren S. 493, 657, 661
Storage 1085, 1169
Storrs, Arthur H. 1829
Storrs, L. S. 1830
Stotesbury Coal Museum 64
Stow, A. H. 1831
Straton, John W. 1079
Stream pollution SEE Pollution
Strikes SEE Labor relations
Strip mining 1443-94, 1907
Strong, Edna 1296
Strong, Henry K. 200
Sturgeon, Myron T. 201
Sub-bituminous coal 882
Suffern, Arthur E. 639, 640, 1080
Sullivan County, Pennsylvania 1703
Sunshine Anthracite Coal Case 1434
Supply 1135
Surface, George T. 1566
Sutherland, Howard 1435, 1911
Swados, Harvey 1297
Swain, George T. 641
Swank, James M. 202, 203
Sweet, S. H. 1081
Swisher, Jacob A. 204
Switch-Back Railroad 1379
Sycamore Coal Co. 50
Sycamore Coal Mines 205
Sydenstricker, Edgar 642, 643
Synthetic fuels SEE ALSO Research 1895

Taff, J. A. 1832
Tams, W. P. Jr. 206
Tankersley, Allen P. 207
Tariff 43, 221, 952
Taxation 764, 768, 977, 1022, 1028, 1060, 1142, 1859
Taxpayers associations 1859
Taylor, George 208
Taylor, Glenn R. 1380
Taylor, John R. 1082
Taylor, Paul F. 644
Taylor, Richard C. 209, 210
Taylor, Samuel A. 1912
Taylor, Warren C. 1298
Teleky, Ludwig, 1657
Tennessee 436, 437, 581, 796, 895, 1178, 1489, 1502, 1602, 1631, 1632, 1663, 1698, 1709, 1765, 1766, 1768, 1773, 1774, 1789,

228

Date Due

MAR 17, 98			